# Armed Response

'I was gripped . . . for the whole of a five-hour train journey. Not only gripped but deeply moved. Roger Gray has written a fine book . . . which gave me an insight into an area of British policing that is beyond the experience and comprehension of most of us. Armed policing may be a regrettable necessity but I came away from the book with a feeling of real respect for the officers involved.'

Barry Simmer (co-deviser and principal writer of *The Vice*)

'The research to play Tony Stamp never ends. To find an author who knows his subject, can tell his story with humour, total understanding and with such passion that you just get so enthralled that you can't put the book down till you have read that particular chapter, is a rare find. But then this author is different. He was there actually doing the job, the training, and being among the first to carry guns as a special unit. His experiences, and those of his team, are told without bravado.

If you want to know why the British Bobby, so beloved of the world, now has a need to carry guns . . . read this book.'

Graham Cole (Tony Stamp of *The Bill*)

'Much more than a fly-on-the-wall documentary . . . His vivid action-by-action recall opens a rear window on how the unit, called SO19, dealt with such cases . . . True crime where the finger of the law is on the trigger!'

*Publishing News*

'Tells the real story of one of the most respected units in the police force today – and tells it straight.'

*Quality Times*

'True-life tales of terror, death and courage from the Armed Response Unit.'

*People*

# Armed
# Response

*Roger Gray*

This paperback edition first published in Great Britain in 2005 by
Virgin Books Ltd
Thames Wharf Studios
Rainville Road
London W6 9HA

First published in hardback in Great Britain in 2000 by
Virgin Publishing Ltd

ISBN 0 7535 1049 9

Typeset by TW Typesetting, Plymouth, Devon
Printed and bound by Mackays of Chatham PLC

# Contents

This book is dedicated to the
memory of
Andrew Frederick Pearce
Pc. 1238 CO
SO19 Armed Response

for
My father and mother, my wife and my sons
Also to absent friends:
Police Sergeant Barry Mannakee
Police Constable Robert Beaumont
Miss Lydia Lane
Friendship transcends

# Foreword

As young constables patrolling Westminster, and subsequently London's East End, this gifted author and I shared so much. We were educated there in so many of life's skills. Social services, negotiation, and significantly conflict management allied to the reasonable use of force as we were sent out to fend for ourselves. We acquired both cynicism and humour along the way, but we both owe much to belonging to the 'police family'. Our separate paths in the service have relied on those experiences and friendship to shape our future courses.

This book is about those individuals who make up the world's finest and best police service. It is about how they deal personally and collectively every day, with the violence, trauma and abject despair which regularly confronts them, and is so much a part of being 'in the job'.

Historically, one of the main reasons for the success and reputation of the British police is that they have handled life's dramas and troubles without resorting to the use of a gun. That is a fascinating and yet awesome responsibility to place upon any individual, but it gives them an insight enabling them to speak to, and deal with, people in the most dire of situations, without resorting to the use of a weapon.

No one in their right mind wants to see the horrors that are the product of the gun culture that has plagued some American cities, repeated here in Britain. Sadly the first examples have been laid graphically before us, with the tragedy of Dunblane at the forefront. We are, and will hopefully remain, very distant from the spectre of teenaged death and glory gangs slaughtering innocent classmates with a gun bought over a shop counter. Thankfully our legislature prevents that. While it is, and I am confident it will remain, the wish of the vast majority of British police officers to remain unarmed, sadly changes have occurred that require a measured armed response.

Roger Gray provides an intelligent and perceptive insight into that response in the capital city of our land. It tells of the people and circumstances involved from more than one perspective. As you begin to perceive all that these officers face, it makes thoughtful, disturbing, yet inspiring reading.

To those who want to change our police service, I say understand it and hear its heartbeat before you tamper with the finest. At a time when policing attitudes are increasingly under scrutiny, this book is essential reading for those who are truly interested, and want to comprehend the British police officer. Roger Gray has, drawing on his personal experience, *touched the very soul of policing*.

Fred Broughton, OBE
Chairman, Police Federation of England & Wales
November 1999

# Acknowledgements

I would first and foremost like to thank all those people – both police officers and many others – who have opened their hearts to me, sometimes at the cost of great personal distress, to enable me to authenticate the accounts related in this book. Without them these pages would be no more than hollow, one-sided accounts.

I also wish to thank the many people who, in one way or another, have supported me in this venture – and they know who they are. I take great pride in the fact that so many people have trusted me with their inner thoughts and emotions, with confidences that I will never disclose.

There are those in authority who could, instead of supporting me, have been obstructive, but there too the trust was implicit. I want also to thank the infinitely varied entity that is 'the job' for the experience of a lifetime.

Thanks also to Jeff Gulvin for opening a door, to Robert Kirby for planting the seed, to Humphrey Price for having the faith.

And to one in particular I can only say . . . stay lucky!

*If we do meet again, we shall smile;*
*If not, why then, this parting was well made.*

*Julius Caesar*, William Shakespeare

# Introduction

T HE CONCEPT OF ARVS is not in itself new. Armed Response Vehicles have functioned in other police forces for several years with differing remits and in various formats. The Metropolitan Police interpretation is perhaps subject to a range of influences not felt as widely or powerfully elsewhere.

They are and always will be the primary response for any immediately occurring firearm incident anywhere in our capital city. Here reside the seat of government and the heart of the financial world. Both have been terrorist targets in the past. ARVs may also deploy beyond those boundaries to give urgent aid to adjoining forces, when required.

In the summer of 1991 the first of these patrols were mobilised, the product of an increasing awareness that, within the Metropolitan Police boundaries, there was no immediate armed response available to confront rising armed crime, or to prevent the terrible carnage of the type of random shooting and killing visited upon the people of Hungerford by Michael Ryan.

At that time the degree of caution exercised by the Establishment was so great as to be stifling. Weapons were to be kept locked and unloaded in safes in the vehicles, the keys attached to the same bunch as the ignition key. The purpose was to cause the crews to stop and to take time before deploying firearms, a tactic that often did not equate with the situations they very soon found themselves dealing with.

Authority to arm had to be sought from distant, often unreachable seniors. The idea that an armed car could contain and 'freeze' an incident while other resources were mustered was often shown to be flawed as the workload rose, and positive immediate action was demanded.

As reality dawned, new procedures evolved, but the early days were a frustrating time. Among the first crews were ex-soldiers and others with firearms experience gained principally from dealing with preplanned operations.

Many of them had great difficulty reconciling themselves to this often hugely confrontational role. Others, new to the scene – whose first 'tutor' had been the need to cope with chaos, to try to bring order from it – were more chastened.

Instead of bemoaning the lack of resources, information or planning, they would apply what they had learned to the situation as it was. Truly, then, they adopted the watchwords, the methods, of the department. Thinking on their feet they would

*improvise . . . adapt . . . overcome.*

The story told here is not mine alone. Much of my life and many of my experiences do emerge in these pages, however, and, hopefully, through my eyes and my words, you will gain an insight into a unique group of people, a fraternity whose birth and growing pains I have experienced and am proud to be part of.

So come and ride with the ARVs at speeds up to 135 miles per hour, as the klaxon wails and the strands of blue light spread all around you in the night.

Put yourself in the car with the crew as the radio tells them that gunfire is imminent or happening as they fight to don body armour, read the map and ready the weapons.

Share their thoughts while they organise on the move and deploy to meet a threat.

Experience a little of their fear and the immense responsibility of making a shoot/don't-shoot decision in moments that will be scrutinised under the unflinching eye of the law, by those who have limitless time and resource to criticise.

Hear their laughter and profound sadness.

Watch while these exceptional people do an extra-ordinary job!

Today, tonight, tomorrow they may confront anything from a fool with a toy to a terrorist with a Kalashnikov assault rifle, an armed robber or an ex-soldier with a gun. ARVs are trained to deal with incidents that will bring them into contact with everything from social services to the SAS.

This is not a work of fiction but a translation of actual incidents to the printed page. Anonymity has been preserved where appropriate, but this is reality. Nor is this a story of some distant secretive group fighting a despot in a foreign land. These are armed police officers fighting to uphold the law, to protect you or your family. They have passed you in the street but you did not know them. You thought them to be just another police car, maybe 'the traffic cops'. The next time such a car passes, with three men as crew and a large yellow circle on the roof, you will know more. You may even wonder who the crew are!

Armed Response Vehicles have emerged from the shadows as a force to be reckoned with in their own right.

Their workload now exceeds that of all other areas of the firearms department. They have been involved in more exchanges of fire, shot more suspects and received more gun-related injuries. The gun-toting bank robber has more to fear than ever before.

And these are still early days . . .

# 1 Blood Money

'GIVE ME THE MONEY. Give me the money, now. I want the money. Give me the money now.'
    The girl on the fifth till heard the words aimed at her colleague on Till One, but could hardly believe it was all happening again. Only days earlier, there had been an armed robbery that had shaken her very badly. Now it was happening again. More fear. Somebody was going to make her suffer fear again. But with that thought her fear turned to anger. The anger grew strong, so strong that the fear was all at once eclipsed. The anger lifted her from her seat.

'No you won't, not again. I won't let you.'

Not long after the Highgate Village Barclays Bank opened, that morning a duffel-coated man had walked through the door. He wore a woollen hat rolled down to his brow, framing dark glasses. The blue jeans that topped his working boots were supported by a brown leather belt, which trapped the Webley & Scott against his body. It was an enormous revolver, a .455, bigger even than a .45 with bullets the size of your thumb, poised within its chambers ready to destroy flesh, to smash bone.

It was the barrel of this gun that the man at the first till was looking down as those words broke his concentration.

'Give me the money.'

* * *

Early turn has that effect on you. You roll out of bed at 4.30 a.m. feeling like a revived corpse, subject yourself to some running water, swallow some tea and head on in for 6 a.m. By 8 o'clock breakfast calls. Sometime thereafter your flesh makes contact with a black plastic seat, as you stare down through your knees at some journalistic gem, spread out across the cubicle in front of you. It's your one private, contemplative moment of the morning: it should be sacrosanct.

Dave was committed. He was past the news, through the TV programmes and into the sport. One bit of paperwork almost concluded, the other not even begun.

Outside in the yard at Forest Gate, Darren and Sam were digesting their breakfast and preparing the car, when a call to Hackney came over the main set radio.

'Lloyds Bank, Mare Street, Hackney. Central station alarm. Ends CAD 3141. Any Trojan unit?' (CAD stands for Computer-aided dispatch.)

Darren was on to it straightaway: 'MP from Trojan 501, show us assigned.'

Meanwhile, Dave was sitting there, perhaps planning a holiday, his belt rig, holster, gun, radio and paraphernalia draped around his boots, when Darren's fist crashed on the cubicle door. 'Come on, you big tart, we've got a shout.' A low voice from behind the door: 'Fuck!' Dave was not amused.

By the time Dave tumbled out of the back door into the yard the other two were well in harness. He dropped on to the back seat like a stone as the Rover took off towards the gates, its door still closing. They turned into Green Street, left into the Romford Road, away towards central London, two tones howling and blue strobe lights bouncing off windows as they passed. Dave lay sideways across the back seat, trying to make some kind of order out of his kit. Sam pushed the accelerator closer to the floor, a grin spreading beneath his fair moustache, quietly amused by the grunts being emitted from the struggling man behind him.

'Give me all the money,' the woollen-hatted man said again, waving the enormous gun back and forth. The teller tried to reason with him: he had chosen to rob the foreign-exchange till with relatively little British money in it. He grew angry, frustrated and ever more threatening by the moment.

'There's no more.'

The girl at Till Five was shouting at him. 'Get out. Just go away.' Her finger brushed the alarm button.

The crew of 501 heard the initial call to Highgate come through. Nothing unusual there. Every morning a host of calls like this, all 'set off in error', nothing to get excited about. Just like the call to Hackney they were running to now.

The girl at the bank couldn't leave it at that. No, too much anger. The robber left the bank and crossed the road, pausing to look back. She was standing there with the hapless manager, as if morally resigned to follow.

The man fondled the butt of the gun inside his jacket, staring at her with malevolent eyes. The threat was plain. The manager pleaded with her to stop, to leave it alone now. But the anger still burned, and she began to follow.

At a console high in the Scotland Yard information room, an update flashed across the screen. Then the words of an operator over the radio: 'Units to assist, please, an armed robbery. Five seven, fifty-seven, Highgate High Street, a Barclays Bank on CAD 3283.' The response came in from local units: 'Yankee Alpha Two, on way.'

Sam had been pushing hard to get to the Hackney call. He was relishing the drive through his old ground. Up the Lea Bridge Road with some 'lift-off' over the canal bridge to annoy Dave in the back as he rose and fell with a thump in the back seat.

'How's your eggs and bacon?'

'Bastard!'

On up to the roundabout, past the ponds, down Cricketfield Road, passing Hackney Downs and the pub where the doorman was shot to death many years before. The updated call to Highgate came in. Darren, the ex-guardsman, had now got his serious head on: no smile. 'MP from Trojan 501. We can divert from your 3141.' The Hackney call was a dud, just an alarm set off in error.

'Trojan 501, you are assigned. Trojan Alpha.'

'Received, MP. On way.'

Sam was in his element. He had worked this ground as driver of the area car, a fast-response vehicle, before being posted to SO19. He knew the route and the atlas was at once redundant. He knew the short cuts, the bends, even the road surfaces. Warp speed.

They had not yet arrived, however, when the marked patrol car running south towards Highgate was flagged down by the furious cashier and her exasperated manager. The sergeant in the passenger seat was told by the young woman that the robber was a little way ahead in Cholmeley Park, a quiet side road.

The PC began to drive slowly down towards him. They were defenceless. Darren, Dave and Sam still had miles to go, though they were breaking their necks to get there. The stakes were going up.

What was going on in his ex-military mind? The marines, then Bosnia as a mercenary, and even the

Foreign Legion. That kind of conflict was nothing like this. No team to merge with here, just him. No clearly identified enemy – well not yet anyway. No plan, no evac, no reinforcement. Just him. He hadn't fired yet, but the girl would follow. What would he do with an identifiable, uniformed enemy? Reloads hung about his neck in small bags attached to a thin cord. Perhaps he had thought about his plans going wrong.

He began to descend the gentle slope, glancing back with menace at the pursuing girl. Keep walking. She'll give up. Keep walking.

The sergeant spoke, 'There he is.' On the footway to the left the robber was walking purposefully away, his hands thrust deep in the jacket pockets, his head down. The right thing to do was observe, report back, follow. But adrenaline overpowered logic. The sergeant and constable stopped the patrol car and got out. With long acrylic baton held behind his leg, the sergeant recklessly closed with his target, trying to match his footfalls, to get close enough to bring him down. It was foolish to believe that an armed robber would be such easy prey. He was not. When the gap was reduced to perhaps five feet he turned.

Totally helpless, the officer had delivered himself into the jaws of death. The massive Webley was poised to deliver a round, travelling at six hundred feet per second, into the middle of his chest. Designed as a classic 'man stopper' for World War One officers' use, the Webley's destructive power had caused it to be abandoned as 'inhuman'.

There was a pause while the gunman stepped back a few paces: 'Stay back,' he said. 'You've got a job to do. I've got a job to do.' Then the barrel lifted, threatening the officer's upper chest, his face, his head. With an ear-splitting crash, the robber sent a round skywards. The stakes were rising again.

The PC had crouched down between parked cars, calling out to the gunman to put down his weapon. But the gunman crossed the road, leaped over a fence and was gone. They gave chase, leaping the same fence. No sign of him.

Then all at once they heard a sound that chilled them.

Perhaps a dozen minutes had passed as Trojan 501 hurtled through Amhurst Road and up into Stoke Newington, the speeds now falling from the high eighties as the tangle of roads frustrated Sam's best efforts. Then through the one-way system watched by a sea of cosmopolitan faces. Sam turned left into Stoke Newington Church Street, where the sound of the two-tones echoed out over Abney Park Cemetery and the graves of my long-dead relatives. Sam was now pushing the boundaries of his driving skills to the edge.

In Highgate shots were now being fired. The bullets could be heard crashing through the tree tops above pursuing police officers' heads. But there was another sound – it had taken the pursuers a few moments to identify it. A school playground – always full of shouts, screams and noise. Something was wrong, though. Too loud. Too singular. Too terrified. The children had seen the running figure, and then the gun. A wave of fear swept across their number as the revolver thundered, echoing around the buildings.

The two unarmed officers now knew where the robber had gone. They crossed the green together and, reaching the wall at the far end, they could see the figure of the man running down the centre of the road. The huge revolver hung loosely from his right hand.

Life is perverse. You park your car, there isn't one around. You lock it, turn to walk away, and there they are: bloody traffic wardens. The white Sherpa van sidled into the kerb and stopped. It bore only the Metropolitan Police logo on a blue background. The occupants were distinctly more recognisable by their clothing. Their dress code was identical. Dark-blue suits, yellow flashes on the shoulders, silver buttons. A shiny peaked cap with a yellow band, a shield adorning the front. Metropolitan Police traffic warden.

Life is perverse. You park your Sherpa, there isn't one around. You lock it, turn to walk away, and there he is: a bloody bank robber.

Sam hurled the car through Church Street into Green Lanes. His crew no longer cared about the violence of the ride. Shots were being fired. 'Any way you like, Sam. Just get us there.' Down the radio they called, 'MP from Trojan 501. Can we have the helicopter and dogs? And requesting Trojan Delta.' That meant authority to arm and deploy. At that time Alpha meant 'go to the area and assess'.

'Trojan 501 from MP, India 99 and dogs on way to you. Negative to Delta at this time. You are Trojan Alpha.'

The car rocked with enough obscenity and outrage to turn a barrack room blue. 'For fuck's sake, he's shooting at us. What more do they want?' Sam had turned into Green Lanes and then Riversdale Road. Soon he would turn into Blackstock Road. From there it was into Seven Sisters Road then Holloway Road towards Archway.

The distance was closing.

While the two following officers split to the left and right footways in pursuit, the gunman tucked the revolver momentarily out of sight. He moved close to the footway opposite the traffic wardens, and headed further down the road towards them. The driver, a bespectacled amiable black man, passed the keys to a

ARMED RESPONSE

white man in his fifties who had moments earlier been
his passenger. His features were distinguished by a full
beard, flecked with grey. Both were quiet unassuming
married men with wives and families.

As the black man turned, leaving his partner to lock
up the van on his own side, he saw the face of the
young man staring at him. Perhaps because of his
profession, used to attracting less than admiring gazes,
he thought nothing of it.

But something, maybe that intense gaze, made the
black traffic warden look back at the young man. The
robber was walking directly, purposefully, towards him,
still staring at him. As he got to where they were
standing, he raised the revolver, and pushed the barrel
against a point just below the warden's ear. 'Give me the
keys or I'll blow you away.'

'I don't have them. My colleague up the road has
them.' The warden's voice was quavering with fear. In
those moments perhaps the thoughts of his family
swam into his head: perhaps he would never see them
again.

The bearded second man broke in to support him:
'No, mate. We haven't got the keys.' At that moment
they hung in the door, hidden from view by his body.

The unarmed police officers were closing visibly in
the distance. With a sneer the robber made off. Later
the black warden would relate: 'At the time he pointed
the gun at me and said give me the keys, it came to my
mind, yes, I was going to die today. I was going to be
shot.'

As the pursuing police officers continued to give
chase, the robber stopped several times, calling back to
them. 'Don't be a hero. Lie on the ground.' Maybe
through a sense of duty, or perhaps a hypnotic anger,
they both refused.

\* \* \*

The road sweeper's thoughts were on anything other than hijack, as leaves and small branches succumbed to his broad broom. Behind him was parked a yellow Renault truck of perhaps thirty hundredweight waiting to receive the fruits of his labours, as successive shovels lifted debris from the gutter into its broad back. Looking down at his work, he had not seen the robber approach. The sound of the truck door opening behind him focused his attention, and he saw the dark figure of the young man in the duffel coat and woollen hat, standing half in the cab.

'Oy, what you doing, mate?'

'Where are the keys? Give me the keys.'

'There's no way you're having the keys.'

From within the jacket, and from behind the door, the shape of the big black revolver emerged. In subdued tones the road sweeper responded.

'You've got them.'

A local sergeant, fair-haired and quietly spoken, aged about 35, was patrolling in a marked car. He had, like many others converging on the location, heard the original call and some of the updates. His overall grasp of the situation was limited by broken radio transmissions and the need to concentrate on a high-speed drive. When he arrived at Milton Park, turning into Hornsey Lane Gardens, he was confronted by the spectacle of several officers running full tilt through a sharp bend. On the other side of the bend, in the distance, he saw the yellow truck. Unknown to him, Trojan 501 were in the Holloway Road, now several hundred yards away.

The only information he possessed was that there had been an armed robbery, an outline of an attempt to take a yellow Renault truck at gunpoint, and little more. As he closed with it he did not know if the armed robber was driving. The radio broke in: 'Trojan 501, Trojan 509, you have Delta.' Full authority had been given and another armed car was running, but the confrontation that loomed was with the sergeant, now only yards away, and drawing level.

'In the wagon, Sarge, in the wagon.' His local radio barked at him as a PC on foot nearby strove to communicate. He braked heavily, slammed the car into reverse, swinging it backwards across the bows of the truck. Recklessly he leaped out, and ran towards the cab. A spidery scar appeared on the windscreen as a bullet passed through with a puff of powdered, splintered glass. A huge bang concussed the air and police officers all around dived for cover. Still close to his car, the sergeant dived behind it, also seeking cover.

Trojan 501 reached the top of Holloway Road and burst, bellowing, into the small one-way system. Dave and Darren had donned their body armour. The carbines were racked and nine-millimetre rounds slid into the breeches. They were now in the highest state of readiness, requiring only the release of a safety catch, the pressure on a trigger.

Sam fought the screeching, roaring car through the last left turn into Archway Road. Ahead of them to the north loomed the towering arc of Archway's 'suicide' bridge, where from time to time lost souls had plunged to their deaths.

The truck forced its way through the chicane that had been created by the abandoned police car. Another shot rang out from the driver's window, aimed at a nearby PC on the footway. Cowering behind his car, the sergeant watched helplessly as the truck careered on down the hill. It burst into the Archway Road, pursued by a marked police car, lights and siren blaring. In that car behind the robber, unarmed officers flinched as again he fired at them. Ahead of him to the south, the Archway bridge and Trojan 501. They would not flinch.

Over the radio came a voice among many, anonymous, but suddenly clear: 'He's firing at us.' The yellow Renault truck drew closer. They could see the spidery bullet hole in its windscreen, the robber at the wheel. He was jumping up and down in his seat. He was laughing. It was unreal, so much so that all three of them missed one very important detail – something Darren would soon come face to face with.

They could see him now, rolling towards them. Sam faced a dilemma. There was only one break in the otherwise continuous fencing, rooted in the raised central reservation that divided this dual carriageway. Its kerbed edges dared him to cross. To run its length and come back would place them a long way behind.

The driver of the police car directly behind the truck saw the oncoming blue and white flashes, heard the wailing of the Rover. He knew it was an ARV. Kindred spirits, advanced police drivers both, he and Sam saw the problem. The solution, a short break in the railings. He slowed, gesturing to Sam to occupy the space he was creating, opening up a void between the area car and the truck, and timing it to coincide with the gap in the railings. Sam hesitated for a moment, brand-new Rover, high kerbs, suspension, brake lines.

*Fuck it!*

The Rover bucked and crashed over the kerbs, brand-new underbelly searing across concrete, kit and crew thrown around inside. Bump, clunk, grind, a final crash as the exhaust impacted on the kerb and the car settled in the outside lane behind the truck.

No banter, no jokes, not even a comment. This was all deadly serious stuff. Armed confrontation was looming. The stakes don't get any higher. Sam tucked the car in on the left behind the truck, while the unarmed units dropped way back. 'I'll quarter him on the nearside,' said Sam, seeking to use the robber's own vehicle as maximum cover. 'Then he won't be able to shoot at us.'

Darren sat with the Heckler & Koch MP5 carbine across his knees. He knew that it was going to be him: front passenger seat, number-one candidate, he'd soon be in a gunfight with a man who would try to kill him. Sam would have to stop the car. Dave was behind him. Split-second differences, but they would put him there. He knew because he had been shot at before.

He could see along the nearside of the truck as it descended the hill. Behind them the bridge, ahead the one-way at the top of Holloway Road. Sam dabbed the brakes – they still worked. Ahead of the truck, perhaps a hundred yards ahead, the traffic was braking.

Something had to happen. A hand came out of the window holding that huge Webley. The bang was drowned out by all the noise in the car. Sudden smoke heralded the bullet that winged past them. Darren broke his silence.

'Fuck it, he's shooting at us!'

'He's got fucking long arms, hasn't he?' Dave cut in from the back seat. The important point they had missed was that the truck was a left-hand drive. Big Darren was right: it would be him.

Sam moved to the outside lane where the 'quartering' tactic should now work. He looked up. In the huge mirrors he could see the robber's face. The truck was tight over to the left now, the offside lane clear to pass. Through the lens their eyes met – he was smiling. Sam knew what it meant; he stayed back. As the truck slowed the tension rose. Darren's left hand went to the door handle while the right gripped the stock of the MP5. Dave was seated centrally on the back seat with a view forward between the other two. He had cleared the kit away for a rapid exit while Sam tried to gauge where the car should be if it all 'came off'. They had to think about cover, consider their arcs of fire, and the backdrop. If they missed their target, who else might be hit?

The traffic ahead had stopped. It would bring the Renault to a halt. The anticipation in the ARV was rising to breaking point. The truck swung violently to the left. A bus lane passing nearside of a small traffic island offered an escape route around the back of the traffic. The truck seesawed dramatically left and right, then exploded into the traffic system ahead of the lights. Trojan 501 were tight in behind.

The two vehicles swung left into St John's Road leaving chaos and disruption in their wake. Somewhere behind, local units were following. In the distance the wail of the approaching Trojan 509, the other ARV, could be heard, but it was not near enough to help. Darren ran a commentary of the route over the radio. It would not help, there was not enough time.

The speed that the truck could achieve was not great, but its bulk made it a formidable weapon in itself. Sam kept his 'quartered' position as they rolled on for another 250 yards towards an approaching NO ENTRY sign to the right.

The truck swung right, the wrong way down Ashbrook Road, maintaining even, uneventful and unopposed progress for perhaps another hundred yards, until it turned into Fairbridge Road. Here all hell would break loose.

At the T-junction the truck went left. Fairbridge Road is fair game for commuter parking. It was lined both sides with cars, broken by occasional small gaps. The elderly West Indian man driving the ancient Rover towards them had no idea of the terror that was about to invade his quiet world. The truck picked up more speed – the gunman was going to ram his way through. Behind, the crew of 501 braced themselves.

The truck swung to the left as an accommodating break in the parked cars presented itself. Sam could see the black man's face changing from calm to horror as the truck bore down on him as he strove to reach the gap. Seeing where this was all going, Sam tucked the already wounded ARV in close behind the truck. Seconds later the sound of crashing, tearing metal erupted ahead of them. The battered old Rover passed, spinning behind them, as the first attempt to block them failed. To this day Sam vividly recalls the terror on the old man's face.

The driver of the delivery lorry hated Fairbridge Road. Every time he turned up there, it was parked solid with bloody commuters. He was past caring now, though. Bollocks! Let the other drivers wait. He parked the lorry and went into the yard to find his customer. As he came out again, he heard a series of crashes, and the squeal of tyres in the distance.

Abandoning all reason, the robber threw the truck back and forth across the road, smashing into every parked car he passed. Sam stuck to him like a limpet as damaged cars flew by them in slow motion. In the mirror empty vehicles littered the road, some still moving, but somehow they got through unscathed. Then the brake lights. What would he do now?

The robber sat in the cab, looking forwards through the damaged windscreen. He could see nowhere to go. A parked lorry, steel bollards, he would have to shoot his way out. Think, you're a soldier. You've got reloads round your neck. Give 'em some suppression fire to get their heads down. Go to cover. Make an ambush.

He could not know that the men pursuing him were ex-soldiers too, or that they were well armed.

Darren gripped the carbine ever tighter, checking again even on the move. Had it fed the round properly into the breech? Mag secure. Check safety catch. Be ready. His left hand held the door ajar, left foot wedging it, poised for that moment, waiting for the voice in his head. *Go. Go*.

Sam jockeyed for the best place to be when the truck came to an enforced halt, as it now inevitably would. He had to balance cover against access in the last few seconds they were rolling. Was the robber the only one in the cab? Did he have a hostage?

In the back, Dave's mind raced through the same questions. What to do? Go nearside and support Darren? Go offside and support Sam? Would he be able to get out? Would there be room?

Sam was wearing no body armour. He had had no time, driving.

More brake lights. Swerving left.

Truck door opening, the hand, a figure, the gun.

Darren was out, his whole consciousness focused on the gun in the robber's grip. It was aimed at him. What would he feel next? A sledgehammer blow to his chest? Blackness, oblivion? He felt the concussion, saw the smoke, but total focus masked out all else as the bullet flew by, and he heard nothing. His own carbine rose in front of him as the trained gunman in him took over. Safety off with the thumb as it rose, the shout, 'Armed police.'

Today, elderly West Indian men seemed to be everywhere. To his eternal credit, with all that was happening, Darren still saw the man standing shocked in line of sight behind the robber. Even as his finger pulled the trigger he aimed off left and the two nine-millimetre rounds tore into a wall. The old man dropped to his knees, cowering on the kerb. The gunman held Darren's gaze for a microsecond of realisation.

The police had guns!

Sam snatched the keys from the ignition, leaving no means of escape for their adversary. Dave ran offside of the truck with Sam, wearing no body armour, close behind. A split second to clear the cab and then round the front, leaping over the trembling black man and his bags of shopping, to support Darren as the pursuit took yet another turn.

The robber ran left into a wood yard nearside of the truck with Darren close behind. At the gates Darren paused, then, with Dave behind him, he walked in. Everywhere the shouts, 'Armed police. Stand still.' The yard was a wide expanse, a killing zone. Twenty yards ahead ran the man with the gun. The soldier, the trained firearms officer, both spoke in Darren's head as he and Dave screamed after him, 'Armed police. Stand still.' Ahead of them factories, workers. The robber was not going to stop. Breaking into a run, Darren fired two more barely aimed shots on the move.

The man was ahead of them, running towards the safe corner of a brick building. It was a wide-open yard, a desert devoid of cover. He would be waiting behind that wall as they ran towards him. And he would kill them.

Soon faces would appear at every door, foolish with curiosity, innocent faces. The gunman could run through the factories, take hostages. A recipe for carnage. It had to end now.

Darren stopped, pulled the carbine tight into his shoulder as his eye drew the two concentric sight rings together. In their centre the single pole of the foresight marked the destination of the round. His finger pulled ever tighter against the trigger. The recoil slammed the butt against his shoulder. As if the strings of life had been cut from a puppet, the gunman dropped.

Sam was behind them with Dave and Darren, moving on the prone figure, weapons raised, covering, looking for the slightest move, a feint to draw them in, to shoot them. Nothing.

With Dave's MP5 trained on the motionless figure, Darren pulled the enormous Webley pistol from his hand. He lay face down with his head turned to the left, a pool of blood now spreading from beneath it, running into a nearby grating. His hands were knuckle down.

He had fallen dead in the air as he ran. Among the hair on the back of his head a curl of smoke marked the passage of a bullet, a small flap of skin on his cheek the exit of a fragment from it. Although the round had been aimed at the centre of mass and the clearest target, the robber's chest, the dipping movement as he ran had dictated the bullet's destination.

They called back to local officers for a first-aid kit, while beating rotors marked the arrival of the Helicopter Emergency Medical Service (HEMS) chopper nearby. Two police officers brought up the dressings: a man and a woman. Hopelessly inadequate as they were, the dressings were applied. The orange suits and green bags of the helicopter paramedics and doctor appeared through the gates of the yard. To their credit they did everything they could. But every monitor flatlined. Nothing. They rolled him over to attempt heart massage, using shears to cut open his clothing.

In the silence that settled as the last efforts to revive the robber failed, he was declared dead. The only sound that remained was the fluttering of paper money. It fell from where it was hidden in his shirt, blew around a little in the light breeze, and stuck in the blood beneath him.

\* \* \*

At the coroner's court, at an inquest held sometime later, Darren's actions were supported with a verdict of lawful killing. He was moved by the presence of the dead man's family, and the ordeal of giving evidence in front of them. The dead man's father displayed the most profound courage, saying he loved his son as any good parent would, but he apologised for all the hurt he had caused.

As a result of the incident Darren was prevented as a matter of departmental policy from carrying a firearm operationally, reduced to shuffling paper and driving senior officers, for several months. After resuming operational duties he was later returned to ordinary duty somewhere in the Metropolis.

The woman cashier whose anger propelled her to follow the robber was severely criticised by her employers. She suffered nightmares as a dark figure stalked the shadows around her for months.

The unarmed officer present at the time of the shooting suffered considerable aftereffects to the detriment of his work and marriage. He required continuing counselling, as did the traffic warden, who was badly shaken. His family were also affected.

Every year, on the anniversary of the event, someone leaves flowers at the scene. *No one wins, everybody loses.*

A national daily published an article in a supplement after the inquest, referring to the dead man as the 'soldier of misfortune'. In his time he had been a marine, a mercenary in Bosnia and a Foreign Legionnaire – strong clues to his character, yet he had no criminal record. Ex-soldiers and men with military experience have featured in other, not dissimilar, events.

The military authorities would do well to take note, as should we all.

# 2 In the Beginning

**A**LL GUNS ARE DANGEROUS and should be avoided at all costs. That was my father's assertion, which I was to hear many times.

I was born in April 1946, in the front upstairs room of a terraced house about a mile from what is now the principal SO19 base. My late and sorely missed father, John, was born perhaps three or four hundred yards from it in 1917; and his father, probably closer still, in 1884, so I suppose a tenuous link existed even before I knew it. The house I was born in belonged to my grandparents and, although I did not grow up in it, my parents and I remained frequent visitors.

My grandfather was a small, wiry man with a ferocious temper that set him apart (admirably in my opinion) from the rest of the family: Jack Russell-like in character, he was, nevertheless, very affectionate. His sense of what was right and proper seemed to stem from the Victorian era, and the experiences of trench warfare to which he had been subjected.

My grandmother, 'Nan', who was to survive him by decades, was a lovely gentle lady who, thankfully, spoiled me. Even now, in this hi-tech age, I still savour memories of how simple life seemed to be when I was with her. The aroma of tea and raisins that always drifted from the larder contrasted with the smell of coal-tar soap clinging to a sink fed by one cold-water tap. I still see the whitewashed walls, the immaculate outside toilet. In the shed outside hung my grand-father's wartime helmet. Now it hangs in mine.

My mother grew up in that house with her twin brother Les, and older brother Frederick, both of whom became my firm friends. The first floor was occupied mainly by my large – and now only distantly remem-bered – great-grandfather. On the floor above him lived my widowed great-aunt.

Home for my immediate family became one of those prefab temporary dwellings in Hackney, some of which survived for nearly half a century. By the standards of the day, it was long on facilities and equipment but short on insulation. Ice on the inside of the windows during winter nights was not uncommon.

My father was a good provider and my mother an equally good carer and, as a boy, I was left free to roam nearby Victoria Park, which became my countryside.

We were lucky enough to have a car, television and regular holidays when such things were the exception rather than the rule. In 1953 when I was seven, my mother gave birth to my brother Laurence.

Academic I was not, although I enjoyed English and some of the more practical activities, and I left school at fifteen without taking a single exam. I hated to argue or be in conflict, and would far rather walk away, but if the final judgement was to be physical I tended to win far more than I lost. It made me loathe bullies, a stance that in my later life accounts for much.

I worked in all manner of occupations including the building trade and as a mechanic. I have an abiding love of sports cars, and have owned many, includ-ing big Austin Healeys and two E-type Jaguars. Working from home I became involved in a small business venture contracting to fix stonework. That could only be called a qualified success, but it did at least pay for the cars.

In 1965 a friend and I took a holiday, driving overnight to Cornwall. We'd met as schoolboys. Dave was a big man with short dark hair, pale skin, and somewhat brutish features. He would later join the police force, and be best man at my wedding. Dawn broke as we arrived, and we could not wait to hit the beach. After swimming and sunning ourselves, we fell fast asleep to wake hours later, in searing hot sunshine.

His pale skin had succumbed and, if I was red, he was positively glowing. Dressing and walking were an agony for him, and I transported my groaning passenger back to our lodgings. There he spread himself out on his bed like a wrinkled pink starfish. I obtained some lotion and gave it to him. Then, on a pretence, I went out to escape the endless whining.

I drove west along the coast road from Marazion towards Penzance, the sea on my left surrounding the dominance of St Michael's Mount. A chicane in the road demanded that I slow down, and as I did so I noticed two girls on my left, walking slowly in the same direction. One was particularly pretty, still with the last trace of adolescence in her face, and the promise of growing beauty to come. In the following years that beauty did blossom. I had found the lady who was to become my permanent passenger in a particular car. I still share my life with Sue. I still have the car.

In 1967 I decided to put the vagaries of self-employment behind me and, seeking direction and security, I followed the example set by Dave, my pink-starfish friend. I applied to join the Metropolitan Police Force.

The job list I supplied them with must have either confounded them or convinced them that I had a broad life experience, for later that year a summons to attend the old recruitment centre office in Borough dropped on to the hall mat. I duly responded. The highly physical nature of the work I had been doing and the sheer weight of the materials we were required to handle had gone a long way towards building up my stature. I'd never have got into the ballet in any case, so at six foot two and approaching two hundred pounds, I was ready for the job. Perhaps that helped with the physical and medical examinations I was required to undergo on that day.

I have always wondered just exactly what walking naked into a room and being required (by a panel of doctors) to turn and touch your toes actually tells them. While I am sure the reasoning is founded on some medical observation, I have sometimes wondered if it was actually a suitability test for holding conversations with certain types of character. Perhaps it was for generating meaningless public statements or, in a minority of cases, pursuing a certain route to higher office. Thankfully for me, the judgement of type was not what it is today, and I remained with the dwindling group of survivors to go on for X-ray at 'St Tommy's', London's renowned St Thomas's Hospital.

Several weeks later another letter dropped through the letterbox. Attend Peel House, SW1, 22 January 1968. A door was opening into a world of infinitely varied experience that I would share for more than another 30 years.

Peel House, mercifully, with its sombre Victorian façade and pig-pen accommodation, was not to be the final destination. The booming sound of a drill sergeant's voice registered dismay on the faces of several innocents, as they climbed the stairs to seek their fate. Duly sworn in, the Hendon contingent stood by while the remainder were marched into the bowels of that grim building, which today is the 'Black Museum'. There the artefacts and exhibits of London's most vile crimes are displayed to the privileged few. As far as we were concerned, the 'Black Museum' it already was.

\* \* \*

Twelve weeks of legislation, practicals, knowledge, reasoning and bullshit followed. While we were still recruits, the infamous Grosvenor Square riot took place, and we speculated that we might be called out. Grosvenor Square became a catalyst for change: compounded by subsequent events it led to a sea change in police tactics and approach to public disorder. The incumbent commissioner, Sir Joseph Simpson, died; and, of far more significance to me, my father had a life-threatening heart attack.

It was a Thursday, and I had, as was my habit, phoned home. My mother's voice was flat, giving nothing away, and I felt at first as if I had done something wrong. The long pauses, the considered answers were all unnatural, and I sensed something awful had happened. The words 'Your father's had a heart attack' ran through me like a huge electric shock.

I cut short the phone call, and walked stunned into the dormitory I shared with several others. John Allen, a Scotsman of about my age with a slightly high-pitched voice, and sometimes pedantic manner, had the bed next to me. To his great credit, he recognised my distress and offered the first words of support. Within minutes I had reported to a less than sympathetic sergeant my intention to go immediately home. His opinion was, anyway, an irrelevance. Nobody would keep me away.

Dad had always seemed like an icon of all that was tough. Five foot eight, forty-eight-inch chest, seventeen-inch neck, massive hands. His history as a boxer and a wartime airman had always seemed like a steel fist in a velvet glove. In defence of home and family, he was as capable of the violence the East End sometimes required as he was of shedding tears for the distress of a child. I have seen him demolish two men with two punches in an unfair confrontation, and yet with the same huge hands he could repair a tiny watch. I could not absorb this sudden proof of his mortality. His heart attack was like a thunderbolt, and it came at the end of my training, on the run-up to a final exam. A really bad time.

Dad survived the attack but was never the same man again. My colleagues and classmates closed ranks around me and at the end of the course I prevailed. We celebrated with the customary overindulgence, some riotous behaviour, and a huge bollocking from the resident superintendent.

I found I was to be posted to the regal 'A' Division, which meant royalty, fixed posts, tourists, pomp and ceremony. The consensus was, 'Not good. Not good at all!' Others were posted to more active areas, where there would be opportunities to shine, and to gain experience. 'A' Division threatened to submerge the enthusiasm of many a young officer with fixed posts outside Parliament, or some dignitary's home. Limited patrols in a confined area, pomp and ceremony were all to dilute the purpose of even the most determined.

Arrival on 'A', however, was not for me a total calamity, as I got Rochester Row, a busier part of the ground. Cannon Row really would have meant all the things I had feared, but at least 'Roch' had 'the Jungle', a tangle of crisscrossed roads lined with large Victorian houses that provided a measure of real police work, as well as homes for all types, whether the eccentric or the celebrity.

There were also all those bedsit girls, the nurses' homes and little-girl-lost tourists. Yes, it could have been worse. After all, this was the swinging 60s. Poor old Ronnie, a fair-haired and substantially built Scotsman, who had been my classmate at Hendon, got Cannon Row. Two weeks of standing in a sentry box in

Parliament Square saw him on a train straight back to the Highlands.

There was always, though, the dark prospect of a two-year posting to the Palace of Westminster, where you became known as a POW confined within the boundaries of the seat of Parliament, remote from the public we had been trained to serve. Police officers from anywhere on the whole of 'A' Division were liable for that posting. But fate and a certain cunning played a part in negotiations that transferred me to West Ham at the turn of 1969. This was to be a very different game.

The difference was immense, real people from the same background I grew up in. It was here I met Mike Waldren, a man who went on to be a most senior officer in SO19, and the overall supervisor on the first Armed Response Vehicle induction courses. We were then both constables and aspiring motorcycle riders. Jointly we went to Hendon, where he disappeared backwards while performing a hill start, while I, thankfully, prevailed. Somehow, though, I feel he has since made up the deficit, overtaking me in the career lane. Another constable and close friend, then and now, was Fred Broughton, my co-conspirator in many a misadventure. He is now the public face of the Police Federation.

West Ham was to be the most formative experience of my early years of service. The reliefs had more than a fair sprinkling of older and more experienced police officers, some of whom had learned their trade from a generation that had seen active military service in World War Two. They were a tight group, suspicious of seniors or authority. They did not easily accept this new generation that drove as much as walked, that policed by the law and not just instinct. The truth was that we were to learn from each other.

The change that has made police cars commonplace, and foot-duty officers rare, was beginning then, and I drove most of the time. As the fleet of cars grew, the need for more maintenance grew with it. In those days it was customary to appoint a nonoperational police officer to such a role. Charlie was the product of such an arrangement. Failing to care for one of his cars was guaranteed to bring down his wrath upon the offender, regardless of their rank or position. At first I could not understand why he commanded such respect, until it was gently explained.

Charlie was Charles Cox, holder of the George Medal for heroism. He had survived being shot in the stomach while two other police officers had died. In June of 1961 a suspect being interviewed following a domestic assault had produced a handgun and escaped from the police station, then situated in West Ham Lane opposite Portway.

In the pursuit that followed Sergeant Hutchins and Inspector Pawsey were shot and died of their injuries. They were posthumously awarded the Queen's Police Medal, while Constable Les England was awarded the British Empire Medal. Charlie was shot in the stomach, but thankfully he survived.

In all of the time I knew him, Charlie never mentioned his award or his injury. He never once showed a hint of the scars on his body or his mind, but the story was related many times by others and his daily presence brought the reality of the danger we constables faced closer than it had ever been before. Our day-to-day briefings were becoming ever more punctuated with news of armed criminals.

Several years later I was on duty in the front office of the new West Ham building, when one of our most familiar local eccentrics strode in, insisting that there was a dead man in a car in Windmill Lane, a few hundred yards away. Our informant's past record of not being altogether credible meant we cheerfully told him to get lost at first. He was a huge individual with a gruff and intimidating manner and a face like the Normandy fortifications, with a penchant for patrolling the footway opposite the station while punching the palm of his left hand with his right fist. He would occasionally (in the ultimate test of manhood) eat a Mars bar with the wrapper still on, throwing half of it to the ground in a contemptuous gesture.

Nevertheless I went to Windmill Lane, and his description of what he had found was entirely accurate. 'A big hole in his head,' he had said. And he was right. The dead man was Harry Barham, about whom there was to be much speculation in the media concerning his private affairs and connections. He had been shot twice, apparently by the rear-seat passenger. One round had gone through the seat, entering his lower back and passing on down into his right thigh. The other had entered the back of his head and exited through his forehead just below the hairline, leaving (what seemed to me then) a surprisingly neat hole. The bullet had then punched a hole in the upper windscreen and disappeared skywards. Barham was still sitting upright, and who knows how many people had walked unknowingly by?

I learned two things that day: not to underestimate the local oddball, and to have an increased respect for the destructive power of the gun.

West Ham was a good grounding and a place where I learned much about policing in the real world. It was a place where larger-than-life characters seemed to exist, both policemen and villains. I remember being over-awed by the hulking form of Dennis MacNamara, the nineteen-stone Olympic wrestler, credited with the ability to hold a man at arm's length. This was graphically demonstrated in the midst of a snooker match. The table was situated on the first floor of the old West

Ham police station, where a lunch-break game was in progress.

Dennis had an opponent who was proving to be a poor loser and, furthermore, was refusing to honour a debt. A final warning was issued, and ignored. The matter became resolved only when the errant constable apologised, suspended as he was from a first-floor window, his only means of support being the grip on his collar by a powerful fist at the end of Dennis's massive right arm.

Frequently we would encounter firearm-related incidents. For a long time the local presence of John McVicar, career criminal now reformed and a journalist, gave cause for concern. Briefings would warn that he was passing through the ground, and that an attempt to stop him should be treated with extreme caution.

A mere exchange of punches between the bouncers and rowdy customers outside the well-known Two Puddings pub in Stratford Broadway demonstrated how commonplace the use of guns was becoming. A police officer had only just passed the venue when the aggrieved ex-customers carried out a drive-by shooting, blowing out the windows with a shotgun.

Sue and I had married in 1968 and set up home in Montserrat Road, Putney, a road I came back to years later, in far less pleasant circumstances. The transfer to West Ham had meant a house move to Essex. In the summer of 1973, a further move to a larger house further out was required, to accommodate our young son. And Sue was now pregnant again, with what was to be our second boy. I applied for, and was granted, another transfer, this time to the very edge of the Met's jurisdiction, a few miles short of the Queen Elizabeth Bridge across the River Thames. A close friend and colleague had speculated that I was leaving for the good life, to go out to pasture. How wrong he proved to be.

The climate out there was very different again. I quickly learned that people as a whole seemed less likely to confront the police, but the ones who did were often much more of a handful. I also learned that it was wise to try to gauge a situation early, because help when urgently required took infinitely longer to arrive.

I amused myself by best-guessing which were the legitimate cars, and which were stolen, and they seemed to be legion. I became quite adept at spotting them, sitting on their tails until they broke cover, with the result that I was involved in several spectacular car chases. The vehicles on three occasions ended up masquerading as a road sign, a bus stop and a rather large and somewhat unwelcome garden ornament. But for all of that I felt as if I was going stale. It was a chance meeting with a group of more 'focused' officers that led to a posting to the Divisional Support Unit, a trouble-shooting mobile group of eight to ten constables, supervised by one sergeant. There are some that would accuse me of understatement if I say that some notoriety was to attach itself to this unit's name.

The annual Barking Fair of 1975 was an opportunity to earn a little overtime and the variety of a short-term posting to a different area. A local pub, The Brewery Tap, was experiencing a new class of customer, as some of the most violent young men in the district adopted it as their local, and began to wreak havoc. Local police alone could not cope. Merely driving a police car past the premises risked being pelted with glasses and bottles.

The DSU were called in to boost the manpower. Instantly everything began to change. I watched as these carrier-borne officers set on the ringleaders like hounds on hares. Within days it was all over. I felt a sense of pride in this group of policemen who would take no crap, and the value of the team/carrier presence became firmly imprinted in my psyche. During a subsequent operation, I impressed a supervising officer, and the offer to join the unit was made. I of course accepted. The posting lasted, on and off, for several years.

Another unforeseen link with SO19 began here: the man who today commands the department at the highest level was then an inspector with the unit; he is now the commander in charge of specialist operations. To name him would be to erode his personal safety. It was during one of my infrequent breaks from the carrier work that I had another experience marking a further shift in my attitude towards guns.

At the Cricketers pub, Cricketfield Road, Clapton, in London's East End, which at that time had a portion of its bars used solely as a club, a doorman had ejected a man for some form of violent or disagreeable behaviour, and blows had been exchanged. While anger and resentment are often the product of such exchanges, the revenge exacted by this individual was beyond anyone's expectations. He returned and shot and killed the doorman.

I had been posted driving that night, but as a favour had swapped roles and was confined to the station. The shooter had been cornered a few hundred yards away in a small side road in Rainham, Essex, and I could hear what was happening over the radio. He opened fire on the surrounding unarmed officers. One round, fired at the area car driver's face, deflected up the windscreen and into the rubber. I scrambled to unlock the two ancient revolvers that were stored in the station safe. As I did so, the gunman's car screamed past the windows of my office and down the main A13 towards London. It was a pivotal point for me, and I remember thinking how vulnerable the officers chasing him were, how easily that could have been me, and how I would much rather fight fire with fire. It also made me think that what we needed was a quicker way to react to a man like this. Perhaps armed, able to respond, mobile.

Shortly afterwards I was moved a short distance to a local station a few miles further north, where I remained for a further year, interspersed with further carrier work. On 8 May 1975 I was driving a van when the radio sputtered a message for me to phone the station officer. The message was everything I dreaded to hear. My father had collapsed and died. Nothing would ever be the same.

Months later I returned to the support unit. The DSU roadshow rolled on unabated. Every Friday night was guaranteed to produce the requisite number of customers, fighting or flat out, from the ample ranks of the local young-bloods frequenting the pubs and clubs.

We were used for the development of the first public-order-shield tactics (though not credited with the bruises and suffering), and were involved in the first deployment of the shields in public. To the best of my knowledge, one the of earliest – if not the earliest – deployments of polycarbonate riot shields was at the Lewisham riot of 1977. I was there, I had a shield, I was even on the televised evening news! I distinctly remember one fresh-faced, fair-haired youth staring down wide-eyed from the roof of the Co-op. He was witnessing scenes of carnage where smoke and burning vehicles mixed with blood, bricks and bottles. I often wondered what sort of man he grew up to be. In time I would find out.

As well as the riot venues (and there were several), we were used for murder and crime squads, untold numbers of football matches and anything else that was manpower-intensive.

Returning to work in the summer of 1980, full of memories of a family holiday on the French beaches of Aquitaine, I could not have guessed at the horrific news that awaited me. The day had started, like many others, with admin and preparation, then it was out in the carrier. I was driving. As we lurched out of the station yard, the sergeant sitting beside me commented, 'It's a terrible business the murder of –', and he related the names. The effect upon me was immediate. I could not believe what he was telling me. He related the story of the double murder of a police officer's parents in a terraced house in Plaistow. The odds were twenty-eight thousand to one that I should know that particular officer. But I did know him. More than that, he had been and still was a good friend, a colleague from my days at West Ham. His father was an avid West Ham supporter and in that and other connections I had met him and occasionally his mother.

Devout Catholics, they gave much of their time to the church and to charitable works. Apparently, they had a small win, which in their elderly parlance was referred to as a 'big' one. They had been heard to discuss it as such. In a horrific twist of fate, they were overheard by two uniquely evil men called Anderson and Jamieson.

Sometime later, Anderson and Jamieson forced their way into the couple's home. Over a period of hours, they systematically beat and tortured the elderly man and his wife, beginning by killing their pet budgie. The barbarity culminated in a pointless double murder. There was no real money: the 'win' was a few paltry pounds.

In another twist of fate, I was present when Anderson and Jamieson were finally captured, which was not, unfortunately, before they had committed a series of other very nasty crimes, including the shooting dead of an Asian shopkeeper. He had run the Shoebox, a small shop in south London. They killed him as they robbed it.

In support of armed divisional CID officers, augmented by our own inspector, who was uniformed and carrying a revolver, the support group laid siege to a small, terraced house in Cecil Road, Forest Gate, where the two had been cornered. The turn-of-the-century houses had once been quite impressive, and were laid out in short terraces or pairs. Short front gardens ended with low walls marking the boundary with the footway. At the kerbside stood the occasional car affording the armed officers scant cover. Negotiations to achieve their arrest were in progress, when a shot was fired from within.

Wisely or not, the armed police officers assaulted the front door, and forced entry. I heard the gunmen inside call out, 'Don't bring your fucking guns in here!' There is no doubt in my mind that the presence of those armed officers not only made the arrests possible without further loss of life then and there, but also saved the lives of other innocents. Many more might have fallen victim to their saga of utter brutality had Anderson and Jamieson not been contained within that house and arrested. It was the guns they feared; it was the guns that kept them bottled up.

I watched them as they were driven away, and I confess to emotions of hatred and anger as powerful as any I have ever experienced. It was of course, for me, deeply personal.

In 1981, I was accepted for the now infamous Special Patrol Group. They were vilified by every left-wing group, and accused of much that was never substantiated. Many things had been said and written about them, but what I remember was a thoroughly decent set of people, a breed apart perhaps, brothers in adversity maybe. I made lifelong friends.

My partner was a cheeky little Birmingham upstart called Alan Jones, who worked his way deeply into my affections. Later in my service, when he and I were both supervisors in vastly different roles, I in the firearms department, and he as a sergeant on ordinary street duty, he would be shot in the groin.

While he was interviewing a suspect on the Westway, Paddington, the man had produced a handgun and shot Alan at point-blank range. The bullet entered his pelvic cradle, ricocheted down his left leg, and broke his thigh. In so doing, it damaged a major artery. A quick-thinking colleague placed his hat over the entry wound and stood on it to stem the blood loss. He saved Alan's life. The irony that I carried a gun and went unscathed, while he performed ordinary duty and was shot, is not wasted on me.

During the early 80s, IRA mainland activity was prevalent, and we attended the scene of many bomb threats and incidents. I found that being so close to such life-and-death situations focused my thinking, separated the wheat from the chaff. The trivia generated by a mass of legislation, or the minefield of regulations that are the policeman's lot, can suddenly fall away in the face of enormity. For me, when the right or wrong speak loudly enough, they are the only voices I will listen to. When I can put aside the voices that whisper doubt in my ear, and listen only to the one from my heart, I am at my best. This, in the years and incidents that were to follow, would be my salvation.

The only other venues that ever inspired similar emotions were the riot scenes I experienced at Notting Hill, Lewisham and other places. I was bloodied but unbowed on several of those occasions.

The security of central London was often the group's posting. That meant that any bomb, terrorist or firearms call in the city centre was going to be our problem. A pragmatic approach to matters was adopted in those days. Only an inspector's authority was required for an authorised 'shot' – that is, an ordinary-duty police officer trained in fundamental firearms tactics and authorised to carry firearms – to take out a revolver. The SPG interpretation of such matters was hardly clinical. They would book out a big box of revolvers and, if you were authorised, you took one.

It would be stretching things to say that, if someone needed shooting, well, you just shot them, but it was not so very far from the truth. Tactics were not particularly refined, but I began to give them thought. In accordance with a rising need, I was granted a firearms course.

Whatever the later highs and lows of my firearms career, at the outset, I was top student on that course *and* I won the class sweepstake. But as the dilution of the SPG's standing, fuelled by the death of the New Zealand teacher Blair Peach, continued and internal politics ravaged its morale, I grew increasingly disillusioned and returned to district. Before I left, though, I met one other man, then an inspector, who would feature twice more in my future. His name is irrelevant, because he was notorious for his colourful use of language. So to all and sundry he is known as 'Fifty Fucks'.

The return to division had left me in a kind of hiatus. A short posting to the DSU, and it was killed off. A new direction was needed. I was back to ordinary street policing. The lucrative earning situation that had accompanied the carrier work had gone, and I was now feeling like the proverbial square peg in a round hole. The answer? The Diplomatic Protection Group (DPG), study time, overtime, change time. Here we go again.

'I see you were on the SPG,' said the inspector sitting at God's right hand. God was an ageing chief inspector, his expression the one of a chess player whose mind is on a game elsewhere. On his left sat a younger man in an inspector's uniform that I swear he had borrowed from his dad. 'This could be a little different,' he continued.

'Yes,' I said. 'But change can be a good thing, and I like the group environment.'

He coughed and lowered his chin towards his chest, looking at me through his eyebrows. His eyes flicked back and forth between me and the sheaf of paper beneath his folded elbows on the desk. 'Maybe, but this is not the cavalry rushing to the rescue here. You'll have to be polite and tactful.'

I replied, 'I have no problem with that, sir. I've worked central London many times and often overtly armed' – referring to those SPG days.

That seemed to meet with approval as the heads swung back and forth between the three. A few more questions parried with some well-rounded and politically correct answers and the interview was over. Smiling now, the hitherto silent chief inspector broke in: 'Thank you, PC Gray. That will do. And by the way, good turnout.'

I looked down at the immaculate uniform I was wearing, and then at the young woman clerk who had sat throughout by the door. I could not resist smiling at her and with a wink I said, 'Thank heaven for the clothing van.'

I was posted to the DPG in April 1985 and arrived at the now defunct A2 base just off Whitehall, the venue of the original Scotland Yard. The base then occupied the upper floors of a building that was also home to the mounted branch. The pungent smell of horse urine, mingled with the greatest supply of flies I have ever experienced, were for me its hallmark.

Shortly after arriving, my inertia at the thought of studying was overcome by a man who was to become my good friend. His name was Kevin Stimpson. He provided me with the study notes, counselled me in my low moments, and gave encouragement where required.

Another propelling force was a certain Superintendent Evershed, whom I had known for years and who could probably outswear the infamous Fifty on his best day. It all worked and some eighteen months later I was a sergeant in waiting. My one abiding sadness is that my mentor failed on the turn of one question, and we didn't go forward together.

The DPG left me with lasting memories of being close to current events and celebrated people. It was Maggie's era and, being both in and around Number Ten, I could chart international events by the comings and goings through that big black door.

I have cherished memories of good friends like Kevin. There was also Charlie, the German-speaking man with a gentle sense of humour, always there to prod me when my studying began to wane. Brendan the red-faced Irishman performed practical jokes that would drive Kevin to distraction, and Martin ('Monty') was a man with a warmth of friendship rarely found. There was the quietly courageous Bob Beaumont, who silently bore an illness that was soon to steal his young life, and Mick, or 'Jack Russell', so named for his dogged determination. These are names and faces that will remain with me always; there are so many others, but they know who they are.

A new relief sergeant (who was to become my soul mate) arrived halfway through the two years I was there. His name was Barry Mannakee. Barry had come to us after a merciless witch-hunt had evicted him from his cherished post as close-protection officer to the Prince and Princess of Wales, a position to which he attached enormous pride. He was, as far as I am concerned, one of the most loyal and genuine men I have ever been privileged to know. Outrageous he could be, but the whispering campaign waged against him was as cruel as it was unfounded. I know what he had to say, not in any public statement, but in the talk between friends while we sweated in a gym, or drove home from work.

Despite speculation in the media, and by a certain despicable American author, I know the real manner of his death. I saw his injuries and I carried his coffin. He was my very good friend. I am proud to have known him and I shed tears at his loss.

Those who speculate at his expense are both beneath contempt and, on their best day, not even a pale reflection of him on his worst. A few days after the motorcycle accident that killed him, and just before his fortieth birthday, his daughter made him a grandfather for the first time.

Another friend both then and now was Barney. You will read of him again as a story of real suffering and genuine heroism unfolds. But, for now, let me introduce him. Barney liked good food and good beer, and he harboured an ambition to be a hotelier. A merciless and accomplished cartoonist, he lampooned everyone. His liking for the good life gave him a certain silhouette and a fearsome reputation for unrivalled flatulence.

Barney also had his own gun, which was unique because the issue weapons were old .38s, booked out on a first-come-first-served basis to police officers who then went out to guard the persons and residences of various dignitaries, statesmen and politicians. It wasn't so much that Barney always opted for this particular weapon, as that no one else would have anything to do with it.

You see, Barney was in the process of relieving himself after one particularly searing curry. Having done the paperwork, he stood up hoisting his strides with him. Sadly, the recalcitrant Smith & Wesson became somehow engaged in the fixtures and fittings, disgorged itself from the security of its holster and fell with a clatter and a plop into the unflushed receptacle. Poor old Barney was very alone while he cleaned that gun, but the reward thereafter was that it remained his and his alone.

In March 1987 I transferred, on promotion to sergeant, from the DPG back to the East End of London. I was to work the East Ham and Plaistow division. The fact that I had spent ten years or so bouncing yobs around did nothing to prepare me for the vagaries of the charge room. Here I was responsible for the administration of all the prisoners. They might be handed over to me at the start of my shift by the previous sergeant, or brought at any time during my eight or more hours of responsibility. Every matter relating to welfare, visits, charging, bail, legal advice, transport or property would be my responsibility. I have always hated paperwork, and here I was sitting on a bloody mountain of it.

Perhaps my future path was mapping itself out already, however, as the first prisoner through the door on my first day as custody sergeant was a man arrested after discharging a machine gun at the premises of a rival gang.

When I had worked at West Ham I had certain reservations about Plaistow. Notwithstanding the people I met and liked there, the posting confirmed my fears. I confess I didn't like the place. Crises came and went and I survived.

The liking I had developed for weight training continued and I ran a little, that never being my strong suit. I think perhaps that the training helped to overcome the grey porridge of daily duty.

On the evening of 6 February 1988, I was taking one of those rare opportunities that provided light relief from the inevitable and ceaseless custody work. Les Drummond, the duty officer of the hour, accompanied me as we seized the chance to just cruise the streets. A chance to quietly survey the manor, perhaps to show our faces to the public in a relaxed way. But it was not to be.

In a small flat high above north Woolwich, a domestic situation echoing a thousand others was taking on a whole new dimension. A man I shall call Terry was locked, yet again, in a dispute with Carol, his common-law wife. What he wanted was to be back in the council flat from which she had him legally excluded, and to have her and his infant daughter back in his life.

Sadly, Terry's negotiating skills were somewhat lacking and, in a rising rage, he produced a small handgun, placed the barrel in the baby's mouth and threatened to kill them all. Carol believed him. Terry won the battle but not the war. While he slept in that golden afterglow, Carol slipped out of the door, forced to leave the infant child behind. North Woolwich police station was but a few hundred yards away and she arrived there dishevelled and desperate.

Within minutes the radio in our car crackled into life, and Les and I had our quiet patrol summarily ended. As duty officer and section sergeant, we knew this, fairly and squarely, was our responsibility. Within minutes we arrived.

The number of authorised 'shots' available that night was quite limited. None of the training and regulation that followed my later induction into SO19 was yet available to us, and I ventured that our outline knowledge and the use of good judgement would be the watchwords.

There were four 'shots' available: Laurie (another sergeant), two constables (Colin, a bearded Cornishman, and Dave, the tall, wise-cracking overtime hound) and me.

Laurie, who would go on to join SO19 with me, was a buoyant and capable individual, stocky and youthful in appearance, with a distracting ability to separately articulate his eyes. Disquieting as this may have been, he was a target shooter, an overall first-class shot, and a very capable police sergeant. Dave was a wry but sound individual who knew how to keep his head, and Colin was the soft-spoken and unshakable voice at my shoulder whenever required.

The four of us gathered in the charge room, while out in the interview room CID officers and women police officers fussed around Carol. I caught her profile, about twenty-two years old with long dark hair. She was heavily made up and the mascara had run from her eyelashes, but her expression was now impassive. I wondered just how much all this affected her, and how deeply. Her life had been threatened, her child was still in jeopardy and the man she had once loved might conceivably die by our guns. She answered questions and drew diagrams of the flat, while speaking in ringing East End tones, punctuated by the odd obscenity and ruinous grammar. But her voice never once faltered or quavered.

The nearest thing to a safe area were the old cells at the rear of the charge room. There we successively checked and loaded each of the old, Model 10 Smith & Wesson revolvers, in the darkened corner of the huge communal cell.

Primitive but reliable, the revolvers have their origins in the old Wild West. Limited to six rounds of .38, with a muzzle velocity of about 900 feet per second, they came a poor second to the seventeen-round capacity of the Austrian Glock, with its nine-millimetre bullets, travelling at 1,100 feet per second. Still, I never met a man who could outrun either of those.

Then, holstered up, we returned to the front office, where Les was mustering his forces. I was collecting my thoughts. I needed to, because I was the armed-section sergeant, and this was going to be my show.

Les returned from the huddle around Carol and looked at me across the ancient office desk, fixed my gaze for a moment and said in subdued monotone, 'Knowledge and reasoning, Sarge. You are on duty when . . .?'

This was how so many promotion exam questions began. I looked back at him wearing one of his rare grins from below his shock of black hair and thick eyebrows. Then I replied, 'Yeah, thanks, Boss.'

The four of us studied the local beat maps and quizzed the local officers. The block of flats involved was seven storeys high and our target premises were on the sixth. The flats were built in a splayed H section, with four flats on each level. Each one formed a leg of the H. A lift opened on to a central landing in the bridging section, and a staircase ran the full height of the block at the far end away from the police station.

This meant that we could approach from the station, which was only perhaps three hundred yards away, from the blind side of the target flat, accessing through garages and walkways. Only the final approach to the main door at ground level was on view, and then only if he hung out of the window to look.

Cordon tape now secured the area and uniformed officers took up discreet positions to create a semisterile area, screened largely by adjacent low-level accom-modation. It was after midnight now, and the time was on our side. In daylight hours it would have been a manpower-intensive, logistical nightmare. What worked against us was that every sound carried and echoed.

While the four of us slipped into the ground-floor lobby, the information room assigned an operator and console, and the link between a force-wide channel and the local system was opened up. Territorial support-group units were located and ordered to make their way, ambulances and dogs summoned and a mobile scene-control vehicle dispatched. The scene was set for a hostage drama in a grand style.

The firearms branch, then known as PT17, were notified, and marked police cars allocated to pick up the officers and 'fast-run' them into central London, to open up the base and kit up. Meanwhile, we amateurs began to clear the landings. One by one, floor by floor, covering each other and moving slowly forwards and upwards.

We had brought the lift down and jammed it at ground level to prevent surprise and cut-out noise. Clearing a staircase is always testing because the angles are constantly opening up, with potential ambush points. We rotated our roles, changing from leading to supporting to give each of us some respite. I controlled the pace and commentated our progress over the local radio link to the control below. The climb and the constant concentration were draining.

Slowly, we cleared to the sixth floor, encountering only one elderly couple, who scared us much more than we did them. But I suppose they *had* lived through a war. We sent them down to the waiting uniform officers below. Once outside the flat, we cleared the landing and contained our target premises. Slowly and very, very quietly, we began to evacuate all the flats and those on the floor above.

Time went agonisingly slowly. Two hours slipped by.

Amazingly, and to their eternal credit, no one muttered one word of complaint. One family gave over their home and telephone for use as a forward control, which would prevent noisy radio transmissions being heard by our suspect. It was now so quiet you could literally hear a pin drop.

Colin went down to the flat immediately below to get a look at the general layout and make a diagram. He would then use that and Carol's drawings to make a plan for PT17. When we thought we had done as much preparation as possible we settled down for a wait, two down on the descending staircase, me, big Dave with Laurie and Colin on the rising set.

On the floor below were two uniform officers in support. Mark, a tall, slim, younger man with the nickname 'Leary', and Bill, whose handle was 'Wickets' because of his divisional number – 111. He was a man most adept at control work and, ably supported by Mark, used the control flat as an information filter and communicated the results manually to me. At about 3 a.m., while briefings were still going on and responses being refined, and before PT17 could arrive, Dave indicated what we all heard or sensed – movement within.

Lights flickered at the foot of the door and shadows traversed in unison with his footsteps. Kitchen noises, taps, the toilet flushing – all the hopeful sounds of normality.

If I had heard the distressed cries of a child or perhaps some kind of preparation, barricades, fire or what have you, we would have been faced with a huge dilemma. None of us were even remotely trained for any form of rapid entry. We had no means to force our way in. This was a flat, remember, offering no alternative point of entry, and we had no means to create a distraction. It would have meant simply running and kicking the door in, if we could. We had no other options. If he started hurting the child we would have no choice but to try.

(It's worth mentioning at this point how much better things are now. ARVs would be there, containing, making plans, considering options and properly equipped. In those days it would take PT17 hours to get there. Armed Response Vehicles count arrival times in minutes, often in single figures – it's a brave new world. But a gun can still kill in a microsecond.)

Terry, bless him, was going to spare us from all of this. I had just dropped down one landing to inform control of his movements, when the latch was heard turning, and I was summoned rapidly back to my post.

There was utter silence now, as Terry was allowed just enough time to clear the door sufficiently to prevent his return. He was a skinny, harrowed-looking individual in jeans, a white shirt and a lightweight bomber jacket; and so strangely preoccupied with his thoughts was our man that he failed to see four armed police officers, half concealed, just a few yards away.

Dave was the first to break the silence. 'Armed police,' he shouted, and then, 'Stand still.' Like the proverbial rabbit in the headlamps, Terry stared into the beam of a spotlight. Then to my absolute horror he began to move his right hand behind him, towards the small of his back, still wide-eyed and open-mouthed. The cold reality of where this was all going swept over me.

Dave called again, his voice rising. In the still night air the drama was audible to all and sundry below and, unknown to me, senior and CID officers were already running up the stairs.

At that point in time closer would have been OK, but to enter the 'plot', the immediate area, was dangerously wrong. Dave was now desperate to get this man to comply. Just the one voice, I thought, and resisted the urge to cut in.

'Stand still. Armed police. Do what you're fucking told,' Dave screamed at him. Still Terry didn't comply. His left arm arched in a parody of some western gunfighter, and his right hand began to ease out from behind him. Four barrels were levelled at his chest as his right hand emerged holding a small revolver. 'Oh for fuck's sake,' muttered Colin.

I could contain myself no longer, and Dave and I were both shouting that same sentence at him. 'Put the gun down. *Put the gun down!*'

My finger took up the pressure on the trigger and the hammer began to rise. Close to mine, and parallel, was another .38, and I could see in my peripheral vision the initiation of hammer movement. It all seemed to be happening so slowly, and I knew that this man was about to be ripped to pieces by perhaps eight bullets. Then suddenly he buckled and half dropped to his knees, his gun hand pointing downwards. The screams to drop the gun finally registered, and he allowed it to fall, clattering to the floor.

The hammers on the .38s returned gently to their resting places. Terry had just been closer to God than any archbishop. I screamed at him, 'Get down on the floor. On your face, now. *Now!*' I kicked the gun away, all four of us still pointing the weapons at him. And then I was pitched violently forwards as a wave of CID officers hurtled blindly and foolishly into the fray. Controlled danger collapsed into semihysteria. If that had occurred split seconds earlier, the hair's breadth left on those triggers might have been breached with tragic consequences.

The little girl slept on, unknowing and unharmed. Luck had been with us and luck had been with Terry.

His luck also held at court for, although he was charged with making threats to kill, which can carry a ten-year sentence, the court saw fit to put him on probation for two years.

I was not displeased with our performance, however. Looked at through today's eyes we would perhaps get picky, but *then* it was a result. After all, it was a good day. Nobody died.

PT17 turned up in an armoured Land Rover, heavily laden with bodies and kit, and in fairness they congratulated us. I have no doubt they would have done things differently if the saga had run on, but the opportunity to abseil off the roof, use distraction devices or whatever was denied them by the long-winded clumsiness of the system. This was to be something the ARVs would put right. And how!

I found I was flavour of the month (well, perhaps the week) and then normality returned. An opportunity to step out of shift work and 'have a life' for a while, training probationary police officers, was offered and accepted. But, in truth, I was still a square peg in a round hole. Fortunately, the staff I had with me were so supportive that it made it all worthwhile. There was Mick, an immaculate Scotsman whose dress code and efficient style would endear him to me thereafter. Never mind his off-duty penchant for more jewellery than a gypsy fortune teller. Then there was big open-hearted Chris Joslin, who was always on my side, and there was Ken.

We would attend endless football matches and numerous public-order events, including the poll-tax march in south London, where I was treated to my final disorder injury. A piece of concrete the size of a cricket ball thrown from a baying crowd on Brixton Hill hit me square on the chin, leaving me cut and bleeding.

Following the infamous poll-tax riots in Trafalgar Square, there was a need for us to be debriefed, and I, my staff and several junior officers were. There was something familiar about one of the interviewing Metcalfe Enquiry officers. He was a fair-haired, fresh-faced young man. The face that had stared down from that roof in Lewisham, and would appear again at SO19 as an SFO (Specialist Firearms Officer) sergeant. This was Steve Collins.

Faces came and went as induction after induction passed through our doors. Fortunately, some were to become friends and none became enemies. It was Ken who made the first overtures concerning the much-vaunted new Armed Response Vehicles, the new arm of PT17, later to be SO19, and started a chain of events that would alter the direction of my life and career in a way no one could have predicted.

I had known Ken from a decade before, when we had both been members of the same Support Unit, albeit on different carriers. Not so much friends as just aware of each other in those days.

At Plaistow he had come to me in need of a change from the routine of relief work, and was attracted to the idea of 'puppy walking', training new recruits. I welcomed his experience and became his sergeant, to be referred to ever after by him as 'Boss'.

Ken is a tall man with a loud and smart-Alec sense of humour, which disguises the fact that he is far deeper and more complex. It took him a while to submerge his streetwise persona into the quieter more considered requirements of his new task, but he did. As with any pressured vessel, though, a safety valve would blow off every so often with something loud, obscene or outrageous. But then life needs its characters and he came through strongly on commitment and loyalty.

One particular day early in 1991, he came into the office waving a copy of a Special Police Order. It began: 'Following an exhaustive review of the deployment of armed officers within the Metropolitan Police, a number of fundamental changes are to be made to the current strategy . . .' It went on to relate how the distribution, authorisation and training of authorised firearms officers would be affected:

> The ARV will be a patrolling vehicle that contains an armoury. The vehicle will be crewed by three officers trained in the use of the weapons, the

equipment in the vehicle and the tactics suited to their role.

ARVs are to provide immediate response to incidents where firearms have been, are being, or are suspected of being used, or may be used or where there is reason to suppose that a police officer may have to face a person who is armed or otherwise so dangerous that he could not be safely detained without the use of firearms.

The SPO went on to underscore that the ARV's role was one of containment until other specialist firearm support arrived, 'unless exceptional circumstances necessitate immediate action to save life or prevent harm or injury to any person'.

Additionally they could 'provide valuable assistance with accident prevention and traffic enforcement as an adjunct to their primary role, and will be expected to do so.'

Bah, humbug!

Ken's 728 (application form) followed swiftly, and above the desks that made up the centrepiece of our office appeared an exploded diagram of a Heckler & Koch MP5 carbine. Thereafter, in his shy retiring way, he would stand on his chair bellowing, 'Uzi nine-millimetre. Stand still, you mother!' We expected nothing else.

In a quiet moment, a day or so later, Ken came into the office as I mused over the same police order. 'Go for it, Boss,' he said. 'You know you want it.'

I replied: 'They want class-one drivers, and I don't relish having to go back to driving school.' (Actually I was wrong about that.)

Ken just grunted. 'It'll be too late soon, you'll be sorry,' he said and went into his Uzi routine.

At home that night I voiced my own misgivings to Sue. A quizzical look invaded her face, and tersely she responded, 'What's the matter with you?' Her reaction surprised me. 'I never thought I'd see you turn into a desk jockey,' she went on. 'Do it. You were always happier on the carriers and in the thick of it. *Do* it.'

I couldn't really argue with that. My application received positive support, the incident at north Woolwich doing me no harm. Several weeks later I found myself sitting in a canteen at Old Street, one that is now so very familiar to me, awaiting the summons to be 'boarded' (interviewed) for the job. A clerk scuttled in and called my name.

She conducted me down one flight of stairs and through the security door into the corridor, off which then all the supervisors' offices were located. The voice of a man I would come to like a lot resonated through the open door: 'Sergeant Gray'.

Entering, I saw a ruddy-faced, red-bearded man in an inspector's uniform. Then, in a parlance that would become as familiar to me as it was to untold firearms officers, he said, 'Come in, old man.' It was about 10 a.m. and the traffic noise intruded through a small opening in a window fronting Old Street. I remember worrying that I wouldn't clearly hear the questions.

The inspector carried the nickname 'the Cat', although I have never used it. It will nevertheless preserve his anonymity. He was sitting behind a large desk, expressionless. Hovering nearby was a man I had met many times before. Tall and tending towards slim, with a long college-type haircut and an aquiline nose. *Superintendent* Fifty's path and mine were about to cross again.

'A bit fucking old for this game, aren't you?' he said, looking for a nerve.

'I can keep my end up, sir,' I replied. And then, 'There's some bigger, some smaller, some faster and some not. But I get by.' He grinned.

The Cat surprisingly broke in: 'You need an older head to slow these youngsters down.'

Result, I thought.

'What do you know about tactics? What are the first and basic things that spring to mind when dealing with an armed suspect?' Fifty barked.

I knew what he wanted. 'Identify, locate and contain.' I paused. 'And thereby neutralise.'

'Yeah?' said Fifty, who was now finding his rhythm. 'And are ya' gonna contact him or leave him there to get old?' I could feel him digging a hole for me to fall into.

The inspector added, 'Yes, what would be your alternatives? What other options do you have?'

I tried to remember snippets from the manual of guidance, desperately worried that they wanted something I hadn't perhaps counted on. I stumbled out, 'Contact. Subterfuge. Raid.'

That did it. 'Raid, *raid*?' Fifty stormed, eyebrows travelling ever higher up his brow.

'Well, the right people might exercise that option,' I countered, rowing for the shore. And before the next salvo could be launched I added, 'And until then I would improvise, adapt and overcome' – quoting the department's watchwords.

There was a moment's pause and then a smile. Although this all had a deadly serious purpose there was definitely an element of a game here. The inspector looked up from the desk while Fifty stood off to my right, moving occasionally.

'You're in the street and there's been an armed robbery,' the inspector said, 'and your suspect is out and he's brandishing a shotgun. He turns away from you and walks towards a busy supermarket full of people. What are going to do?'

'Challenge him,' I replied.

'What if he doesn't stop? What are you going to do?'

'If I can't stop him by challenging him, he's not going into that store with all those people. I couldn't lose control of him.'

'So what will you do, Sarge?' said Fifty.

'Shoot him, sir.'

'What, in the back?' Fifty sounded horrified.

'Yes,' I said. 'If I have to shoot him with good reason, back or front makes no difference.'

He subsided, almost smiling again. 'What about if it's coppers he was approaching, what difference then?'

'None,' I said. 'It would make no difference. I would stop him.'

'*What*? In the *back*?'

'Yes, if need be,' I replied.

Then they asked me about legislation, procedure and the pressure that would be placed on me as the sergeant supervising the crews. They asked if I would give ground to senior officers pushing me to bend the rules. I countered, 'I've done enough custody work to have learned how to say no to anybody.'

They looked at each other and Fifty grinned. 'Good answer.'

My warning to attend an induction course at Lippitts Hill a fortnight later followed shortly after. I was one of only six sergeants to be selected, from the eighty who'd applied. It felt good.

# 3 Prelude

THE COMRADESHIP was going to be the saving grace. If that had not existed things would have been dire indeed. Lippitts Hill was the province of those who had their feet firmly under the table. D6 had in time become D11 as the need for growth from the firearms equivalent of a village store to a shop in the high street had forced change. Then as that wind of change blew again it became PT17, as at that time it still was. Within the wire-fenced perimeter of the old anti-aircraft battery, then prisoner-of-war camp, the spirit of D11 was alive – if not too well – haunting every corridor. To confuse friend and enemy alike its title would later change to SO19. They tell me that's progress!

Laurie, my partner in the armed incident in north Woolwich, had succeeded with me. He and Steve, another sergeant, would be my travelling companions on the daily trek around the M25 to where the camp nestled in the folds of a vast forest. At the entrance, then and now, sat the huge figure of a seated man carved from a concrete block by a former POW. The figure always looked as though he were pondering his fate. How very apt.

The site had once been three fields for purely agricultural use, until the rumblings of war turned it into an air defence facility for the all important munitions factories nearby. When war broke out it defended the airfields scattered around its feet on the London borders. Within the grounds, then and today, is the 'bunker' formerly used for aircraft co-ordination, and latterly as a gym and venue for numerous mock armed searches. The old off-camp munitions sites were to provide for countless training exercises. They will be remembered (certainly by me) as an inexhaustible reserve of rabbit droppings and nettle rash. Ammunition, explosives and associated materials used as far back as the Gunpowder Plot, and most major conflicts since, had been supplied from there and a residue still remains.

Today the wealth of undergrowth and forestry is giving way to new industrial and residential developments. Perhaps the many blast walls should be left though, at least until after all the boilers have been lit.

The POW-camp make-up of 'Lippitts' is still very evident. The dormitory layout of the wooden hut residences speak for themselves. Off to the left, inside the gates, are the ranges. Far distant and higher up can be seen the more modern silhouette of the helicopter facility. The sound of a wailing siren heralds the rising beat of helicopter rotors.

Abruptly it appears from behind the glass and concrete of its residence to dominate the scene with noise, and the smell of burning kerosene. Then it powers off towards the city, on a clear day visible on the horizon beyond vast reservoirs. The owners of increasingly expensive houses, no doubt the patrons of the equally close riding stables, complain bitterly and regularly of noise and disruption, despite the camp's primacy of decades. What ever happened to squatter's rights? Nearby, the barking of police dogs leads you to where their small training facility lies nestling to the right against a high hedge of fir trees.

'Crack, crack' from the ranges invades the ears, gunfire telling all that training is in progress, while men clad in black overalls double past in groups, their belts hung with endless kit. White vans slung with ladders and ropes are filled with strange devices, all painted a depressing and nonreflective matt black. Sparsely populated flower beds sit outside the focal point of the canteen, where old friends meet, but others wearing nervous expressions sit in groups, brokering new friendships while they wait to be trained, scrutinised and judged. In a small annexe at one end, instructors wearing blue berets huddle over steaming coffee cups and endless clipboards.

As far as I was concerned Lippitts Hill was going to be the centre of the universe for the next two weeks, and to this day remains the centre for Metropolitan Police firearms training. What seemed evident from the outset was that for many we were seen as trespassers on hallowed ground.

Laurie, Steve and I parked near the gate and followed the handwritten signs, PT17 STUDENTS, to a group at one end of the canteen, gathered around the tables marked ARV COURSE, a visible statement of what was, then, resented change. We clustered around it feeling like a race apart. Oh dear!

The detractors were in truth a vociferous minority but, as we all know, such people's voices are those most clearly heard. They would continue to dog the footsteps of ARV growth for years, but they would not halt it. The three of us mingled with the group as I met people, some of whom are with us today, others now barely remembered. Those doomed to fail.

Steve's enthusiasm was infectious. He had tried and failed to get into the department before. To him success would mean euphoria; failure, despair. He saw this as a lifeline. Both he and Laurie, as gun owners, had acquired skills that were to serve them well. The intervening ten years of neglect since my basic course with the SPG were going to turn this into hard work for me.

Other faces present on that day were 'Bobby Back Doors', Matt and Demps, dubbed 'Badger' for his hair colour. First lesson of the first day was 'ARV authority levels'. A stick to beat us with. A muzzle lest we bite.

The rest of the first day consisted of footage of the terrible carnage caused by Michael Ryan during his orgy of violence in Hungerford, an incident we all perceived as pivotal to the creation of armed response, and the topic of conversation over lunch. Some input on equipment and weapons was followed by a trip to the range, where the cracks began to show. I went home chastened that night. This, as they say, was going to be a whole new can of worms.

The next day dawned bright, and the prospects of the coming hours were discussed. This was to be an introduction to our 'primary weapon'. The Gurkha has his knife, the archer his bow, the fusilier his rifle. The ARV man has his MP5. For me it was to become a working relationship: good to have the gun around but we never really got on.

The three days that followed were purgatory. Magazine in . . . make ready . . . selector lever to fire . . . stoppage . . . selector lever to safe. I had that one all the time. What's this bloody stoppage lark? Revolvers don't 'stop'.

High port, kneeling, prone. Selector to safe between positions. Click . . . What, no bang? The rounds not fed, the working parts have not gone forwards . . . Stoppage . . . selector lever to safe . . . mag out . . . no . . . action to the rear. Cock, lock and look. Turn it over, shake out the misfed round, it's stuck. Now, mag out . . . clear it . . . mag in . . . strike the action forwards. The shout 'Back in!' Then bang . . . bang . . . click . . . Fuck it . . . *'Stoppage.'*

Actually, it's a damn good weapon. Derived from a machine gun. The Metropolitan Police version as carried by ARV crews fires single shots of nine-millimetre, soft point ammunition in common with the Glock self-loading pistol. These rounds are designed to spend all their energy within the selected target, creating maximum knock-down but, more importantly, to avoid overpenetration. Put simply, they're designed not to pass through and strike a second person.

Its accuracy is like a surgeon's knife compared with the mallet that a handgun can be. Within the confines of a suburban environment, that accuracy could actually save innocent lives, placing the rounds precisely where they were intended.

As I said, though, the MP5 and I just never really got on. Another two days of stoppage drills left my hands bleeding and my confidence at an all-time low. Thursday was classification, a multiskill, multipositional shoot under pressure. Why? Because the chief instructor would be there.

Mike Waldren had moved on well in the promotion stakes, his failure as a motorcyclist at Hendon leaving not the slightest stain on his copybook. He had mainstreamed in the firearms field, and was now a chief inspector. The presence of one of my own contemporaries at my shoulder served to intensify my fear of failure as the first-range orders echoed across our lines.

'This is a ten-round shoot loading with magazines of six and four,' Dave, the instructor, barked. I could feel the eyes behind me, just over my shoulder. Dave went on, 'A pair of shots to be fired, sense of direction on each exposure of the turning target. There will be one extra exposure for the reload.' He paused, then, 'Muffs and glasses . . . and, with a magazine of six rounds . . . load.'

I jammed the long magazine into the aperture under the gun, praying to myself, 'Don't jam, you bastard.' On the instruction 'Make ready', I struck the lever to drive the action forwards with the ball of my now very sore left thumb. Never mind the pain, just work. It fed. Dave went on, 'The first exposure is a trial exposure, do not shoot.' Clank. The same nasty paper bastard with a carbine that I would meet many thousands of times turned to face me, and then turned away again with another clank. 'Stand by . . . Stand by.' Then the instruction 'Watch your front.'

I looked down at the MP5 'Don't you dare, you arse. No stoppages.' The paper bastard turned to face me . . . clank.

I threw the carbine up into my shoulder, knocking off the selector lever as it rose. Bang, bang . . . Here we go!

The guardian angel of old police sergeants looked out for me. Fifty rounds with eyes burning into my back. Several reloads later, fired from multiple firing positions, and I had prevailed. Then the revolver, and it was over. I had qualified on both weapons.

Tomorrow, though, would bring new challenges: rifles, rendezvous points, briefings and concealment. Then there would be a full exercise down on the old munitions site, known by its initials as PERME (Propellant, Explosive and Rocket Material Establishment). I was to be subjected then to a new test of endurance – well, actually, not quite so new. 'Fifty' was going to be there.

Friday began with the rifle demo, which was an eye-opener, as down the full length of the fifty-metre range the sniper did exactly that to the 'bastard with a carbine', assuring us that the same was possible over three times that distance.

It made us aware that the only possibility, when faced with a high-velocity rifle, was either to duck or try not to bleed on the carpet. Then it was 'First steps at the scene of an incident' and rendezvous points. That's something that takes years of street experience – you never stop learning. Lunch passed with most of us in a better frame of mind than of late.

In two battered old Chryslers loaded down with kit, weapons and bodies – standing in for real ARVs – we limped off towards PERME. At that time our contingent of the Met's vaunted Armed Response – dressed as we were in odd tracksuits and overalls, carrying a mixture of old kit in beat-up and aged cars – looked considerably more like New Age travellers in migration!

The sergeant's role was a murky compromise. We were not to become fully fledged tactical advisers for a long time to come, or to receive training beyond that of our own men. Senior officers seemed to be at odds in these matters and, in this absence of clarity, the sergeants suffered.

'You're just one of the troops, like everyone else.' That huge anomaly rang in my ears so many times, as instructors strove to make this assembly of men a functioning unit. If you stood back and presided over failure, you showed a lack of leadership. You could not dominate the scene, and if you tried to find the middle ground you were indecisive.

The exercise that had been planned was one of containment, followed by movement across country after some alleged terrorists, these roles played by instructors who will never get their equity cards. Sergeant or not, in this scenario I was controlling my group in the usual step-by-step fashion for which I am now famous. Cover and movement, I thought. I made measured progress while the fourth sergeant on the course, a south London man, went off hare and hounds with another group.

By the time we had fought our way through the undergrowth a mock massacre was in progress while he took his troops up under the guns of the 'terrorists'. Blanks were being fired in all directions while student ARV crews were being captured, or slaughtered wholesale. The voice of Dave, the instructor, came over the radio in a poor imitation of an Irish voice. He told me he had taken a sergeant hostage and was about to shoot him. The sergeant was Laurie.

The whole situation was lost irretrievably. It was then that a tall figure stepped out from behind a brick-built office. 'You're the fucking sergeant, you sort it out.'

Hello, Fifty!

I shrugged. 'Can I have a unit at point six on the red,' I began, using military-derived codes to identify and place my men. Down the radio the instructor's 'Irish' accent could again be heard, 'Oim gern ta kill this fookin' serjunt in wern manit.' Fifty had that grin on his face again. But it was almost the weekend. Nobody was going to upset me now.


I tried to put it all out of my mind for those two days, but it was not easy. The time flew, and before I knew it Laurie's car was outside the house with Steve in the passenger seat. We were off again. The tone of the conversation was not optimistic.

Monday morning involved an input concerning fire fights, provoking much thought and discussion, and led on to vehicle tactics later. This could be condensed into 'They always shoot at the car, so piss off quick' – without the car, that is. In fact, it went on to cover stopping and deploying from the cars, while covering each other's movements, and engaging hostile targets.

The afternoon covered weapon retention. The gentle art of not giving your gun to the opposition. The instructor was a former Special Forces man, fit as a fiddle and a damn nice bloke. He was, nevertheless, to bring me to the point of retaliation. I became his stooge in the demonstration of how to retain your weapon when attacked from the rear.

I duly tackled him, reaching under his right arm to seize his carbine. He pivoted the weapon backwards, forcing the butt downwards while my hand remained trapped. The result was enormous leverage being applied to the bones of my right forearm. The pain was indescribable. Slowly the use returned, but, as the day wore on, I suspect we both knew what response any more such agony would produce. My pain threshold along with my restraint would accept no more.

The week continued with more exercises and input. Negotiating, air support, scene assessment and first aid all featured. Somewhere along the line there was a fitness test.

Years later, when a great stock of old records had been computerised, and the old files made available to us, I saw the results. 'A fit man', the instructor had felt moved to add as an extra comment. As the oldest man there I was pleased. The signature belonged to the man who had caused me so much pain.

As the week drew to a close the feeling grew that we were about as welcome as vagrants at a WI meeting. When the three of us left my home on that final Friday morning the mood was subdued. We took a cross-country route to somehow slow the pace and stopped by a parade of shops at Steve's request. He returned holding a brown paper bag, refusing to disclose its contents.

The day dragged by with more search techniques. We covered the practices to be implemented were there a shooting, but the shadow cast by the prospect of the pass-or-fail verdicts to be given to each of us at the end of the day prevailed.

Mid-afternoon saw the whole course grouped together in the old gymnasium, presided over by Dave the instructor, while we awaited our fate. Down a corridor, just a few yards away, the chief instructor held court with his subordinates.

Steve broke the silence. 'Just in case any of you lot ever feel like being nice to anyone, I bought you this.' He threw Dave the brown paper bag. There followed a rustling of paper, as from within it the instructor pulled a lemon. Steve added, 'You can suck on that.' Dave was for the first time speechless. Behind me someone snorted as they fought to suppress laughter. A light-hearted moment temporarily lifted the gloom.

Names began to be called as a new hush descended. The south London sergeant went first. His hangdog expression spoke volumes as he scuttled away. Then a big man called Carl who I liked and approved of suffered the same fate. Confidence, if there had been much, was fading.

Slowly, one by one the names were called. The successes to the canteen, the failures to the gate. Steve's turn came. As his name was called he went ashen. It meant so very much to him after years of trying. Laurie and I sat in despondent silence as Steve emerged.

He walked down the corridor in silence while we looked sadly at each other. Then, from somewhere further down the building, his jubilant voice rang out: 'Yes . . . yes . . . *yes*!' One satisfied customer.

Laurie went next as we wished each other luck. He emerged from the office saying nothing, and turned towards the darkened corridor. I was none the wiser. Now they had all gone, successes and failures both. There was just Dave, the instructor, sitting alone in the gym, turning the brown paper bag and its contents over and over in his hands, and there was me. I sucked in a lungful of air. 'That's my lot, then,' I said.

For the first time he smiled. 'You'll be all right.'

Big Glynn, an instructor who had been a source of encouragement to us all, appeared framed in the doorway, his presence filling it. A voice rang out from the office behind him. 'Come in, Sergeant Gray.' Stepping aside, he winked.

The chief inspector and two instructors sat nearby. As I entered the room Mike Waldren looked up from a sheaf of paper. 'Sergeant Gray,' he said quizzically, and after a momentary pause he smiled. 'You've passed.'

Game on.

## Don't Take Your Coat Off – You're Not Staying!

Monday, 24 June, marked the final and most exciting chapter of my police career. It was to rival anything that had gone before as the most colourful. Certainly it would prove to be the most emotive.

That strange feeling of familiarity was strong in me as I walked through streets where my father, grandfather and our forebears had trodden. I had parked my car in a side road maybe a mile away, using the distance to make time for reflection and calm. I turned into Old Street under the span of the disused railway bridge, long since silent from the rumble of steam locomotives and rolling stock. Then I walked towards the Victorian granite façade of the old police station that was now the firearms branch headquarters, attached to what was then still a functioning magistrates' court.

The steps that led to the large wooden doors were hidden beneath a sea of bags and feet, as seventy-five men, two women and five sergeants arrived in groups of varying sizes. All were trying to gain access through the 'airlock', electrically controlled double doors that permitted only limited entry. The ebb and flow of the crowd was an indication of what was about to become increasingly obvious. The firearms branch was about to be dragged into the nineties.

The place buzzed with activity as men with ruck-sacks and kitbags tried to find a corner to call their own. Not enough chairs, lockers, toilets. Not enough any-thing. It was like the corner shop being taken over by Tesco. Out in the yard a small fleet of Rover 827s obtained at the expense of some traffic division, specially converted for our use, fitted now with gun safes and extra radios, stood waiting.

The base room, small enough to be called quaint, was overrun with activity as disorder rose out of chaos. Just outside, an SFO team lounged glowering at the in-truders who were invading their insular world.

The days of lock up and go home were about to end. In just one week's time, on 1 July, they would be 'open all hours'. They didn't like it, and it showed.

A doughty old senior sergeant, marginally older than I was, handed out locker keys, while individual instruc-tors looked for the new sergeants to muster the reliefs around. My instructor was a well-known, round-faced individual called Rick, who called together the faces that were to become my relief. As the mixed group took its first steps towards bonding, I introduced myself. Ex-soldiers. Ex-cadets. Older men, younger men large and small. And one of the two women. 'Find your locker, dump your kit and we'll meet outside.'

First faltering steps. 'Shall I get some teas, Sarge?' Sam cut in. 'Yes, OK, mate. I'll pay.' It was expected. I knew I was going to like Sam. His fair hair and military moustache were a façade behind which there was almost an innocence.

The good, the bad and the ugly were all there. There was no doubt that that the new unit had drawn some of the strongest-willed, most motivated characters to be involved in what was then an unknown quantity.

Apart from Sam there among them was big Darren. His bearing marked him out. There was Sandy, our

woman officer. Demps (a.k.a. the Badger) was a diminu-
tive Action Man figure with a scalp of grey hair that was
occasionally as entertainingly short as his fuse. Then
there was Simon, or 'Dutch', so named for his family
origins, and posh Bob with his gentle eloquence, Frank
the joker, with his heavy northern accent. Their characters would all slowly emerge.

The net had, however, been cast wide in the hurried
drive to start up the unit, and not everyone who came
through that door was to remain welcome. There were
those who were skilful at hiding their real characters.
There were those who were skilful at hiding their real
intentions. Sadly, before those big wooden doors had
closed that morning, a few of those people had slipped in.

You can shout 'Team' because that's what you care
about. Maybe, though, you just want to get your voice
heard and your face seen. The greatest number were
there for all the right reasons. Those that were not, time
would expose and fate would deal with. The empire
builder would be humbled, and the liar disgraced.

Outside the base within the hour, the big old green
buses formed up, and we filed on board, bound for
Hendon. There, in a huge hall, we listened while voice
after official voice echoed words of support, tempered
with caution.

One senior officer after another marked the occasion
with a speech laced with constraint. The overriding
impression was that we were just passing through. The
speculation was that the Armed Response Vehicles
would quite soon be devolved, subdivided about the
Met. That would mean localised parochial control. It
would also mean the loss of opportunity to become a
cohesive unit, with all the advantages of mutual support
and standardised practices. All that would be steam-
rollered by cost, demagogue senior officers and,
inevitably, rivalry.

There were many of the old school who would be glad if this assault on the previously closeted Firearms Branch were to slip silently away, and leave them alone to posture and retell old stories. Though, for a long time, that threat remained, to this day it has not become reality.

By mid-afternoon we had been fed and watered. We returned to Old Street aboard the creaking buses, spending the remaining time throwing kit into lockers and assessing our new colleagues. They were indeed a mixed bag.

Tuesday heralded a mass migration to a military range on the south side of the Thames Estuary, where there was a large enough facility to reclassify this vast number of people on both handguns and carbines. A task not possible on our own domestic ranges. We had been told to be wet-weather-equipped and, regardless of the time of year, that proved to be good advice.

Constantly subject to conditions rolling in off the sea, as shipping slid by in the distance, it could be described as inhospitable. A block-built facility provided the only respite available and was controlled by an individual who ruled all that he surveyed like a dictator, and had the power of the keys.

Wave after wave of us went forward to shoot until the handgun classification was complete. The flasks of coffee and the sandwiches provided a welcome reminder of greater comfort awaiting us elsewhere.

Wednesday was reserved for classifying on the carbines, by which time I was beginning to identify personalities. Standing, kneeling and lying, we fired endless rounds until the sky opened, washing the patches off the targets, making scoring impossible, and caking us in mud.

As the day turned to farce, dripping wet, we cleaned the guns in the 'block house' and mounted the coaches for home.

For me, names were becoming attached to faces. Darren began to emerge as a formidable adversary for any man. Tall and powerfully built, was this ex-guardsman. Dutch was notable for his quiet, measured ways. I knew at once that I could trust him. Posh Bob's suave and gentle ways charmed us, and everyone else, completely. Norman, built like a square-rigged sailing ship, was another ex-soldier. Immensely strong, he engendered the same measure of trust as Dutch. I always thought that, in a game of last man standing, it would be him. Then there was Sandy, whose gentle ways belied her great strength of character.

Opinions were being formed. I would have to juggle all of these against a background of supervisory mistrust and a murky set of operating rules. And I would be alone. It was not going to be easy. We would not be allowed to deploy without consulting an SFO inspector, and would then require the authority of a commander to do so. A chief inspector could assume that responsibility in an emergency, if he was willing, and if we could reach him! The inspectors were not required then to work nights. If we were confronted by an immediate situation in the middle of the night, it meant both of those ranks would be asleep in their beds.

The waiting involved drove some to distraction, almost rebellion, giving the barrack-room lawyers among them endless ammunition. Overriding the system brought immediate sanction. All of this, though, was still to come, and thankfully, but slowly, as the ARVs matured, things got better.

Thursday was to be the team-building physical day at Lippitts. Exercises involving ingenuity and endurance were the tone of things. Typical was the obstacle course situated at the far northern end beyond the helicopter pad. This was to be negotiated without allowing a huge wooden log to touch the ground while it was passed over streams, under obstacles, and over a rope bridge. This could be achieved only with application of mind and muscle, and the previous similar experiences of those ex-military men. Other tests of a like nature would follow – and then the run. I was dreading the run.

The loop runs perhaps for three miles starting and ending at the gate. It climbs and falls several times and culminates in a long torturous climb back up a merciless hill to the camp. I tried to measure my pace so that I would last, and the tactic worked. As we climbed the last hill I had enough wind to run ahead, then drop back to encourage those really suffering. Above others was a voice, gruff and assertive, seeking centre stage. It was calling 'Team! Team!' One of those that slipped in the door.

Friday was reserved for a full dress rehearsal for the photographers. We were in clean and pressed uniforms, as, three lines deep and three tiers high, we smiled while the camera flashed repeatedly. Flanking us were two of the cars that would carry these officers into the history of 'the Met'.

## The First Foray

At about 6 a.m. on 1 July 1991, there was a furore of activity about the Old Street building as preparation for the first ARV patrol was completed. The old Smith & Wesson .38 revolvers were booked out individually on the strict understanding that they would not so much as be loaded, let alone worn. Similarly, belts and holsters were to be kept in the ballistic bags in the rear of the cars. There was to be nothing to indicate these were weapon-carrying vehicles. In fact so anonymous were we that the information room at Scotland Yard did not recognise our call signs when the cars answered the first armed calls.

The weapons were to be kept in their unloaded state in safes separating the carbines from the handguns. They were to be locked at all times, and then opened only on the authority of some remote and vastly senior officer, when strict criteria had been met. The keys were to be attached to the same bunch as those for the car's ignition, the intention being to cause the crews to stop the car, and take more time before deploying effectively. This procedure was also intended to delay their response, giving supervisors 'control' over their deployment – something of a conflict of interest, you might think, when you consider the reasons for the whole concept.

The system was unworkable and led to much 'rule bending'. The locks on the safes would jam with repeated use, either refusing to lock or, worse, refusing to open, and they would be left unlocked. The design of the safes, although refined many times, proved in-adequate, leading to the loss of magazines and ammu-nition beneath the seats, such things often occurring in the most heated of circumstances.

There were not enough radios for crews to communi-cate effectively at the scene of any incident. There was no separate vehicle for me as a supervisor. I and the other sergeants were forced to go as fourth man in already overcrowded and overloaded cars.

Untrusted, untested and overscrutinised, we went forth to break new ground. I knew it was inevitable that the Met would have great difficulty accommodating this radical departure. I was aware that winning the ground would take time and be very painful. Such is birth, but new babies still arrive, don't they?

There were many among our ranks whose patience was short and would cause me concern as they strained at the leash. Only time would bring change. On Wednesday, 3 July, my relief went out on their initial late turn, as I waited with my heart in my mouth for the first call.

Within a short time it came. I found myself at what was then City Road Police Station, where, after consulting distant seniors, we ground slowly into action. The frustration showed; the local inspector responded by giving me his entire confidence, saying, 'Well, you're the firearms expert.' I made plenty of mistakes, but that was inevitable.

The ARVs were up and running. Within days pivotal events would occur, the first policy changes begin. Before I was done I would carry the first responsibility for the initial firearms response for the whole of London. Suspects and my men would be shot at differing incidents. Tragedy and triumph awaited, but for now we were just the 'new kids on the block' . . .

# **4** New Kids on the Block

THE TWO MEN PAUSED outside the post office while their gaze swept up and down High Holborn. One carried a large parcel wrapped in brown paper. No one took any notice. Why should they? After all, it was the logical place for them to be with an article like that. No one had taken any notice when they had 'walked the plot' a few times before, and driven around it several times before that.

They weren't taking any chances. If there had been the slightest hint of a police car, a uniform or anything to threaten their perceived safety, they would have cancelled in a moment. But no, they were safe. Or so it seemed.

It was such a big parcel, though. One that would force the cashier to open the security gate to take it through. Pointless making all that fuss – after all, it was a great big box and all it contained was one solitary gun.

The woman stood impatiently in the slowly shrinking queue. Just some registered mail to send and then she was off for the rest of the day. An evening meal then the theatre beckoned. She was dressed in a new red suit, which she thought really looked good on her. 'Makes you look slimmer,' someone had said. That had elevated it to the status of prized possession.

About to go into the post office were two men who would have no respect for such pride, a conflict of interest that was to prove enlivening.

* * *

Three weeks had passed, and the presence of these armed cars on the streets of London had penetrated the consciousness of the copy-hungry media, generating increasing amounts of attention. Several articles appeared in various publications and numerous requests began to be made that would open up the previously closed doors as never before.

The attention was welcomed and reviled in equal amounts dependent on who you spoke to last, but the 'open-door' policy being adopted by the Establishment at that time encouraged co-operation between the department and the press.

Tuesday, 23 July, was a late turn for the crew of Trojan 503. They were being prevailed upon to co-operate in a fashion that took things one stage further, and might today be considered wholly unacceptable. The editor of London Weekend Television's *Crime Monthly* and a cameraman were in the building on 'attachment', and the powers that be, anxious to win public approbation, had decreed that they would be allowed free access, including riding in an operational Armed Response Vehicle.

The crew were less than impressed with that prospect. Their rear-seat man, a dark-haired officer, who revelled in the nickname 'Chuck', articulated their protests to Bob, the easy-going sergeant. But to no avail. The voices of authority had spoken and their will would be done.

With the crew's protests still ringing in the sergeant's ears the car swung out of the yard. The driver was Andy, a strongly built man; Sarah, a young Scots woman and the second of those joining on day one, was the operator. Chuck, to his annoyance, was crammed in the back with the cameraman and editor, together with all the equipment. Comfort would have to be a secondary consideration.

The idea was that the car would go to Kensington to give a short presentation to local officers, to broaden the barely understood perception of the new ARVs to a group of ordinary beat officers. The same input then filmed could be used to advertise the unit's presence publicly through LWT.

They would get footage all right, but far in advance of the mundane presentation they were anticipating.

The atmosphere in the car as it swung out through the big steel gates into Hoxton Street was nevertheless hospitable. While the crew were basically disapproving, there was no point in rudeness. They accepted the situation grudgingly and got on with the job.

Chuck was an old hand at negotiating his way around central London, the product of his earlier service.

The route they agreed was to have taken them through Oxford Street to Marble Arch and then on to Kensington, but somehow it got lost in the translation.

'Left here,' Chuck called from the back seat, as Andy sailed past the appointed junction.

'Bit of a late call that,' Andy countered, restrained from a more colourful response by Sarah's presence at his elbow and the strangers in the back seat. 'How about this one?' He proceeded to make a turn that was going to take them where Chuck least wanted to go.

'Nice one, Andy. You dozy git.'

Andy bit his lip, replying only with 'Thank you.'

'Andy, you made a right cock-up of this!' The Rover swung left into High Holborn. Andy frowned.

'Look, I'll just get down to the Aldwych, round the one-way and head into town, OK?'

Chuck grunted his approval while Sarah quietly smiled to herself. In the back the editor and his cameraman perspired in the summer warmth. Their equipment weighed increasingly heavy and the wish to escape the heat of the car grew by the moment. Crushed against the door, Chuck cursed his sergeant.

The two men took a final look around. Nothing. Now they were going to 'take this one down'. The first, noticeably darker skinned than the second, slipped in through the door of the post office.

The people waiting to be served were typical of the queuing British, polite and orderly, so no one was going to argue with the two men barging their way to the front. The first hoisted the large parcel on to the counter adjacent to the scales while the second turned away and leaned on the writing counter, complete with chained pens and sponge pads. Now the people at the counter had their backs to him. It was as he fingered the large knife under his coat that the woman in her new red suit joined the end of the queue.

Through the glass and bars of the counter the clerk could see the man smiling at him. 'It's a heavy package, brother,' the first robber said. 'This going to cost me?' He pushed the package towards the security gate. The second robber slid his hand over the grip on the knife. The woman in the red suit barely had entered the foyer when she saw him, saw the knife, and moved closer to the door.

Trojan 503 was rolling towards the junction with Drury Lane as the lights changed to red. The traffic had backed up, and the prospect of waiting in the heat of the queue appalled them. In the back the TV crew cooked. Not very far away, someone else was becoming averse to remaining in a queue.

As the barred security gate opened, the robber galvanised himself to action. His hand ripped into the parcel, and came out holding the gun. The second man pulled the long knife from under his coat, and the gunman followed the parcel, vaulting through the security gate.

'Stay away. I take what I want. Don't touch no alarm.' He slid his hands along the counter, scooping anything of value into a green canvas bag. Then he plucked the cash from the drawers. The second man waved the knife in the air so that all could see it, then pointed it at the customers. 'Get down on the floor. On your faces. Now.'

Not in her new red suit. No way. Seizing her opportunity, she ran into the street.

The traffic had moved. The ARV was close to the lights when they changed again to red. 'Bollocks!' Andy spat the word out under his breath. Despite the heat, Sarah had her window up in an attempt to hear the radios against the traffic noise. They were all shaken from their discomfort by the young woman in a red suit, suddenly tapping at that window.

'Officers, there's an armed robbery going on. There are two black guys in the post office.' The girl indicated the post office just behind them. 'They're robbing the post office now. One's got a gun and the other one's got a knife. The one with the gun's behind the counter. The one with the knife's holding everyone on the floor. He told everyone to lie on the floor but I ran out because I had my best suit on.'

Andy swung the car into the kerb as Chuck jumped out of the back seat and Sarah began to call frantically for armed support. They could see that no one was going in or out of the post office, but a small crowd had formed at the door. The implications were both grave and obvious. The film crew had been suddenly elevated to where they must at once have both longed and yet dreaded to be: on scene when it happens. Sadly, it was their presence that denied access to the carbines behind the back seats.

A moment to push home a magazine and slap the action forwards in a lethally accurate carbine was replaced by the cumbersome need to place six separate rounds in a much less accurate revolver. The revolvers were in a small safe on the transmission tunnel just behind the front seats. While Andy went forwards, unarmed, to check the scene as per his training, Chuck tucked himself in behind the car and loaded the handgun from a plastic box, round by round. He did it by habit, without looking down, watching Andy's progress towards the post office. Later, at the Old Bailey, he would have to repeat the act.

From the window of the post office Andy signalled back, his right hand making a facsimile of a gun: the confirmation of a firearm seen. At the car Chuck was weighing his options when they were swept aside as the two robbers ran headlong from the door. They ran in a curve around the ARV and the two police officers gave chase. Sarah, in the operator's seat, was forced to remain on the radios, unable to leave the two carbines in the car. At the same instant the TV crew seized their opportunity and began to follow Andy and Chuck. For the first time in anger, the ARV's call went up. 'Stop. Armed police.'

Near the junction with Drury Lane, the robbers turned into West Central Street with Chuck and Andy in close pursuit. Clumsily, a good distance behind, the laden camera crew were following.

The man in front had been the one behind the counter. As he ran he held the green canvas bag with the proceeds of the robbery in it, and the gun. Behind him ran the man with the knife.

As they turned the corner a getaway car waited with the engine running, a third man at the wheel, his face a mask of shock as everything he didn't want to see came towards him. Two men who could now incriminate him chased by police officers in uniform, one with a gun. Just to make it worse there was a cameraman to record it all.

Something about getting out of bed on the wrong side!

The gloves the robbers were wearing were their final undoing. The moment their mortified cohort gave them was not enough as they fumbled at the door handles with clumsy gloved hands. Honour among thieves there was not as the driver abandoned them to their fate, shrieking tyres announcing his exit.

The pause for the car was enough. Chuck and Andy were on them. Shouts of 'Armed police' followed, as the robber with the gun surrendered to the revolver held almost against his neck. Nowhere to go.

'Against the wall. Get against the wall, now.'

The robber leaned against the wall assuming the 'position' as he was subjected to the same fear and humiliation that moments before he had been happy to impose on other, totally innocent, people. Chuck stood off, covering with the gun, as Andy pinned the knifeman against a wall, an act of singular courage in itself.

By now the air was alive with the sound of klaxons as all manner of help began to arrive. Armed officers from the Diplomatic Protection Group were on the scene and, of all things, a vehicle clamping unit helped to handcuff the robbers.

All the time the camera rolled. The Armed Response Vehicles had truly arrived in the public eye.

In the charge room at Holborn police station, about £11,000 was recovered from the bag, together with the gun. An armed operation on another post office nearby came up empty, giving rise to the suspicion that an operation on this team had 'got it wrong'. Due to Andy's keen eye the getaway car was stopped close by and the driver arrested.

At the Old Bailey the gunman, Richard Williams, pleaded guilty to the offence, asking for sixteen other offences to be taken into consideration. His lifestyle, which involved expensive cars, designer suits and society girls, had been supported by a string of successful robberies, some netting as much as £60,000, £80,000 and £120,000 over a period of two years. He was sentenced to thirteen and a half years' imprisonment.

For the knife-wielding man, Renée Thomas, this was a first for this type of offence. He was sentenced to seven years. The getaway driver, a man grossly misnamed Able, got three years.

In follow-up operations on a variety of premises, further quantities of cash and firearms were recovered. Williams later escaped from police custody by faking a dental emergency and escaping through a toilet window to the embarrassment of his police guard.

During a subsequent armed operation he was found by one of the department's most formidable firearms officers, cowering in an expensive cabriolet with yet another society blonde. He was, I understand, quite submissive. To the best of my knowledge he remains in prison as I write this. I would be interested, though, to know the type of visitor he gets nowadays. The incident elevated the ARVs into the public arena, if only for a while, and precipitated a change: the guns remained in the safes, but at least now they were loaded. The first of many small changes that slowly empowered the ARVs.

As I had predicted, change would come as reality slapped the 'Colonel Blimps' of the force coldly in the face. Of course it would not change quickly enough for some. Two steps forwards, one step back *is* frustrating, but at least it was in the right direction. Soon enough other events would exert their influence. Big Darren and I would both be involved.

# 5 The Sins of the Father

IRULENT ANGER FLOWED through his body, carried by his blood to every part of his being. His heart-beat, violent in his chest, pounded through the pulsing veins at his temples as the same thoughts returned again and again. He could see her in his mind, her warm thighs clasped about another, younger, man.

His home, his children touched by another hand. The bed that had been his only refuge, where for a while at least her softness took them far away from the violence, the anger that had been his whole life. In the darkness as he had lain in that cell, his only home for so long, he had seen them a thousand times, endured a thousand agonies as in his head she had moaned in ecstasy.

A flash of colour invaded his transfixed eyes, a shadow as he passed below the glazed structure of a motorway bridge. His thoughts returned to the present. 'Shit!' He had meant to tuck in beside an artic, to screen the stolen car he was driving from eyes that would know, pursue him, bring the whirlwind of a car chase as every police car around descended upon him. They loved a chase, the Old Bill, and there they were now on the exit ramp of the services he had just passed beneath.

As he stared back through the mirror he could see the Vauxhall all dressed up in its ridiculous motorway colours. Then the headlights of the huge lorry flashed repeatedly in his mirror as he weaved dangerously close into its shadow, the bullish horn blasting through the car, drowning out the rap music from the stereo. In the mirror the radiator loomed large, the word VOLVO clear in the reflection. He stamped on the accelerator.

A holdall on the seat beside him fell open, a box of shotgun cartridges scattering on the floor, the metalled grey of the shotgun barrels illuminated with each flash of the motorway lights. In the nearside mirror, far behind, the shape of the patrol car remained unmoved.

He grinned to himself. Wankers. Uniforms. He hated uniforms. Pulling the bag closed over the gun as the yellow lights flashed by in the low early light, he returned to his anger. The sign overhead spelled out a fatal destination, white letters, white arrows stark against the blue background: M1. LONDON 60 MILES

'Shooters Hill,' said Matt firmly.

'Nah. Croydon,' said Barney. 'I'm the only qualified chef around here. Best canteen's Croydon.'

'Night-duty curries, garlic bread, yes, Croydon. But breakfast, Shooters Hill,' cut in Skid. He had the casting vote they would go to Shooters. They were the crew of Trojan 504, the ARV responsible for a large quarter of south London. Skid (brakes are for wimps), tall and fair-haired, was driving; Matt, a pragmatic, logical man, obsessed with fitness, was in the front seat. In the back was Barney. You already know Barney.

As the car pitched down the ramp leading into the car park at Shooters, Barney was already showing his usual early-turn symptoms.

'Hurry up and park, will you? I'm busting for a dump,' he grumbled shifting uncomfortably about the rear of the car.

'Best you let him out, Skid,' Matt warned. 'If he farts in here the car will be uninhabitable for a week.'

Barney's ample frame disappeared towards the building as he called, poker-faced, over his shoulder. 'The best things in life are free.' As always, his digestive tract from end to end played a principal role in the day's events.

Matt settled in at the table behind a newspaper. Skid followed from the counter cursing under his breath as the tea and coffee escaped over the rim of the cups, little rivers running races to the edge of the tray. Barney burst in beaming, visibly more at ease.

'I'll have the full cooked breakfast if you please,' he said, grinning at the short West Indian woman whose famed egg-and-bacon specials would draw the crews here most early turns.

'That will be three specials, then.' She turned, smiling, towards the kitchen. A mutual affection existed between her and the ARV crews of 'C' relief.

Always a little banter, always their patronage. For her it was a matter of professional pride. This morning, though, the cosy arrangement would be interrupted, the meals returned. Not through complaint, but something more sinister.

As it grew light, the last, long, curving approach of the M1 cut a swathe through the suburban housing as he approached the exit at the North Circular Road. As he passed through the confused tangle of roads and roundabouts, under a railway bridge, signs told him this was Cricklewood. A roadside coffee stall beckoned, as suddenly he remembered how long it had been since he had eaten. He tucked the stolen car in behind the open-fronted caravan that steamed with the promise of food and drink.

He approached the counter. 'Couple of bacon rolls and a mug of tea, please, mate.' He reached into his pocket for the paper money crushed against his thigh.

Opening his hand he also saw a scrap of paper, an address. As he paid for the food he flattened the grubby piece of paper on the counter for the apron-clad man to see.

'Do you know where this place is, mate?' He spoke with a strong Birmingham accent.

'You come a long way, son. But it's a distance yet. Right across London. Best wait till the traffic dies down.'

He had been waiting for years, waiting since the judge handed down a sentence of eight years for the armed robbery that had gone so badly wrong. Waiting for parole while her visits had grown less and less frequent, waiting while the demons of doubt came at night. He had waited while around him hard men crumbled as woman after woman betrayed them. He waited even after she was pregnant again. They'd had but one moment together and she was pregnant. An infant child now. It wasn't his. He didn't believe it was his. Every conversation with every other inmate fuelled that belief. The waiting was nearly over, now, though. Another hour or two he could stand.

As he leaned against the car in the safe embrace of the shadows, he consumed the last of the food. He glanced around. There was no one. From within the car he brought out the shotgun, broke it and slid cartridges into the twin breeches. With a hollow clunk the gun snapped shut greedily swallowing the rounds. Then, with it safely back in the bag, he looked once more at the directions the man in the apron had drawn for him. He studied them with the darkest hate a man can conjure written on his face, in his heart. Hatred for his own family. He would not wait much longer now.

Bob, the inspector, was leader of this group, designated Red Team. A gentle-voiced but assertive man, he had been present on my induction course, on that accursed run. Training is an essential part of the specialist firearms officer's role, to which he was now committed. Nevertheless, it was often interrupted by other demands. This time, though, he was determined to get a couple of hours on the Lippitts Hill range, with his team. Graham, a fit, smiling man with a thick dark moustache, and Dave ('DC'), the sergeant, had all the weapons, ammunition, earmuffs and targets ready. Breakfast had been devoured in the nearby canteen and they were all set to go.

At Shooters Hill, the eggs crackled in the huge blackened frying pan. As the Trojan 504 crew waited, all but salivating, the man from Birmingham was guiding the stolen car towards the abandoned South London Fire Station. Ahead of him was a mini-roundabout, and he paused to check the directions, pulling two wheels on to the kerb. As he sat there a marked police Astra glided by. He didn't care now: he was so close they could not stop him. He would shoot them. The car drove on.

Many miles away, high on a forested hill on the northern borders of London, the first shots of the morning rang out as Bob, DC, Graham and the rest of Red Team began their practice. A siren wailed a mournful warning echoing about the range. India 99, the force helicopter, appeared overhead and dropped steadily on to the landing pad.

In a small, terraced house close to the abandoned fire station another breakfast was over. The woman had fed her children, a boy of about four and an infant girl. The woman, wearing only panties and a housecoat, was about to get dressed.

She felt safe here, so far from Birmingham, in a house the refuge had found for her. She had left the

Midlands once and for all, trying to escape his violence, his obsession, the jealousies, threats, the bottomless pit of fear. She had seen him hurt others, hurt them badly.

Now that hatred was for her, but he was far away. She had consoled herself with that thought. He could not know where she was. What she did not know, could not possibly know, was that someone had betrayed her.

Barney rubbed his hands gleefully as the steaming meals appeared on the canteen counter. Skid ordered a fresh round of tea and coffee. Across London Red Team were 'patching out' the targets after the first shoots, marking the scores.

Outside the south London address, the stolen car came to a final halt. The driver got out and walked towards the house. In his hand was a sports bag, in the bag the loaded shotgun and an axe.

At home in Birmingham she had been more careful. Even when he was in prison, as the threats grew, the anger flared, there were still his mates. Never answering the door, the phone. Always someone to check first. Constant fear, day and night; waking, sleeping, fear. Here, at last, she had learned to relax a little, to trust.

The doorbell rang. At the door a silhouette, the figure of a man with a bag. No surprise: they came to this old rented house from the council, fixed the electric, the drains; they came from the welfare. Smiling, she opened the door.

What words can describe total rancorous hatred, utter bottomless loathing, vengeance craved for more than life, fearless even of damnation? All this was written on the face that confronted her.

What words can describe the fear that assailed her whole being as he threw back the door, drawing the axe from the bag?

Next door, a neighbour was casually watching. He saw the man knock, heard the door open, then he disappeared from view. And then the screams, terrible, terrified screaming. The woman, naked now but for a tiny pair of pants, ran out into the front garden. In a moment the man had caught her, hand at her neck, forced her to her knees. Then with a vicious curving swing he buried the axe in her skull. The horrified neighbour watched, transfixed as the now limp form was dragged back to the doorway, the axe embedded in flesh and shattered bone. Shaking himself from the horror of this surreal, macabre vision, he reached for the phone.

The call from the panicked, muddled neighbour brought local police to the scene within minutes. As the officers walked up the path he was ready, waiting at the window, staring at them over the limp, half-naked form of the woman, now propped up in a chair in the bay, her skull cloven, the axe still embedded. When he was sure they were close enough to see it all, he raised the shotgun, fired and blew her stomach apart. Fresh blood, tissue, intestine mixed with fragments of shattered furniture, sprayed the walls and window.

The policemen stood rooted outside in sheer disbelief, horror turning instantly to fear as the gun arced above the woman's head, the second barrel threatening now to take their lives. He levelled it at them, eyes full of hate, of fury, a madness dripping with the darkest emotions known to man. Behind them, back down the path, was life, their connection to it a filament, a strand of consciousness that this man could break in a moment. Just one thought. The faintest pressure of his finger. They turned and ran.

At the car the driver threw himself on the radio pleading for 'urgent assistance' – the classic call for help.

\* \* \*

The meals had made it to the table and newspapers were discarded as the serious business of eating began. They were barely passed the first few mouthfuls, Skid, Barney and Matt, when the multichannel radio on the table spoke. The driver's terrified voice. At once there were empty seats, meals forgotten. They were gone. All they knew was that shots had been fired at or near police. It was enough.

Skid pushed the ARV to the very edge, howling and bellowing through the pitching roads of Forest Hill, cursing every obstruction, damning every traffic-calming 'speed bump' that broke the flow as he did what he was best at: making lunacy an art form, then calling it skill.

In the house the little boy cowered. He had just witnessed his mother's horrific murder. Now he watched the man who had killed her striding insanely from window to window, cursing, muttering. His father, whose hands had once tenderly held him, now threatened his life, the life of his infant sister. As the trembling boy looked on, his father took clothes, blankets, pieces of carpet, piling them here, piling them there. Then the boy recoiled at a sudden flare of light: matches. He was going to kill them all, to fire the house. To burn them to death.

In the yard at Old Street, Clarky, Mac and Dixie were changing cars. They contrasted with each other well. Mac the grizzled ex-soldier, balding, tattooed, a thick black moustache, veteran of more than one exchange of fire. Dixie, smiling, the epitome of Mr Nice Guy, thoughtful, helpful. Clarky, analytical, precise.

They transferred the kit from a dirty, expiring Rover to a clean one fresh from the workshops. Another mechanical horse to be ridden into the ground. As the events down south came through to the north base at Old Street the baseman called out for them to respond.

Moments later they were running, pitching the fresh car straight into the fray as with screeching tyres Dixie threw it broadside into the traffic. Bawling tones, strobing lights, he threw it under the old bridge and right towards Bishopsgate, heading for London Bridge and the south. No 'perhaps' about this call. This was serious stuff.

In the bungalow, the small centrepiece administration building that provides a backdrop to the seated concrete figure presiding over the gates of Lippitts Hill, the telephone rang. Moments later, the blue-overall-clad figure of a senior instructor appeared breathless on 'A' range where Red Team had found their rhythm. The *crack, crack* of the carbines descended into withering fire as a hand fell on Bob's shoulder. The realisation that something major was occurring spread infectiously across the range. Then the bellow of the range instructor: 'Live round unload.' Even as they waited to know why, experience told them to prepare. The weapons must be clean. Matters of evidence should there be a shooting: who fired, who didn't? The *rack, rack, clack* of the carbines being cleared, the more metallic ring of the pistols.

In the Air Support Unit a few short yards from where Red Team were preparing, another phone rang. A man in a different kind of uniform, a pilot, spilled his coffee as he ran to the freshly fuelled helicopter. Moments later the abrupt whine of the starters echoed into the open hangars and the blades, lazily at first, began to rotate above him. With a cough the motor caught, a puff of kerosene smoke on the wind. The 'Paraffin Parrot' was preparing to fly.

There was no way the team could get there by road in time to be effective, yet the carrying capacity of the helicopter was limited. Bob, DC and Graham would be flown in, the remainder of Red Team following by road. They threw the bulk of their kit into 'Bill', the much-abused old Sherpa van, and headed south.

Ducking under the rotors, the three men with a minimum of kit climbed aboard the waiting helicopter, the beat growing stronger as the revs rose and the checks were completed. Then at once it lifted slowly till it cleared the buildings; dipping its nose, it raced south.

The helicopter would cover the ground in distance-shrinking minutes, but now, at the scene near the house, every second became an age for the hard-pressed crew of Trojan 504.

Skid had descended the hill in fine style to arrive with a tyre-squealing flourish on the forecourt of the old fire station, tucked safely in cover behind a high wall.

What they were then told by the assembled local officers was the definitive ARV nightmare. The worst-case scenario with the bare minimum of manpower. It was make-your-mind-up time. Far away but closing fast, Clarky, Mac and Dixie were trying hard.

'Shit!' In a tyre-smoking, screeching four-wheel lockup, Dixie drifted sideways across a junction as Mac winced. Clarky cowered. Then, spinning the steering wheel, Dixie stamped on the accelerator and they were rolling again. No time for banter. Nobody cared. Must get there.

Matt took the front, tucking himself in behind the garden wall of an imposing Victorian house which fronted the target address. All around now, the sound of two-tones as more and more uniform units arrived. Dogs, handlers, an ambulance. From the house, faintly, he heard a baby cry.

Inside the house the fires were beginning to catch. The curtains moved at the window, the face of the small boy appeared. Then behind him, in the shadows, the man with the gun.

Ferried by a local car, Barney had negotiated the whole block of houses to make his way up a ragged, dirty alleyway at the back. There he settled in to watch and wait, carbine in his hands, presiding over the rear windows, the door. He too heard the pathetic cries of a very young child.

Skid, still with the adrenaline of the drive coursing through him, now had to put on another set of emotional clothes and become the calm, organised voice of control, the man everyone, regardless of rank, would expect to have all the answers. The man to run both radios, the log, and also in this case peer over the wall and cover the side of the house with a gun.

They desperately needed more manpower. Seeing the problem, a dog handler slipped into the containment beside Matt to support him. The gunman appeared again, this time at the first-floor bedroom window. Under his arm was an infant girl, in his hand the gun, in his shadow the small boy, the shield between him and Matt.

'Let the children go, mate. No need for them to be hurt.' Matt opened the dialogue.

Insane rage still burned. 'I ain't coming out,' he screamed. 'I'll kill them. I'll kill you. What I got to lose?'

Distantly the tones of Trojan 507, Clarky, Mac and Dixie, could be heard. Somewhere over the Thames, India 99 swept towards them.

Matt called again, despairing for the children's lives, but the response was, 'Fuck off. I'm going to die anyway, so who gives a shit!' The gunman disappeared, heading for the back of the house to confront Barney. Among the local officers were Matt's trusted former colleagues, men qualified to use revolvers. He appealed to a local senior officer. 'Some of your blokes are AFOs.

Authorise them to arm and we can use them.' Pressed to make a decision, to assume the responsibility, the inspector crumbled. He refused. They would have to cope.

Trojan 507 swept on to the forecourt next to the car where the hard-pressed Skid was now standing, torn between his gun and the radios. As they did so, a very senior officer foolishly if courageously appeared at his shoulder. The perfect target. Skid's shocked reaction was to tell the man to 'fuck off back behind the ambulance' some fifty feet away. To his complete amazement, like a lamb, he did so.

Running, Mac filtered around the old Victorian house to support Matt at its front wall, confronting the smouldering building. Dixie and a local took over the control to free Skid. Laden with a heavy ballistic blanket, Clarky laboured to the rear, supporting Barney and bringing much-needed cover from fire.

Matt was in an agony of indecision as the helicopter passed overhead, now close enough to hear the conversation on the back-to-back radios the ARV crews were using, close enough to look down on the house as the pilot prepared to land. Bob was immediately aware of what fuelled that agony. Over the radios, the words; from the windows and the tiles of the house, smoke. The house was rapidly catching fire.

Aware of the irony, Skid from the forecourt of an abandoned fire station called for the brigade as at the rear Barney and Clarky flinched. As the heat in the rear bedroom intensified the glazing burst with a shattering bang that sent them diving for cover. The fire, hungry for oxygen, consumed the curtains in a moment of flaming, ferocious breath, then began to lick hungrily at the guttering.

The boy had appeared quaking at the front window. He began to point at Matt, then Mac, speaking over his shoulder to the shadowy form behind him. The gunman was marking his targets, preparing for the final flourish of a gunfight as fire consumed them all. Matt took another moment to think. What could be gained? What could be saved? No chance for negotiation. Balance the risks. Save whatever life was possible. The children, the innocents. Shoot him. Get them out. Sniper-initiated assault. Extreme decisions. He whispered his plans over the radio.

To his right Mac made a last-ditch attempt to negotiate the children's release. From his position to the right the angle was extreme, his vision limited. 'Come on, mate,' he yelled. 'Let the boy go. He's done nothing wrong.' A parade-ground voice ringing clear across the no-man's-land. At Matt's bidding Stuart, the dog handler, hoisted the big ballistic shield vertical. Skid handed over the control to a bewildered local. Dixie was at his back, by the wall, ready.

The carbine was now resting on the shield. Calm, slow. Matt could see all that mattered, the window, the man, but shadowy. Stuart was to call him forward, to bring that head to the window, framed, illuminated, easy shot. Everything . . . now . . . slowing . . . down . . . Couldn't hear Mac's booming voice – only the voice in his own head. Check the action . . . forward . . . good . . .

Mac called again: 'Let him go, he's just a boy. It's not his doing.' Inside, for a moment the hatred faltered. Mac was getting through. At last a positive response. But was there time?

The burning house, the baby, the woman. The baby's cry echoed in the now quiet, empty street. Remote from them, traffic, the radios. In the breeze, the crackle of the blue and white cordon tape, distant faces.

Matt's master eye drew the sighting rings of the MP5 together as instinctively the selector lever went to 'fire'. The single finger of the foresight ranged about the window, then picked up the silhouette of the man as he moved to the light. Steady. Steady. Focus. Sights clear. Target blurred. Steady.

'All right, I'll let him out, but you fucking stay back!'

Mac responded: 'OK. But don't show the gun. Do everything slowly. No aggression. Let him out the front door. Somebody will meet him.'

The smoke was billowing out of the rear window, flames dancing between the roof tiles. Out of other windows – more smoke. It was taking hold. Matt nodded. Stuart cleared his throat. At this rate the boy would never get out in time. The baby would have no chance. If there was still any for the woman, it would be gone.

In a cloud of dry grass cuttings and fallen leaves, the helicopter settled on the football field of the park, where the local van that had tracked their progress stood by. The slowing rotors passing above them, Bob, DC and Graham, laden with kit, were running. The back doors of the van enveloped them as, with a squeal from the protesting tyres, the Sherpa roared off.

Behind them the rhythm of the rotors beat harder again, as the helicopter lifted skywards; turning and dipping, it powered back towards the house. Moments later it appeared above the scene churning the rising smoke into curiously shaped spirals.

At the control on the fire-station forecourt John, the swarthy Irish sergeant, and Laurie were arriving. The figure of the man was clearly outlined in the window, no sign of the infant. Stuart took a breath to speak. Matt took one as well: he held it, taking up the pressure on the trigger. Keep pulling, slowly, slowly. Sight picture. Wait for the bang. Keep pulling.

Mac called again, 'Do exactly as I tell you.'

The man's voice rose. 'No, you listen –'

Then a bang, loud, shocking, and the figure in the window disappeared mid-sentence. A second bang. Silence.

The baby's cries stopped. Breaking in Matt's head, the worst of all thoughts. 'Fuck it. He's killed the kids.'

Stuart turned to him, the shock standing out on his face. Over the radio, suddenly, voices: chaos, everyone speaking at once, cutting across each other's signal. Matt broke in on them all: 'Stand by. Stand by.' He turned to the stunned dog handler. 'I haven't fired.'

Then moments later, near the door, Skid and Dixie saw the small boy at the downstairs bay window, his face stained with tears. Shocked, bewildered, he raised his arms, opening his hands in a gesture of despair. Unarmed senior officers ran forwards. From somewhere in cover a voice called to them, '*Stay back!*'

While Matt, Dixie and Mac stared tensely through the sights of the MP5s, Skid and a nearby local officer began to plead with the boy. One pane of the sash window was open. Through the square opening the child was framed, a pathetic, terrified innocent. Skid looked straight into the boy's glazed and shocked eyes. Yet they could not – dare not – go in. A moment's emotion, a rush forwards into the building could be fatal. Where was the gun? Where was the gunman?

The boy could see and hear Skid calling, entreating him to come out, to climb through the window. Safety, the voice of authority, the means to step away from these awful sights, awful feelings. All of those things were embodied in the voice of the policeman who called to him so passionately. That extended hand meant safety, an end to this terror.

Skid beckoned and finally he responded.

Inside the house, below the windowsill, concealed by the back of the chair, was what Skid could not see. He was asking the boy to climb over the disembowelled, cleft-skulled, lifeless puppet that once had been his mother. Knowing no other way than to obey, the boy did as he was bidden. He clambered, half slipping, on to the blood-soaked body, then the sill, then dropped to the path outside. He froze.

'Come on, son. You can do it. Walk to me. Come on, you can do it. Walk to me.' Skid coaxed, voice firm yet gentle.

The boy's fragile form seemed diminished by the backdrop of the house, dwarfed by the events around him. Other voices, emotional, loud, calling him to come forward, registered as panic on the tiny face. Suddenly he was a prisoner of his own fear; confusion roamed in his eyes.

Skid fought for his attention, but could not hold it. Stepping out from cover he made that awful decision all of us dread: to risk his life for another. He made his way down the path, the longest walk of his life. His right hand held the pistol, raised to shoot the first threat from the house. His left hand beckoned to the helpless boy. 'Come on, son. Come to me. You're all right. Come on.' The boy eased forwards while Skid braced himself waiting for the explosion that could destroy him.

The distance between them closed slowly as, agonisingly, the faltering steps of the small boy pulled Skid further down the path, nearer to the danger. With his whole being crying out for the security of that plain brick wall that seemed so very far behind now, the fingers of the police officer and the small boy touched. In an instant he was scooped up into the security of Skid's arms as he backed away from the window, a weapon in one hand, a child in the other. Embodied in that moment was everything SO19 exists for – a weapon to protect the innocent.

Matt, Dixie and Mac breathed easy, returning their MP5 selector levers to 'safe'. As they relaxed a little from the 'aim' there was still no sound from the other, younger, child. Throughout the whole grisly incident there had been the sound of the baby's distress. Now there was nothing save the radios, the cordon tape, the distant traffic. And the malevolent crackle of the fire. It had lost the boy, but it still had the baby, it still had the man, it still had the hunger.

At the control the Sherpa van had come to a halt where a visibly shaken Skid took a moment to collect his thoughts. The small boy, now in the hands of the ambulance crew and a sympathetic woman officer, confirmed what the crews believed. Mummy was dead. Daddy had killed her.

Responsibility now fell on Bob, as the inspector, and the two other members of SFO Red Team. The local commander was happy to allow him free rein, but the issues and the urgency were clear. Bob was in command in seconds, the briefing on the hoof.

'The information I have is that a man and a small child are inside that burning house. The other person, a woman, is believed to be dead. I intend to effect a hostage rescue by frontal assault, to force an entry with a view to saving life and securing an arrest. The emergency services are on standby.

'The fire brigade will only enter on my command. I will then hand over control to the local scene commander [the local inspector]. I'm sorry, but time precludes a more detailed briefing.' He looked at the sea of faces surrounding him, hanging on his every word. Senior officers, fire brigade, ambulance, ARV crew, his own two men. 'Skid, John, Laurie. You'll supplement the entry team with me, Graham and DC.'

In the house the fire raged, smoke still funnelled skywards. There was no more time. 'Form up,' Bob commanded. Distantly the helicopter circled.

As Bob, with Graham carrying the heavy door ram, approached the glazed aluminium door, the remainder covered the windows with carbines, faces intent, looking for the slightest threatening movement.

A flurry of activity, Graham's arm swinging back, the sound of rending metal, breaking glass. They were in. The call 'support' brought the remaining entry team moving forwards, weapons raised to cover the windows. Arcing MP5 carbines swept the hallway: cover this door, cover that. Eyes everywhere, looking for movement. Nothing. Practised moves fell into use. Bob the stairs. Skid, Laurie and John the lower rear. DC and Graham the front room.

A nod and the two men entered, eyes, guns sweeping over the contents. DC called, 'Close.' The signal to clear the room. And then Graham's voice: 'Jesus bloody Christ!' They both saw her, a mind-numbing mass of blood and bone that had once been a woman. Blood ran down the mask that had been her face. The source, a cleft in her skull, the axe still buried there.

Her abdomen was gone. Where the shotgun had done its work, an awful furrow marked a path to where that obscene litany adhered to the wall.

The flames were now as much a threat as the hidden gunman. In the hall a small seat of fire was burning. But more threatening was the smoke that lurked at the top of the stairs, curling in the breeze like some malevolent spirit, daring them to come further. As the threat of the flames grew the remainder of the ground floor was quickly cleared, then slowly they began to climb. The heat was becoming unbearable. Bob led with Graham at his elbow. DC was close behind with John and Laurie in support. As the guns at arm's length ranged about, responding to the opening arcs of vision, breathing became laboured, eyes watered and smarted.

Close-quarter stuff. Handgun territory. The super-accurate carbines were suddenly too clumsy, too awkward. Glances now, no spoken sounds. Hand signals to cover here, move there. The occasional creak of a floorboard, the rattling, metallic sound of the carbine slings. The crackle of the fire, their own heavy breathing.

From the gunman, from the baby, nothing.

The bathroom at the rear of the house presented itself as over the radio DC gave a warning to Barney and Clarky. 'Units at the back. Expect movement, level two.'

The bathroom was clear, empty. They turned to the first bedroom, the room where the fire demon lived. As Bob reached for the door handle Graham stopped him. Patting the wooden surface with his palm, he winced. It was red-hot. Bob clenched his jaws and with a gloved hand and a grimace he turned the handle. The door opened a fraction and searing smoke and fumes were breathed out as if by some demonic reptilian entity. A sudden flash of orange light crossed the walls and ceiling. In a split second they had shut the demon in. Bob's hand, Graham's hand, fighting the door closed. If there was anyone in there, they were already dead.

There were still two rooms to clear, a small front bedroom, and the main threat: the room where the gunman had last been seen.

Confrontation of whatever kind was imminent. As the last and most tense episode began, they braced themselves for the worst. Graham and John the large room, the smaller one Laurie and DC. Bob covered, and the smaller room was cleared first. Only one to go now. Only one place he could be.

An exchange of glances, of nods. Ready. Then Graham, followed by John, burst into the room. They stopped, crouched, covering. He lay beside the bed, far from the window he had dominated. His right thigh was almost gone, ripped into a bloodied pulp by a massive shotgun wound. The lower leg was still supported by the bed above him.

His motionless face was a death mask, flecked with blood from a colossal stomach wound. Where his stomach had been was an enormous bloody cavity while beneath his back a pool of thick blackening blood spread across the floor. Nearby a sawn-off shotgun, but, more abhorrent than all of this, there lay, doll-like across his stomach and half in the wound, the gasping, heaving shape of a semi-naked child fighting for breath in the swirling smoke.

The most humane, most natural reaction drove Graham instantly forwards, registering above the horror, the appalling sense of massacre. The smoke, the guns, the man, the fire. All secondary, forgotten, dismissed by a single thought. Save the child. He lifted it from the wound in the gunman's belly, then turned rapidly out of the room. Across the landing, through the heat, the swirling smoke, baby against his shoulder. Downstairs and out into the air.

Near the wall, a uniform, a nice clean uniform. A senior officer into whose arms the baby was entrusted. Behind them lay the tangled broken flesh that had been its parents. Parents it would never know. Nearby the brother with whom the burden of that day would perhaps for ever be shared. A terrible legacy.

Turning back towards the house, Graham spoke: 'Take the child to the ambulance. Tell them smoke inhalation.' Then he disappeared back towards the fumes.

Then, in his ears, suddenly, an obscenity was generated by revulsion: 'Oh, fucking hell!' The child had emptied its bowels down that nice clean uniform.

Upstairs, hands clutched to mouths against the thickening fumes, the team made the most basic check for life signs on the obviously dead man. Then rapidly they rechecked the house, before handing over to the fire brigade as a matter of extreme urgency. The fire demon would be robbed of new trophies, at least for today. But then another demon had carried away two lives, tainted for ever two others, and affected many more.

As the hissing water drove out the heat, turned the smoke to steam, those involved stood down. The distant crowd watched in awe as the guns were cleared and put away, the shields, the ballistic blankets returned to storage.

Quietly now the boys grouped round the front of a car to reflect. The scratching hissing sound of a burning match on its way to a cigarette met with the inevitable black humour. 'Mind where you throw that.'

Many questions will remain for ever unanswered about that day's events. Perhaps it's better that way. Why did this man develop such a fervent hatred for his own family? How could he – even for a moment – desire to destroy his own children? And why, if he chose to end his own life, did he do so in mid-sentence?

Although all too late, he was beginning to respond to Mac's pleas to spare the children. Why inflict that terrible leg wound? Why a stomach injury? That could only have prolonged the agony. If he *had* chosen to die, then just one shot to the head would have done it. Quick and easy. Final.

Could the little boy somehow have struck the shotgun, causing him such injury as to make the second shot a mercy? Nobody will ever know.

A murder enquiry was nominally and rapidly opened, then closed with the obvious conclusion. At the inquest held later a female officer related that the small boy had told her *he* had killed Daddy, an assertion the coroner, quite rightly, dismissed as the fantasy of a child who wished to have protected his mother.

After all, how could such a small boy fire such a huge, destructive weapon. Below the age of ten there would be no responsibility in law, and again in law such an act by an adult might well have been judged as lawful.

However, I am convinced the coroner's judgement was the right one, rendered for the right reasons.

Truly though, in this case, the sins of the father had been visited upon the children.

At the conclusion of the incident, as the fire brigade damped down the last of the embers, as the helicopter powered back to Lippitts Hill, the remainder of the SFO team arrived too late. The on-scene debrief concluded the business. At a nearby police station the notes of evidence were completed and Trojan 504 was back in the game.

As they rolled out into the street, dazzled by the late-morning sunshine, Barney spoke into the radio: 'MP from Trojan 504. Show us back on watch.'

'Trojan 504, your message received.'

They drove north for a while, then Matt spoke, as if to relieve the eerie quiet that had fallen over the car. 'Right then. So where were we? Oh yes, breakfast.' The haunting, reflective silence was broken.

'Shooters Hill?' Barney asked.

'Rolling,' said Skid.

As they entered the canteen for the second time that day, Mary, the short West Indian woman, was clearing away the sea of plates that was testament to her popularity. 'You still doing the breakfast specials?' Barney enquired.

'Look,' she retorted, lifting her eyes from the cloth that washed the table before her. 'Breakfast finished at eleven o'clock. You know that. Eleven thirty now, it's much too late.'

Matt let his most hurt, puppy-dog expression slip across his features. 'We've been so busy, Mary. You saw us run out of here. Do us three specials. You know I love you, don't you?' A smile crumpled the lines in her face. She had always intended to cook for them, just wanted to hear the words.

A short while later the newspapers were again discarded as the serious business of consumption began. After all, for her as well as for them, it was a matter of professional pride.

This incident stands prominent as one of the most violent, most significant of the early days. Along with others it provided the impetus for change, driven by immediate need. The original statement, 'There will never be a need for ARVs to perform a rapid intervention', began to carry the proviso, 'Only in the most dire circumstance . . .'

# **6** The Weekend Warrior

IT WAS THE SAME BUS STOP he used every day to come home from work. Mr Average. Nothing seemed to break the monotony of his existence. As the bus lurched the last few yards to the same familiar venue, he tucked the rolled newspaper under his arm, steadied himself against the rail and made his way along to the platform. Nothing much in the paper. Oh yes, it was Remembrance Sunday, a day we should think of men in uniform with respect and humility.

He loosened his tie as he walked, the only concession he would make to the warm air. He straightened the suit jacket as he turned left from the Uxbridge Road, taking the same route he did every day. He hadn't been to work today, though: instead he'd been visiting his mother. It just felt as if he had been to work.

The bus passed through the junction behind him on its way to Shepherd's Bush. As the roar of the diesel faded he heard shouting somewhere ahead. Two large white police vans, like the ones he occasionally saw laden with men, dominated the road. An ambulance stood close in to the kerb. In the centre of the road he saw what looked like a traffic police car. Suddenly his interest quickened. Perhaps this was a particularly grisly accident. Whatever, it was something different.

He drew closer, still walking on the opposite kerb as he always did on the way home. There was more shouting, now a series of bangs. A figure, a policeman, no hat, ducking down behind the traffic car. He was holding a machine gun. No, it couldn't be. There were policemen running everywhere, hiding behind walls, taking cover.

Nothing like this could ever happen near him – they were probably filming or something. Unchecked by the numerous police officers around him, their attention focused elsewhere, he walked through the middle of a gunfight. Total scepticism his only shield as live ammunition cut the air around him. Then he turned the corner and was gone.

It had been a singularly uneventful late turn. I had spent the better part of my time planning yet more duties. The sergeant, at that time, was the only immediate supervisor on duty with the ARVs during any unsociable hours, and the sole administrator of the day-to-day management.

The time passes slowly on a Sunday afternoon when you know everyone else is somewhere having 'a life'. Not surprising, then, that I was pleased to see my old mate, Laurie, walk in the door, to take over the night duty. I briefed him on the events that had occurred since he was last here. He would see my late-turn cars in, as was the custom.

In the locker room I did my best quick-change act and headed downstairs. I crossed the base room, noticeably devoid of any oncoming night-duty crews. As I made my way towards the door Laurie emerged from the base room, looking concerned. 'Your relief's exchanging fire.'

'Yes, OK. Pull the other one.'

He repeated. 'Your relief's exchanging gunfire. I think one of them's been hit. I'm not joking, Roger.'

'Jesus, you mean it.' I was now changed, ready to go home. 'Grab a car, I'll change back and be with you in a minute.' This was the first real gunfight the crews had been in. My relief, and someone had been hit. Barely a year had passed, but we had the first gunshot casualty.

We had a car. It was no more than an Escort, but it was marked, had two-tones, blues and a gun safe. It was no Rover 827, but could reach a hundred miles per hour, and it was equipped. Good enough. Once again I threw my kit into the back seat where it had resided for the previous eight hours, and ran to the big steel gates. Laurie, who had his driving head on, pulled out into Hoxton Street. Moments later we were passing under the old railway bridge towards the city. The wail of the klaxon echoed from the height of the surrounding buildings. Sparkling blue reflected from every window. 'MP from Trojan 500. Reference your Acton call. Show us assigned.'

Earlier that evening things had reached crisis point in the west London house. The trouble had been festering for years, as the young man's increasingly obsessive behaviour affected every aspect of his life. It had begun as a burning interest in all things military. Through cadets into the Territorial Army. The combat magazines, weapons catalogues.

Increasingly, fantasy was blurring with everyday life, a singularly dangerous situation when a young man's existence is split between day-to-day boredom, and the role of a TA intelligence officer, to the SAS.

His father, with whom he lived, had been a military man – perhaps that played a part. The remainder of the family, his mother and sister, were both increasingly affected by the growing aggression he displayed. A big man in his late twenties, he was a formidable adversary.

There had been previous incidents of violence, and the police had been called. This time he was to be 'sectioned', placed in a secure unit for psychological assessment and care. Often, though, we confuse disturbed with stupid. This man was not stupid.

The doctor had been led into the lounge by the time the social workers arrived. His father was in conversation with them as the young man came down the stairs, wearing the appropriate dress code for the occasion. He was decked out in full camouflage gear and wore the beige SAS beret. In his hands he carried a huge, ceremonial samurai sword. Seconds later he was alone in the house, the others driven out, terrified, into the street. The police were called, the message going out over the radios shared by the ARVs.

Big Darren was operator in the car with Simon at the wheel, and Sandy, in the back, 'maps' on that shift. As Simon filled the fuel tank, Sandy devoured yet another tube of Smarties. She seemed to have a particular weakness for them. Darren heard the call. 'I know that address,' he said, drawing on previous experience of the area. 'That bloke's a real nut and he'll go for it.'

Simon quickly signed for the fuel, and they turned in the direction of Acton. These were still early days. There was still a marked reluctance to assign ARVs to all but the most obvious calls.

The crew decided that discretion should be used. They would be near enough to help, far enough away to be merely observing.

The running time from town can be quite short, using the Westway and the Rover's prodigious speed. Once down into Acton, a left turn and a little more mileage brought the scene into view. Simon rolled on towards the parked carriers of the Territorial Support Group (TSG). As he did so Sandy glanced to her right. Framed by the lights behind him, in the doorway of an imposing, if somewhat eccentric-looking, terraced house, was a very big man. She could see the uniform, the beret. She could see the sword.

'I think that could be him.'

The man was standing, feet apart, the sword set point against the ground, both hands resting on the hilt at chest height. A fixed sneer on his face. A challenge. Ahead of the car on the right, an ambulance stood by, along with the two TSG carriers and local officers' cars. As little more than observers the ARV crew had themselves assigned to the call. They were to maintain a 'vicinity-only' status. Well, that was correct, just that it was the *close* vicinity.

Simon swung the car through a U-turn behind the waiting carriers. The man's father was speaking with the local duty officer. In a more sombre mood still, the TSG officers began to don all their protective kit and ready the shields and batons. A knife was one thing, a sword something else. A Met officer's forearm had been sliced clean off by one not long before, and I don't suppose that was far from their minds.

When kitted out, the huddle of men clutching shields, helmeted and with polycarbonate protectors strapped to their limbs, listened to their inspector's final briefing. In the ARV there was talk of the mutilated police officer. Quietly, they slipped the handguns into their holsters. Sandy cleared the path to the safe containing the carbines. Emphatically this was a TSG job, nothing to do with the ARV. They were just there to watch, to support.

The TSG formed up and moved forwards. Simon started the engine; there was no protest as he selected 'drive' from the automatic gearbox. He didn't even touch the throttle as, on tickover, the Rover began to track the walking officers.

Feeding the steering wheel gently through his hands, he guided the car out into the centre of the road. Keeping a respectful distance, they shadowed the group.

\* \* \*

Laurie had saved up a month's supply of adrenaline, and he was brimming with it as we hurtled through London. The City was left quickly behind, as we descended the looping road down behind the old Mermaid Theatre on to the Embankment.

All I could think of was that my crew had been shot. Every idiot who knew how to delay us seemed to be practising his art. Parliament Square came and went as we barrelled on past the bridges. Lambeth, Vauxhall, Battersea and Chelsea all blurred by, at the boatyard we swung towards Earl's Court. At the junction with King's Road the lights were red as we approached. Then red and amber, green a split second before we crossed. Off to our right the man who was running the red changed his mind but the one following didn't. 'MP from Trojan 500, there has been a damage-only accident,' I began. Later there would be a God Almighty row because we did not stop. We could not. Injured metal is one thing, injured flesh another – but some bureaucrats don't see it that way.

Simon stopped the car short of the address, allowing the TSG officers to get ahead but able to watch them form up. The strange, often eccentric and individual make-up of each of the front gardens of the houses denied them sight of what their suspect was doing. Simon allowed the Rover to trickle gently forwards again.

It would soon make little difference as, from behind the low walls and conifers, came a loud bang, and the TSG officers 'bomb-burst' to cover. Frantically, a uniform PC beckoned the ARV forward. 'Shit, he's got a gun.' Simon spat out the words, as he slipped the Rover into reverse. But Darren had already gone.

I saw the Range Rover in traffic livery parked by the side of the road and, as Laurie paused, I related the accident to them and the reason for our haste. The two traffic officers looked unmoved. I could not see the young sergeant's chevrons hidden behind the door pillar; sadly, as it would turn out, he couldn't forget them. We took off again preoccupied with our own concerns. We were now very close to the scene.

Darren had slipped into the garden of the adjoining house and, using the high conifers as cover, he peered over the low brick wall. The man in the camouflage gear and beret was looking directly at him. In his belt was the huge sword, in his hands a Lee Enfield .303 rifle. He raised it, aimed at Darren and fired.

The shout of 'Armed police' came instinctively from his lips, as Darren then pulled the trigger of the .38. He got two shots off as the gunman ducked back in the doorway, the sound of the rifle bolt going forwards clearly audible. Darren backtracked out to the street.

Sandy was trying to extract the carbines from the safe concealed behind the centre armrest of the rear seat. The gunman suddenly appeared at the gate, aimed at her and fired. He hit the windscreen and pillar of the car. On the side of her head the blood had begun to flow but adrenaline killed the pain. She must get the carbines.

Simon had gone to the rear quarter of the car, covering with a handgun down the road towards the house. Remember Mr Average? Around the corner he was getting off that bus, now walking towards a gunfight.

The MP5s were mounted on a slide that pulled out from the back seat, but it allowed the magazines only to be balanced on top of, and not locked into, the guns. As in this moment of truth Sandy pulled the slide out, the magazines fell, disappearing beneath the front seats. The gunman returned to the doorway, reloading the rifle as Darren took cover at the front wall.

He called towards the door. 'Armed police. Come on out!' The rifle rose, spoke flame, and a searing pain scorched its way across Darren's face. He could feel no blood. A scar on the wall told him he had been lucky. The pain was caused by ricochet fragments of masonry. The man had fired towards his voice. Again the sound of the rifle bolt.

Sandy recovered one double magazine, and with both carbines went back to Simon, still covering from behind the car. Regardless of the risk (as she did not know where the gunman was), her fear was compounded by the thought that the carbines might fall into his hands. Knowing he had shot at her already, she nevertheless stayed till the guns were secure.

They split the double magazine, loaded the MP5s and, having made them ready, went forwards to support Darren. Sandy turned to Simon.

'I think the bastard's shot me.' She was bleeding, the source as yet unknown. As Simon turned he saw a bespectacled, middle-aged man in a suit staring at him incredulously.

The man paused for a moment and then, with his rolled newspaper tucked under his arm, walked off along the pavement through the middle of a gunfight.

In the hallway of the house the gunman had reloaded his rifle, readying himself for his next victim. The element of surprise was slipping away from him, however. And the crew began to function as the trained unit they were.

Identify. Locate. Contain. Only the third element remained to be achieved. Simon moved off to find a route to the back. If they could keep him in the house, perhaps a peaceful resolution could be negotiated. This, though, was not a peaceful or negotiating kind of man.

Back at the TSG carriers, a distance from the house and near the junction, his father grasped what was happening. The boom of the rifle had been contrasted by the sharp report of a different weapon. The police had guns; they were shooting back.

The make-up of houses was a nightmare. Simon's efforts were frustrated by blind alleys and high fences. Frantically, he searched for a way round the back, but there was none. Darren, with the bleeding Sandy at his side, braced himself for the next exchange. His face still aching from the ricochet, he called again. 'We are armed police officers. Put the gun down. Come out, you will not be hurt.'

Simon ran back to the street. He had to let the other two know the rear was insecure. Hypnotised police officers still stood close by, potential targets all. Some had taken cover while others had ceased to function, transfixed by what was happening. He had to get them out. He called to them. No one listened.

Perhaps thirty yards away the father broke free from the shocked TSG officers around him. He began to run towards the house. There were no cordons, nothing to stop him. Of the dozens of uniformed officers, none had recovered from the shock of gunfire sufficiently to block him. Only three minds were truly functioning, but then this was their game.

Simon tucked in against the wall of an adjoining house. He identified an area near the front gate, took account of the backdrop, checked the sight picture of the carbine and waited. If the gunman came out he would not make it to the street to threaten or injure again. Simon would shoot him.

Behind the front garden wall, Darren tucked himself in, covering the front door with a revolver, while Sandy had moved almost to the gate. Using a brick-built pier rising up from the same wall, she took careful aim at the centre of the door. The shadow of a man carrying a rifle moved along the hall towards them. Again they called,

'Armed police. Put the gun down.' The shadow did not hesitate. He was there again, framed in the doorway. The calls of 'Armed police' from both officers reached a new pitch. Very deliberately the gunman lifted the barrel and took aim at the police officers, now tucked in behind cover.

The rifle boomed, its orange flash bright in their eyes as they returned fire. As both would later recount, an eternity seemed to pass. The gunman staggered but did not fall, then a darkened figure burst through the gate past them both.

The ex-soldier in the gunman's father knew that, if the rifle was raised again, the police officers would once more open fire. He threw himself forwards, rugby-tackling his son to the floor. Darren and Simon were through the gate after him with Sandy close behind. As they pinned the still-fighting, uniformed figure to the ground, local officers ran in to support. Sandy restrained the distraught, angry father, as his son was handcuffed and rolled over. Blood spread from a bullet wound in his abdomen, but it had no apparent effect on him, as still he struggled. A good supply of ammunition hung from his waist. He had meant to make a fight of it.

While the crew from the ambulance stationed nearby tended to the gunman, my three officers walked, stunned, back to the waiting TSG carriers. As they did the blue flashes and wail of the ambulance marked the gunman's exit towards the nearest hospital. In the warmth of the carrier, the first opportunity to find the source of Sandy's bleeding revealed puncture wounds in the left side of her head.

The old Lee Enfield rifle had been converted to fire shotgun cartridges. While she had fought to recover the magazines, several pellets had passed between the open door and the windscreen. They will remain in her scalp for the rest of her life. If the shot fired at Darren had hit him, death, blindness or disfigurement could have resulted. While they waited, somehow the father made his way to where they sat. He burst into the carrier and punched Darren in the face. To his great credit Darren did not react, nor ever seek redress. TSG officers restrained the distraught man.

It had taken only moments for the gunman to recover that gun from wherever it was hidden. I pose this question. Who knew of its existence and whereabouts? Who could have prevented all this from happening? Whenever that man suffers from the gunshot injury, as he will all his life, whose conscience should that be on?

Had the ARV crew not prevented this man from going mobile, perhaps the disbelieving man on his way home, and others like him, would never have got there. Maybe several police officers could have met a similar fate. Prevention would have been better than cure.

Both of the final rounds fired at the suspect had struck their intended target. The one that penetrated damaged his liver. He will suffer ever after. The second hit the scabbard of either the sword or a bayonet he was also carrying. Apart from the blunt trauma at the time, that round did him no permanent damage.

An evening paper reported the event by saying, 'In scenes reminiscent of the Hungerford massacre ...' The incident was never allowed to approach that scale, contained, as it was, by an ARV. That is precisely why they were created.

A neighbour said to a local reporter, 'He was shouting, "Fuck off, you pigs." You think, Big man, big gun, that's it, and you go. I rushed back inside and the police shouted to everyone to get back indoors. The police behaviour was exemplary. They did everything by the book.'

Well, they would: they were my people.

* * *

There are many questions posed by this incident. How was a man of this disposition allowed access to military know-how and weaponry? The consequences of there being more sophisticated firearms that night do not bear thinking about. While people of a disturbed mentality should be of concern to us all, the totally innocent should surely deserve the first consideration.

Laurie and I arrived at the scene not long after the event. Simon remained with the TSG while we attended the hospital. Sandy lay on an operating table as doctors unsuccessfully probed and cut her scalp, but the pellets remain there to this day.

The remainder of the relief gathered in the corridor outside. Posh Bob held her hand and comforted her. Later she quipped, 'I'm not sure if he was comforting me or I was comforting him.' Even in this age of equality, chivalry is not dead and men still react emotively when women are hurt.

Laurie and I were summoned to the local traffic garage, where the young sergeant and his embarrassed driver were waiting in an office with their inspector to ambush us. Laurie was accused of failing to stop and report a traffic accident, even though I had called in over the radio and accosted the two officers in the Range Rover.

Because he was young, the sergeant seemed to feel that I (another sergeant) had not shown enough respect for his shiny chevrons, which had, in fact, been obscured by the vehicle's door, and so complained to the inspector. No apparent importance was attached to the fact that this had been a live-firearms incident, or that police officers had been injured. 'It wasn't life-threatening' was the response from the inspector.

In what is truthfully an exception, I lost my temper. All respect for seniority paled against the enormity of what had occurred. I felt the hot rush of real anger as I launched the first salvo. 'I do not choose to insult other officers,' I began, 'but when one of my people has been shot I don't care . . .' I didn't need to go any further as the inspector raised his hands, palms towards me in a gesture of peace.

'All right, Sarge,' he began, as a silence descended that brought matters to a swift conclusion. No more was ever heard.

Years later an ARV would buckle a wheel on the way to a man confronting police officers with two live hand grenades, the pins already removed. After rolling on gently for the last mile they also were criticised.

Sometimes I wonder . . .

# 7 Have Gun . . . Will Travel

THIS EARLY TURN would make a lie of the weather forecast. As the first sunlight had cracked the dark skyline Keith and I were already rolling towards the base within the comforting warmth of my car. By the time we reached Old Street, his head was rocking gently around his shoulders above the tightly folded arms, as the warm bed he had left such a short while before called to him again. He had taken over as the 'C' relief inspector perhaps two years before. A tall, slim, dark-haired man, he had a strength of character quite beyond that perceived on mere first acquaintance. We had become, and remain, the very best of friends.

The cobbled ramp rocked the car as we approached the gates. Keith blinked his eyes before stepping out of the car to open them. It was promising a glorious sunny morning although 'some showers' were forecast. Rarely was there such an understatement. It was 5.40 a.m.

Once the usual early-turn tea and banter were over we headed east in the supervisory Volvo estate. Now Keith could drive for a while as I relaxed. Our first port of call was breakfast, urgent now as Keith has the consumption speed and appetite of a vacuum cleaner.

Every relief has its favourite breakfast haunts. For 'C' relief it was Charing Cross or Belgravia, if they were north. Shooters Hill for the south-base crews, until the corporate hand closed its doors for ever. Then Croydon or Brixton became the choices.

Keith and I had our venues as well. The small canteen behind the tall façade of Thames Magistrates' Court would often draw us. It was never crowded and it even boasted a small sun terrace; we kept that one to ourselves.

Moira, a slim black woman, her hair heavily flecked with grey, would always make us hugely welcome, giving me the expected greeting, 'Hallo, Sarge, how's your lovely big son?' referring to my eldest, now heavier and taller than I was. He had occasionally worked there as a custody officer. Always for me there was a big hug.

But this time we were too far north, so we swung off the road into the car park next to the shiny sides of a catering van, steaming with tea and coffee, and sending forth the aroma of sizzling bacon. This was another of our better-kept secrets. It lives among the green expanses on the north side of Hackney Marsh.

Dismay registered on the faces of the local relief scattered around the collection of plastic tables presided over by the drop-down counter of the van. We were evidently trespassing on hallowed ground.

The presence of an unknown inspector and sergeant did not bode well. Tea, coffee and rolls were either hastily consumed or abandoned. Before we were out of the car they were gone. Shrugging our shoulders, Keith and I walked to the van to order mugs of tea, and the best bacon rolls for miles. If only they had waited!

As we sat at the tables enjoying a few moments of life's simple pleasures, down south storm clouds of different kinds were gathering. Men with guns would again bring fear into innocent lives and ARV crews would be tested for 'all-weather availability'.

Somewhere in deepest Surrey a lorry driver was about to have his day ruined. In the back of the five-ton lorry he drove was a large quantity of spirits on its way to a bonded warehouse. There were those who intended that it would never arrive.

As the lorry slowed through a small village, cars swung across its path, and men with guns burst from the doors running back towards him. They shouted, swore and threatened. The lorry lurched forwards again moments later. Bound, gagged and terrified, he shared space with the spirits in the back. The engine note rose in the darkness. Then a change of pace, more speed. The lorry violently rocking. He could hear the clumsy grinding of gears as the driver panicked. A rending crash as a shaft of daylight lanced the darkness from a hole in the lorry's body. All around the sound of breaking glass, raised voices. Then a face, a uniform.

The local police had been lucky, and got to the lorry before it could be spirited away to some anonymous yard and the load swapped. The lorry driver would probably have found himself on a remote stretch of road somewhere, and the lorry perhaps never seen again. Fate, though, had intervened. The crashed lorry had spilled its expensive load into a roadside garden, and the armed driver had run down through a small industrial estate, over wasteland and down an escarpment on to railway lines. Unwittingly, he had crossed the borders and was in the 'Met'. The territory of our ARVs.

The bacon rolls had served their purpose well as, satisfied, Keith and I headed east towards where the edges of London merge with Essex. With phone calls and notes to make, Keith had relinquished the driving seat by the time we crossed into Romford section. There, just a short way from the M25, Keith's phone rang, as simultaneously the radio barked out the same information. Our intruder from Surrey was 'on our patch'. We accepted the call as spots of rain splattered on the screen like breaking eggs. Just a few, nothing to worry about, but they were so big!

We burst on to the motorway at junction 29 having trumpeted our way through the small town to get there. Intermittent heavy showers wet the screen as I drove the car ever faster over alternately wet and dry roads. Over the radio came the voice of the operator, passing information gained from the mixture of our own cars and the Surrey units still in pursuit, resolved not to let this bastard go.

Barney was there again, along with 'Shaky Jake', ex-soldier and ex-boxer, all thick dark hair, black moustache and eyebrow scars, and John Hayes, a tall willowy man with the reputation of being just a little accident-prone. In a car park beyond the industrial estate they were being briefed as preparations were made for an 'open-country search', a skill in itself. Nearby a handler prepared a long search leash for Bruno, a brutish German shepherd with not perhaps the most forgiving disposition. His colleague prepared a harness for a gentler second dog.

As I approached the expanse of the Queen Elizabeth Bridge I found myself pressing the accelerator ever closer to the floor, the speedometer needle sweeping towards the nineties.

Over the radio came the update from the scene that the suspect had been sighted and lost, and a cross-country search was in progress. The road rose ever higher ahead, as, hundreds of feet below us through the lattice of the bridge, I could see the Thames Estuary with shipping and jetties spread out. On the windscreen spots of water the size of fifty-pence coins began to spatter.

I had 'everything on', the strobing blue roof lights, alternate flashing headlamps. The horns wailed far ahead through the clear unobstructed air.

Perhaps at the tollbooths they could see us coming, or maybe the control we had passed moments before had called ahead, but they were ready. Beside me Keith's apprehension was growing.

'Are you going to slow down?'

I honestly have no idea what speed we were doing, but it was far in excess of the statuary fifty miles per hour. At the booths ahead the uniformed staff scurried back and forth directing traffic with small 'lollipop' discs, clearing a path straight through the toll. I took a deep breath before answering, 'No.' The pat-pat of the huge raindrops against the glass began to increase.

We drew ever closer. Descending the last few hundred feet off the bridge, Keith hooked the radio handset back into place, then put his telephone in the door pocket. As I lined the car up with the narrow passage between the booths he braced a foot against the dashboard.

The staff stood wide as the world went into fast forward, paused and rocketed behind us. We were suddenly through, hurtling out towards Surrey. As we emerged from beneath the canopy above the toll, rain began to defeat the wipers. Keith was silent for a long while even as further updates came over the radio. As we crossed the junction with the A2, he made his considered response. 'You', he said pausing for effect 'are a fucking maniac.'

While the lorry driver fought to steady his shattered nerves within the warm confines of the attendant ambulance, close by the other ARV crews deployed from their cars.

On the forecourt of a conveniently situated service station Jake had swung the heavy Rover through a wide tyre-scuffing arc. Its nose dipped under braking as in the same instant the engine fell silent. Close to a nearby fence the two dog handlers waited. As the ARV crew dragged the guns and kit from the car, all around unarmed local units arrived. A second ARV roared in behind them and made ready. Beside me in the car, as we passed above the Swanley junction, Keith made a pronouncement that would come back to haunt us: 'I know where it is: it's just off the M23.'

As we thundered on through the rain the perverse weather that day began to play havoc with the visibility. Rain varied in strength from drizzle to stair rods that turned the scene ahead of me into oily broken images.

At the scene light spots of rain barely hinted of worse to come in the warm humid air. Dressed only in shirtsleeves beneath the heavy body armour, laden with kit and having been briefed by a local sergeant, the crews moved forwards.

Through the garden of a local house, over a six-foot wall and under high chain-link fences they struggled on as Bruno homed in on a scent and they followed. As the handler's confidence grew that they were on to the armed suspect, a harrowing sound reached Barney's ears. Somewhere close a high-speed train clattered by. He turned to face Jake and John Hayes, as with mutual glances they recognised the severity of their situation. Trains, electricity, dogs, armed suspects, and now rain. Steadily increasing rain.

'You drive, I navigate,' Keith asserted. 'I know what I'm doing.' I could not believe that we had come so far and travelled so fast yet not had sight of our destination. We were now a good distance down the M23 when I protested that we *must* have passed our turn-off, and grudgingly he conceded to a U-turn that took us back several miles.

Still no suitable exit or road sign presented itself. 'And they call *me* pathfinder,' I quipped. He turned to look at me from where his eyes tracked the passage of his forefinger down the page of the atlas. 'Bollocks, just bloody drive.' I had to smile. Distantly thunder rolled threateningly, forked lightning flashed on the horizon.

The crews had followed the dog and handler through a derelict light-industrial area, over shrubland, through the garden of the house. They had negotiated the wall and fence to be where they were now. That was no improvement in the situation. As the same storm we were watching drew closer to them, they stared down an almost sheer railway embankment.

The rumble of thunder competed for supremacy with the passing trains. The noise conspired unsuccessfully to drown Barney's words: 'Well I'm buggered if I'm going down there. That's the end of that.' Bruno, the big German shepherd dog, suddenly pricked his ears and, throwing himself against the leash, began to bark, loud and aggressive.

From the driving seat of the Volvo, I protested. 'Look, we've covered this ground already.' We were on the M23 now going north, back towards the M25 whence we had come. 'It's not here, you've got it wrong.' I protested.

Keith's explosive response followed. 'No, I haven't. I've driven this route dozens of times. It's here. I *know* it's here.' I turned the Volvo around again and headed south once more.

The dog was on a search lead. Yards of leather strap that allowed him to range around, to explore every scent. The handler had a light grip on the leather that slid through his hand at about a six-foot length from the dog. The remaining twenty feet lay coiled around Barney's and John's feet, poised as they were perhaps a hundred and fifty feet above the railway. Below them a sea of bricks, broken bottles, trees, scrub and rusting barbed wire.

Far down the M23 I pushed the Volvo on to ever greater speed, ignoring the intense rain as the urge to get there almost overpowered me. As the horns wailed and the blue lights circled above us, a small sign presented itself briefly in the flashing headlamps. It said BRIGHTON 8 MILES. I turned to Keith and smiled again. 'Fancy a paddle?' There was another of those long pregnant pauses. Then came his response: 'Fuck!'

The dog handler called suddenly, 'There he is, about halfway down the slope.' Jake took a few cautious steps forwards and down. Bruno launched himself towards the threat. The coiled lead tightened around Barney's and John's feet. Ian, the driver of the second ARV, stood beside them, his crew a few feet behind. The scene was set for disaster.

Jake felt the soft ground beneath his feet begin to fall away, and he fell back, hoping to spread his body weight, to prevent a slide. The panicking dog below him began to frantically back-pedal, but could not prevent his own accelerating descent. Behind and above him Jake heard cries of alarm as the dog's lead tore Barney's and John's feet from under them, and they joined the cascade of uniforms. Ian and unarmed local officers somehow became involved, lost their footing and followed.

Jake's efforts to prevent his slide failed, serving only to slow his progress as he spread his arms and legs like a demented starfish – but to no avail as he gradually gathered speed. Below him the dog's fear was turning to anger, as the handler's demanding voice called him back.

Barney and John adopted the same 'starfish' tactic. All three grabbed desperately at shrubs and small trees, as they rushed ever faster down the steepening slope. Far below, threatening, the trains rumbled by. Pieces of uniform were ripped off. The seat of Barney's trousers, the whole of one shirtsleeve. The plastic butt of his carbine and its magazine were torn away, and lost somewhere among the undergrowth.

They began to bleed where the brambles and barbed wire tore at their flesh, as they overtook and then re-overtook each other in the headlong descent, like snow-boarders, going ever faster.

For Jake, though, there was a worse threat as the angry dog scrambled back up the slope. He was looking for someone to blame. Jake's open legs and his unprotected crotch drew ever closer and he selected his target. In a desperate bid to stop himself, Jake dug his heels into a patch of soft earth. Brambles tore again at his uniform, helping for a moment to slow him, and he slithered to a halt. He lay there, his splayed legs the only means to prevent him sliding again as Barney and John hurtled past. The dog, though, was not deterred. Much later Jake was to quip, 'It was a small target, but a good one.'

Barney's ample form crashed through the undergrowth as he approached the last twenty or so feet. The bottom of the embankment terminated in a six-foot-high concrete support wall that prevented the earth from 'creeping' towards the actual railway lines. From its highest point he found himself launched into the air. He landed with an enormous crunch on the gravel, his back to the lines. Around him policemen began to fall out of the undergrowth – 'like apples in an orchard' was how he described it.

For poor Jake, in so many ways things were definitely going downhill. Bruno and he now had eye contact as the dog closed with him. Far behind them in a rising pitch the dog handler, from somewhere above the cascade of blue uniforms, screamed repeatedly 'Leave-leave'. In a sudden darting movement the dog sank its fangs into Jake's unprotected left inner thigh.

His agony rose to smother the pain inflicted by a multitude of cuts and scratches as, unsatisfied with the grip it had established, the dog worked its way further up Jake's thigh towards a more significant trophy.

As thoughts of shooting the dog or beating it with a long baton crossed Jake's mind the handler was suddenly there, launching an unprecedented attack on the errant animal.

Succumbing to the rising pain Jake closed his legs and slid further downwards, dropping on to the railway near where Barney and several others stood.

Looking like soldiers from a ragtag army, with ripped uniforms, lost and broken equipment, they stood silent for moments while the increasing rain diluted the blood from hundreds of scratches, until it looked like the scene of some major blood-letting. Then, as policemen often do in adversity, first one face, then another, cracked into a grin, then a chuckle. Finally they descended into peels of laughter.

It was time to reorganise, to reassess. Somewhere, perhaps nearby, was at least one armed man. At their feet water lay in pools, splashed by fresh rain. While the control fought to get the power turned off, across the deadly live rails a further embankment of equal height challenged them. To the left at perhaps 150 yards hence was a viaduct bridge on top of which, some 100 or feet above them, more police officers, and, significantly, the fire brigade, looked down. To the right at about 200 yards was the dark and menacing mouth of a long railway tunnel.

The group waited for long minutes while the railway authority stubbornly refused to turn off the power. The thought of disappearing in a cloud of smoke appealed to no one, and prevented the further use of dogs, perhaps to Jake's relief.

From high on the viaduct the fire brigade indicated a heat source registering on their small, hand-held thermal-imaging equipment. Down the radio, the control confirmed 'power now off', as a passing train sidled to a halt, most unhelpfully, in the middle of the search

Bobby Back-Doors' ego will suffer ever after, but it could have been a lot worse.

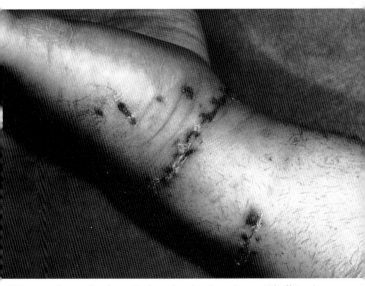

This scar shows the damage done by the American pit bull terrier, Bullseye.

*Above*  The ex-soldier, mercenary, legionnaire and now bank robber, lies dead at the end of a terrifying chase.

*Right*  The Putney Incident. The Soldier lies dead in the front garden of a suburban house.

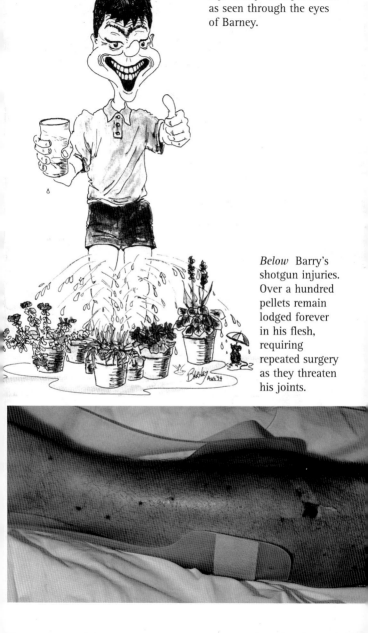

*Left* Barry Oldroyd-Jones, as seen through the eyes of Barney.

*Below* Barry's shotgun injuries. Over a hundred pellets remain lodged forever in his flesh, requiring repeated surgery as they threaten his joints.

*Above* The Gang of Four (*left to right*): Andy Pearce, Chris the SFO Officer, Shaky Jake and Phil 'Twelve Hits'.

*Below* The Relief near the end of my time with SO19.

*Above* A Method of Entry man uses an enforcer to break in; other members of SO19 stand by to enter and clear the room.

*Below* Be warned: this car door shows you why you shouldn't hide behind a car when you're being shot at.

*Above* The original weapon issued to ARV crew – a Smith & Wesson model 10 revolver (*top left*). It was to be replaced by the more sophisticated Glock 17 self-loading pistol (*top right*), shown with the German-made Heckler & Koch MP5 9mm carbine (*bottom*).

*Right* The original members of the ARV team. Me, second from right, front row . . . the good-looking one.

*Above* Day one of the Armed Response Unit; the first car rolls out of Old Street.

The car, the tools, the man.

area. The driver dismounted, going forwards with a bridging device to ensure the power could not be switched back on. Bloodied and torn, they began to search again. Barney checked his carbine, butt broken off and magazine missing. He knew that same embankment would have to be searched exhaustively for the lost ammunition.

Aboard the train startled commuters watched the small group of battered police officers combing the tracks around them. An area of dense undergrowth was identified by the brigade as having a body-heat indication, but proved so inaccessible as to be dismissed. 'The only thing that could get through there', John concluded 'is a hedgehog.'

Deep rumbling thunder announced the arrival of the full force of the storm. Rain lashed the scene as, forlornly and far away, Keith and I despaired of ever finding our way there. Over the radio came yet another call. This time to Enfield in north London, where police had laid siege to a man with a shotgun. After threatening the occupiers, who had fled, he had challenged, 'Come and get me.' But now all was quiet. Was he alive or dead? They had to go in, and Keith and I were miles away.

They cleared first one side of the train, then crossed over the tracks to clear the other. John's accident-prone reputation surfaced. He slipped off the edge of a railway sleeper, badly twisting an ankle. As he lay agonising on the coarse gravel around the lines, others ran to him. In seconds the ankle ballooned. Keith and I were back on the M25 doing 115 miles per hour in driving rain, desperately trying to circuit almost half of the motorway length to where we were now required to be.

John sat helpless on the lines, waiting for the pain to subside as Barney and the already wounded Jake stood ready to lift him to his feet. Ian the driver took John's carbine and slowly, with help, he rose to his feet. He hobbled towards the train. A woman of about fifty, accompanied by her strikingly attractive daughter, watched through an open window.

The thunder reached a new crescendo, flashes of lightning dramatising the scene. The rain beat ever harder until it ran in little rivers down his face. Totally dejected, John lifted his eyes and said to the two women facing him, 'If you've never seen anyone struck by lightning then keep watching, because the way my luck's going I'm going to get hit any moment.'

As the crews satisfied themselves that their armed suspect was at least not in the immediate area, attention fell on the uncleared tunnel. Lifted into the warmth of the train, John settled down to shiver, finding himself seated opposite the two women. They sat surrounded by the bagged and wrapped purchases, the product of a long and expensive day's shopping. John smiled and spoke again. 'I really thought I might get hit by lightning there,' he said.

There was a long pause. The younger woman winced; the older one's face became grave. 'My husband was killed by lightning,' she retorted.

His torment was over though. As the power was switched back on, the train began to roll the last mile to the next station. Once it was in the tunnel, the driver called back to John that a shadowy figure lurked somewhere within. John was reduced to standing on one leg while staring into the darkness through an open window, pistol in hand. Within the tunnel the radio was useless. Obliging fellow passengers, including the two women, strained their eyes in the darkness but no one was ever found. At the station, the irony of it turned all involved into friends, as John mounted an ambulance and the women went on their way.

Jake and John found themselves at the hospital together, where advice and painkillers were administered and, to add to Jake's misery, a large needle penetrated his buttocks, to prevent tetanus. At the scene Barney and Ian worked their way back up the slope, taking nearly an hour to reclimb a descent they had made in seconds. The magazine and ammunition remained missing. They sat, wet, dishevelled and miserable, on a pile of bricks at the summit.

An abseil instructor arrived to mock them, but immediately agreed that ropes were the only realistic means of descent. After two attempts, the ammunition was recovered.

After having their scratches attended to by nurses, who hailed them as heroes, the crews headed back. As they arrived at Old Street, looking like vagrants, Barney stepped out of the car to swing open the huge green steel gates.

A very senior officer confronted Barney. 'What do you mean turning up for work like this? You're an absolute disgrace.' Barney's unprintable response quickly cleared up the matter, and elevated everyone's mood.

After further terrorising Keith on a return journey around the M25 and through the Dartford tunnel, I pulled up at a suburban house in Enfield, in time to organise an armed search. As we stood by, John Brannigan and a team of specialist firearms officers effected an entry and arrest.

One that got away. One that didn't.

At the parade that preceded the next tour of duty, I was subjected to untold derision. Keith had told the relief we had got lost as a result of *my* directions. I suffered mockery ever after. On the occasion of my retirement the relief kindly bought me several cherished gifts. At the presentation, one of those gifts was a street map of Brighton.

## The Great Banstead Lorry Chase

It was a Saturday-night duty spilling over into the cold turkey of an uneventful Sunday morning. The evening had its share of run-of-the-mill calls, but now things had just gone completely dead. John Brannigan was 'strapping' with us that night, as we were short of supervisors – just the two of us, and the expanse of the Metropolis as our responsibility. It wasn't, however, making many demands. ARV work can be like that: long periods of inactivity, then suddenly the whole world goes mad.

John is a swarthy dark man, his hair matched by a thick black moustache. Solidly built and a six-footer, he has a deep voice and a ringing Irish accent, complemented perfectly by a dry sense of humour. Early on, it became obvious that we would be friends. He came into the department after me, and was obviously hungry to go further. Tonight, though, we two sergeants trawled through Brixton heading back towards north London.

John had been driving for several hours, and the undemanding Rover 827 was lulling him gently towards sleep. I recognised the symptoms. Flickering eyelids, occasional deep sighs, and I knew it was time to give him a break. Little encouragement from me was needed for him to stop. He relinquished the driving seat, and I found myself quite happily behind the steering wheel.

Soon after that I was also talking to myself, as his chin dropped towards the folded arms, and his eyelids succumbed to the leaden weights that were drawing them downwards. Not only is a Rover 827 easy to drive but it's also pretty damn comfortable, and warm, and when you're tired . . . Well we're all human!

The two radios nestling in the dash had been quiet for far too long. 'For the attention of all cars, 3 and 4 areas,' barked the lower set. Well that, in general terms, was where we were. 'Attention called to a blue seven-tonne lorry, index mark . . .' The radio operator went on to relate that the three male occupants had been involved in an armed warehouse robbery, using guns and knives.

They had pistol-whipped the warehouseman, and stolen a lorry laden with a large quantity of high-value electrical goods. The warehouseman's family had apparently been threatened. This was common practice, intended to slow down the speed with which the theft would be reported. This bunch were really nasty bastards.

This, to be honest, was all rather unexciting, not because we didn't feel for the poor bloke, but because it wasn't so very unusual. The robbery had taken place in Surrey, a fair distance from the Met, and a long way from where we were. Additionally, only a fool would keep a thing that identifiable, that visible, on public roads for any period of time.

'No,' I thought. I was visualising a lorry lurching off down some farm track, perhaps to a darkened yard, where its contents would be spirited away. Then perhaps to be dumped or burned. But only a fool would still be driving it, and into London. Never!

The radio crackled again. 'Reference your . . .' and the voice of a police officer somewhere relayed the reference number and the index mark of the lorry. 'We are behind this vehicle now, just passing the old Mortlake Brewery, travelling east.'

It was coming towards us, albeit a good distance off. I snatched up the handset. 'MP from Trojan 500, show us assigned.'

In the passenger seat John snuffled, the rising tempo of events penetrating his sleepy consciousness. I stamped on the accelerator and swung off left from the Elephant and Castle. The big old engine growled from the depths of the car. The gearbox snatched a low gear, and the usually genteel Rover showed the other side of its character.

John's head rocked back, hitting the restraint. 'Oh shit!' he protested, rubbing his face with the palms of his hands. He picked up the handset of the radio. 'What the bloody hell's going on?' he demanded, dragging himself back to reality. 'Snap out of it, mate,' I said. 'It's game on and it's coming our way.'

He turned on the Met sound. The long mournful wail echoed far ahead. Strobing blue lights glittered atop the car, the familiar patterns of flashing blue bouncing back from every reflective surface we passed.

I guessed the lorry to be heading towards Wandsworth. Now in the small hours of a Sunday morning, the traffic was light.

I headed towards the river at Lambeth, passing the Imperial War Museum on our left, the 'lab' [forensic science laboratory] and what was later to become the south base for the ARVs. The wide one-way system allowed me to use the full width of the road. I drifted the car through the curves, power firmly on, tyres protesting loudly. On through the roundabout at the south side of the bridge, passing Lambeth Palace. On down Albert Embankment, to leave the bright cream eye of Big Ben over my right shoulder.

Mile after mile passed rapidly, as we closed with Nine Elms and Battersea. Over the radio, the driver of the following police car filled us in on the progress the stolen lorry was making. I cursed every obstruction as we closed with the pursuit, luckily, following my predicted route. They had gone through Mortlake and into Barnes, past the building that had once been headquarters to the Special Patrol Group.

Then across Putney Heath close to our old home, still on roads I could picture in my mind's eye, that Sue and I had frequented while we still courted. We barrelled on through Battersea, headed for the huge one-way circuit at Wandsworth, known as Armoury Way.

By now the 'boys' had got the scent, and two other ARVs were hurtling towards the fray. I caught snippets of radio transmissions above the noise – the sirens and the interruptions of the second radio set, barking out messages on another channel, increasing our frustration. John struggled to make sense of it, but the insight I had into the area helped enormously.

Tibbet's Corner, I heard, straight up the hill from Wandsworth, and we would be there. 'The bastards are heading back to Surrey,' I shouted to John. 'I know where they are, and we're on them.' I winked at him. *'Right on them.'*

The last location we got as we topped the hill was Wimbledon Park Side, a long, relatively uninterrupted road skirting Wimbledon Common, with that open ground on its right, now sadly infamous for the tragic, horrific and apparently unsolved murder of Rachel Nickell.

At the last moment I negotiated a slip road, taking us up on to the roundabout to make a joining with the main A3, going south. We burst blaring on to it, while the traffic came to an abrupt halt. A chicane turn to the left, and, oh, what a spectacle confronted us!

The Metropolitan Police rolling roadshow spread out before us. The combination of the lorry's limited speed, and our inability to stop an unwilling seven-tonne monster, had created a convoy the Blues Brothers would have been proud to put their names to. Half a mile of glittering blue lights, serenaded by the cacophony of klaxon horns and sirens, all playing a mixture of tones high and low. They all wanted a piece of the action, to somehow be in on it, but good practice dictated they must wait, and good sense told them that they should.

But why? That seemed to be the robbers' unspoken question. We've got guns, we've got knives, we've got a seven-tonne lorry, and we can go wherever we want.

But this was just the sort of thing the ARVs were created to be equal to.

John's announcement of our arrival was greeted by the radio operator with relief. Our request for other units to drop back, to allow the armed units to head up the pursuit, were emphatically relayed to the other cars in the convoy, and we were waved by. I could see the flashes of the alternating headlamps of two oncoming cars, their roof lines picked out in flashing blue, the wailing tones somehow more intense as they closed with us. Radio transmissions were telling us they were ARVs.

They were as close as they could wish to be, but passing the bandit lorry in the wrong direction. Somehow they had to turn around and get in behind the quarry. Behind us in an unarmed police car the driver understood it all, allowing his speed to fall, and a gap to open.

On seeing his opening the driver of the first oncoming ARV locked up for a highly spectacular, tyre-smoking U-turn. The second ARV following him similarly locked up to avert collision. The cars slewed and snaked, avoiding the T-bone impact that threatened. Before the smoke had cleared they were tucked in behind us. Suddenly it was all control and order. I wondered what the divisional boys thought. They probably loved it!

Now it was down to us: damned if you do, and damned if you don't. The big old lorry rolled on through the twisting bends, passing into Wimbledon itself. On down the hill, through the new development that is the centre of the town.

On it rolled, past Wimbledon Theatre towards Merton, sullenly resisting any effort to stop it. Divisional cars of all shapes and sizes began to appear at junctions as word spread, but nobody had the means to stop this giant. Foot-duty officers hurled everything from abuse to refuse at it, with absolutely no effect save for our suffering the backwash.

The pace was really rather sedate. After all, this lorry was no lightweight and, having not long stolen it, the boy needed time to familiarise himself.

Behind us was Trojan 504 driven by Barry OJ (standing for Oldroyd-Jones), slim, dark-haired and frenetic. Beside him was 'shaky Jake' my ex-marine, ex-boxer Scottish stalwart. In the back was the infamous 'Jonah' himself, 'Lucky Bob'. I could see him in my mind's eye, his Lee Van Cleef features pressed downwards towards the atlas, plotting the route while his adrenaline levels rose.

The car following that was driven by Chris, an ex-SFO officer. He had forsaken that role for the immediacy of the ARVs. A good head on nomadic shoulders. Their operator that night was Kevin ('Granny'). In the back seat was Martin, 'most reliable', left to wrestle with the maps and kit.

The glittering convoy rolled on towards Merton, crossing into the main road at the High Street. John fought to pull the body armour over his head, the sticky Velcro pads grabbing at the car's upholstery.

The lorry swung left at the dictate of a small one-way system as he then lifted the radio handset from its hook. Then he gave clear instructions in that deep Irish voice. 'Trojan 541 from 500, put the block in.'

There was no way I could reach my body armour, or that we could retrieve the radio operator's lone carbine, slumbering in the safe behind us. Instantly I knew the danger. If the lorry stopped, the first confrontation would be with us. We would be projected into a face-to-face exchange, armed only with handguns. 'John,' I mused, 'if there *is* a gunfight right now, well, it's going to be you and me first!'

Behind us Barry had reacted. In my mirror his headlights swung wide and the Rover drew level with us. In the huge mirror dominating the side of the lorry's cab, I could catch glimpses of the driver's face, and I could see his wild-eyed expression.

In the same instant, Bob's face rose to fill the space between Barry and Jake in the front, whispering to Barry with the ominous resolve that is his trademark: 'Don't even think about it.' He was right. The conflict would have been anything but even.

For the seven tonnes of Luton-bodied lorry was suddenly alive, like an angry dinosaur. The robbers were happy to play a waiting game while the police stayed back, but not now. If we could stop them, we would nick them, and they were having none of it.

The lorry had swung left into the High Street, and was about to turn right with the one-way system as Barry overtook us. If the danger had not been evident enough, the lorry itself became a huge threat. As Barry dropped back, aware that they would be crushed if they tried to pass, the huge vehicle dominated the centre of the road.

Every hint of approach was countered by a wild swerving. As I ventured towards the centre of the road to look beyond the lorry, the driver braked, swinging the vehicle wildly as it pitched back and forth, its huge bodywork assuming dramatic angles of lean.

Over the radio the voice of a car much further back continued to describe the route, while the armed cars sat impotent on the tail of the 'bandits'. We had the means and the will to deal with the suspects, but how could we stop this giant? Over a separate wavelength the ARVs conversed, voicing this opinion and that, swapping ideas. But the lorry rolled on. Behind me the two armed cars jockeyed for position.

On we went, through the red traffic lights at the end of the one-way system, to burst back on to Morden Road going south, as the lorry's rear nearside wheel mounted the kerb. The whole thing tipped violently and dangerously over to the right as behind me police cars sat two abreast. Still the eyes in the mirror, the occasional swerve, as the driver reminded us of the threat. If we tried to pass he would attack us with seven tonnes of steel. A few ounces of lead would be no contest.

The road rose over a railway bridge and I realised that the offices of the makers of ITV's *The Bill* were within sight, and I wondered what they would have made of this!

As we descended towards a small roundabout at the junction with Morden Road and St Helier Avenue, there came another voice among the many, jamming the airwaves.

'MP from Oscar. We are close by, seeking permission to deploy Stinger.'

Hope! Stinger is a device not unlike a garden trellis that can be thrown out on the road surface, expanding as it goes. It presents hundreds of hollow and razor-sharp metal quills facing upwards. Any vehicle passing over them will have its tyres punctured, and they will progressively and safely deflate. It would be the answer to my prayer – *if* they could get in front.

There was a pause, then the reply, 'Yes, understood, Oscar, but stand by, permission is required from a chief inspector.' We were in dire straits, and the bureaucrats were at it again!

Behind, through my mirror, I could see Barry now playing a waiting game while beside him, even at this distance, Jake's Celtic fury clearly burned bright on his features. Behind him Lucky Bob's deadpan face would now be pale with pure menace. Parallel with them, Chris piloted the second ARV. This would be a reckoning.

Behind them again was that same roadshow. Dozens of blue lights turned the night into a kaleidoscope of glittering blue. The night air was alive with a crescendo of sirens. In my door mirror I could see one set of lights, higher and distinct from the rest, as the tall traffic-division Range Rover, the Oscar car, broke ranks. He was moving up with the Stinger.

I called to John, still fighting for control over the radio, 'The traffic car is moving up.' He shouted down the microphone 'MP, we can deploy Stinger now, require immediate permission.' We had driven around a second roundabout as the lorry had ploughed straight across, pitching and rolling dangerously. Still first in line, I winced as private cars swung into the kerb, the torrent of noise and lights invading their ears and, through their mirrors, their eyes as they then cowered near the kerb.

The lorry swerved out past them, fearful faces peering up at its swaying bulk, a child mesmerised by the horde of pursuing, glittering, bellowing police cars. The long dual carriageway of St Helier Avenue rose ahead, narrow and hostile, as the lorry dominated the centre of the road, a sudden wild swerve serving to reinforce the threat.

I knew we were approaching Rosehill Roundabout. If the lorry went along the main route, Reigate Avenue, we would have a chance! A wide, three-lane dual carriageway – he would be hard pushed to stop us passing.

The entry to the roundabout was pure theatre, as the huge bulk yawed like a sailing ship. Its first left turn was so violent that the nearside rear wheels lifted clear of the road. I waited for it to pitch right over, to end this nightmare, but there was too much weight.

The chassis dragged its bulk back to the ground as it lurched on around. I tucked the big car in close behind.

This was no challenge to my driving skills, the speeds being quite low – but the stakes were very high.

In our car, a silence, contrasting with the huge volume of sound outside, descended on us. John and I watched the big vehicle continuing on. In my mind ran the prayer, 'Don't turn yet, not yet.' Bishopsford Road was ignored as hopes slowly climbed. Still the lorry rolled violently on, swerving, yet still following the shape of the strange lozenge-shaped island.

Wrythe Lane was ignored as Rosehill came into view. The tension was almost unbearable as the lorry drove towards the exit and then turned away. Reigate Avenue was next, but he could still pass it. John's agonies voiced themselves: 'Take it, you bastard, take it', and then 'Yessss', as the lorry pitched into the main route south.

Now we could take him, as, with the throb of a big V8 engine, the Range Rover hurtled past. Beside me, John's hand brushed his gun, reminding me of how close confrontation was. I felt for mine, its rubber-covered grip a reassurance. Now all we needed was authority to deploy the Stinger.

The pace was building, and for the first time the lorry, now rolling downhill, achieved a significant speed. John pleaded into the microphone yet again: 'MP from Trojan 500, we need authority to deploy Stinger now.' There was an awful pause, as the operator came back, 'Stand by, just trying to locate the chief inspector.' In moments we had passed the Range Rover, its crew poised at the kerb, and the opportunity was lost. Over the radio a voice echoed all our thoughts. 'For crying out fucking loud, what are they doing?'

A valuable opportunity had been squandered, but there was no time to reflect on that. The speeds were now far more of a problem than before. It was easy enough for us to keep pace, but now the road was wide enough for us to pass. The hyped robber at the wheel used another tactic to keep us at bay. As his speed passed sixty miles per hour, he hurtled through a red traffic light.

This was far too great a risk, either to ourselves, or to some innocent. As we jockeyed for position, for a means to halt this lunacy, first one ARV, then another, had taken lead position. We approached the lights, I braked heavily, now lead vehicle again. I brought the massive convoy of police vehicles to a virtual halt. Angrily we watched the lorry pulling fast away. Divisional cars raced forwards to block the junctions, to allow us to close with our quarry.

The front wheels spun as the Rover fought for grip. I had planted the accelerator pedal hard on the floor, and I intended that it would stay there until we were in touch with the lorry once more. At the next junction the lights were again red, but the locals were there already, blocking the opposing traffic as the lorry thundered unflinching through, and closely we followed.

Inside me real anger began to boil. John marshalled the cars behind us, trying to organise some kind of rolling roadblock. Inside our car, over the airwaves, obscenity was rife. Climbing St Dunstan's Hill towards Belmont Rise, the lorry's great bulk worked against it, and we closed with it at 'warp speed'. As the sea of blue lights threatened to wash over him, the orchestra of sirens to overpower him, the robber threw the lorry back and forth ahead of us.

Holding us at bay, he had one lunatic card yet to play. His brake lights were suddenly bright in my eyes, as a roundabout marking the junction with the Brighton Road loomed ahead. Then the lorry snaked as, at once, he both braked and steered. It suddenly swerved to the right, rocking violently as the rear wheels clipped the kerb and the big vehicle half mounted the roundabout, passing it on the wrong side. I couldn't hear through all the noise, as John shouted from the passenger seat. Behind me blue lights danced both left and right, the drivers making last-minute choices.

Ahead oncoming traffic panicked, swerving this way and that, mounting the grass verges to escape this maniac. Then his lunacy plumbed new depths. In the face of half a dozen sets of approaching headlights, the wrong way along the dual carriageway, he drove directly at them.

There was now no way I would let him go, and I followed. Barry's headlights danced in my mirror.

Relentlessly the speed began to rise, as I latched firmly on to the back of the lorry. Behind me, Barry threw the Rover back and forth, then, passing us, ventured forwards, level with the cab. From the nearside window, Lucky Bob's head and shoulders appeared, as he made a clear statement of intent.

A yellow circle of light danced around the driver's window. In Bob's hands the menacing shape of a carbine, its torch mount piercing the darkness. With no other way to send the message, he had chosen to graphically demonstrate the odds. If they chose to make this a gunfight, they would lose.

The bureaucratic wheels had finally turned, and permission to deploy the Stinger given, as along the left-hand lane the traffic Range Rover charged ahead. The second ARV and divisional cars stood back, waiting for what now looked like an imminent crisis. In the lorry, the sight of the carbine seemed to have registered. Ahead the wicked carpet of razor-sharp quills waited, as the Stinger slithered across the road, the now stationary bulk of the Range Rover marking its presence.

Escape was becoming ever less likely, but our robbers were not about to give up so easily. Suddenly brake lights dazzled me. The lorry slowed, then swerved left.

The central reservation was marked out with significant kerbs. They were crowned by unmown grass that made a lie of its height. The lorry's huge wheels rolled easily across, as he chose to dodge the Stinger, to put the following cars at risk of ripping out their underbellies.

I had travelled too far, become too angry, for a gamble of such low stakes to stop me. John cringed as I swung the steering wheel left. The Rover bucked and crashed its way over the island. Ahead the traffic-car crew watched in horror as the dark shape descended on them, silhouetted now by an aura of flashing blue.

Now the determination to stop this was so powerful that, with little time and no gloves, the traffic officer dragged the Stinger across into the path of the approaching lorry. Its slithering shape cut off the last exit for the robbers. His hands became wet with blood. The evil spines had torn open his palms.

I tucked in tight behind the dark hulk; Barry's car lurched across the reservation to fall in behind. 'We must have him now,' I said, as plans for an armed stop formed in my mind, and beside me John began to position our cars to strike. It was still not going to be that easy.

We crossed a bridge that spanned a railway running through a cutting far below. Ahead the traffic lights gleamed in the night, marking where the same bleeding hands grasped the retrieval line, ready to drag the Stinger out from behind the lorry, to allow us to follow, to bring the quarry down. Then the brake lights again, bright in my eyes.

The lorry swung out, first right across the two southbound lanes, and then, in a dramatic 'swan-neck' manoeuvre, turned violently towards the kerb. Beyond the bridge, hidden from my eyes, was a track. Too big to be a path, too small to be a lane, it nevertheless gave the robbers somewhere to run, and they took it. The dark shape rose over the kerb, and then pitched downwards with the descending path, as the big Luton body twisted and rolled.

As I followed, the shape of small trees loomed across a grassy divide, picked out in the lorry's lights. Behind me the bright beams of following cars cut arcs in the air, sirens echoed.

Suddenly we were consumed by a dark tunnel. Taller trees formed a canopy above. The dirt track was transformed into a swirling nightmare of dust, first white, then blue, in the lights, as the big wheels ahead threw it into the night air. My only guide was the rear lights ahead of me, dancing first left, and then right, the lorry lurching obscenely back and forth.

Shocking loud bangs pierced the car. Branches were torn off the trees above by the lorry's tall bodywork, to fall on the pursuing police cars, adding to the confusion. The radios spoke with a dozen desperate voices as I followed blindly. Distantly in the night, more sirens.

Stones began to pummel the floor beneath my feet with a staccato rhythm, as the front wheels fought for grip on the loose gravel. John braced his feet against the interior, his left hand gripping the microphone, the right clamped around the butt of his gun. If the robber braked, I was so close we would probably shunt the lorry. If I backed off we would lose them.

On down this tortuous track we followed, the car absorbing endless blows. Ahead stood an obstacle not even this lunatic could ignore. Steel bollards blocked the way, the track reduced to a forested path. The rear lights, now a frosted haze in the dust-filled air, pitched suddenly right, then violently downwards.

The night was rent with the sound of tortured metal, punctuated by the loud crack of young trees snapping, as the great bulk crushed them. Branches fell around us. I braked hard, the car slewing to a halt, half turned to the right. Before I could open the door, fleeting shapes passed the car. Jake tore past me, carbine in hand, and everywhere the shouts, 'Armed police.' Screaming, barking, excited police dogs dragged their handlers towards the fray.

Old instincts took over, and I found myself running forwards, gun in hand. Off to my right Jake's voice rang through the air, 'Cab clear', as he pulled at the driver's door, jammed against a copse of trees. Bob stood off, carbine raised, ranging around the front of the lorry. Near the roller shutters at the rear, Barry covered with a handgun as I moved to support him. Behind us John directed others, giving updates over the radio as he did.

The thick undergrowth took on sinister, unreal dimensions. The lights swept back and forth, creating dancing shapes from the foliage, casting grotesque shadows. In the treetops above, the rotating blue beams of the abandoned police cars whirled like beacons.

The lorry had pitched downwards in the dust-filled haze, crashing down a slope and through undergrowth until the density of the trees had forced a halt. The passenger door lay open, testament to their escape route, while the driver's door was jammed shut by a host of broken and twisted saplings. The last man out would have to be the driver. He was the man I most wanted to answer for all of this.

As we covered his movements, Jake climbed into the back of the lorry, the sound of the roller shutter loud as other sounds subsided. Around us, a wide-ranging, unco-ordinated search was taking place. Where there was no artificial light, total, evil blackness presided. In the back of the lorry, high-value electrical goods lay shattered, but it was otherwise empty.

John appeared at my side. We joined the main body of the search, where chaos ruled. No means of communication, verbal or visual, could have any effect in this jungle. Only the barking of the dogs and the ranging beams of torches told me where the police line was. A robber could have lain at my feet, and I would not have seen him.

What was bad for us was not necessarily good for them. Off to the right of the main pathway, a thicket of dry brambles and vines crackled loudly. Nearby a police dog began to bay and howl. A bright beam of light panned across and through the foliage, to settle on the thicket, and the movement stopped. I could see no one, but I resolved to play a game of bluff.

'Armed police, stand still.'

In the darkness, someone was trapped. The headlong race to escape had taken him full-tilt into a tangled network that would not now release him, at least not silently. For long moments there was silence, then stark crackling, as the dried vegetation clung to his every movement.

The dog strained at its leash, whining and baying, as a handler closed with the scene. Seizing it by the collar, he shook the dog, cursing it to be quiet. Again there was movement, then more silence. Slowly our man was hoping to slide away. Still I could not see him. It was time for bluff again, and a measure of aggression.

'Stand still, we are armed police. Stand still or I will fucking shoot you the next time you move.' It was total bluff. Shoot him? I had no real idea where he was. There was a surge of movement. In the light of Jake's torch-mount beam, suddenly there stood a defiant figure, a big man in his twenties, facing off the now howling, barking dog.

From around us, armed ARV crews appeared. As more shouts went up, the wild-eyed man moved towards the dog, his staring expression perhaps betraying courage that had been bought. As carbines and handguns rose towards him, I watched in disbelief as he stepped forwards again, and kicked the dog.

The effect was predictable. Now beyond restraint, the dog was on him as he fell back screaming, placing his upper legs within range, and the animal took its revenge. The handler was there instantly, pulling the dog away, and again all reason seemed to leave the robber.

He rose to his feet, seemingly oblivious to the pain, and to the odds. Moving forwards, he confronted Jake, who, with Chris and Barry, was closing on him. Beyond them Bob ran into the fray. Instantly the fracas turned the fight into a total confusion. Cursing and screaming shattered the air, torchlights spiralled around, lighting up a face here, a limb there, the occasional dog, or a tree. Unable to do otherwise, I pitched in.

Thorns and brambles tore at clothing and skin, and I grabbed at an arm. The dog was by now screaming hysterically, and quite useless. A powerful rush of movement knocked me back into dense imprisoning brambles, as the robber rose once more to confront Jake. It was a bad mistake. A torchlight found the man's face, and Jake put him down.

Moments later, both scratched and bleeding, Barry and I led him sweating back towards the car. In his eyes was the clue to where all the strength and aggression had been found. As Barry 'read him his rights', the hulking form of a local inspector moved forwards to receive him.

'Off you go, boys,' the inspector smiled. A huge hand on the end of a heavily muscled arm clamped itself around the robber's wrist. 'Will you be all right with this bloke?' I queried. 'Oh, I think me and Mr Robber are going to understand each other.' He smiled again. A passing local PC glanced at me. 'Don't worry, Sarge. The inspector's a class wrestler.'

As we walked back into the woods, from behind us a scream confirmed yet another failed attempt at escape. Lucky Bob walked towards me, a hand held awkwardly.

In the pale rising light, the skin shone, taut and swollen. In the fight his hand had been broken.

Hours passed as we searched fruitlessly in the darkness. John and I would not have the crews roaming in this blackness, looking for armed men, and we resolved to wait for the dawn. We asked for the helicopter, craving thermal imaging and the 'night sun'. The bureaucrats were there again. 'No craft flying at this hour, it costs too much. Calling out a crew.' Uselessly, and hours later, its rotors beat a rhythm above the scene.

As dawn broke, we called in more manpower. As we slowly cleared the wood, it became apparent where the others had at first run. From the path, Alan recovered a huge and evil knife. All around us were branches, spikes and thorns that in the daylight we could duck or avoid. In a headlong pursuit at night, the possible injuries from the undergrowth or an ambush did not bear thinking about. Losing the other culprits was painful, but it had been the right decision.

The robber we caught was imprisoned. A certain amount of natural justice had befallen him at the jaws of the dog he foolishly chose to fight. As for his compatriots? That wood was a terrible and dangerous place through which to flee.

Who knows what injuries they did or did not sustain? Perhaps fate dictated that there was a little natural justice for the lorry driver they had so cruelly pistol-whipped and terrified. For all I know they might still be lying out there in that wood. If I am honest, were that the case, I wouldn't lose a moment's sleep.

Bob's 'lucky' reputation was further enhanced. He sat in the hospital waiting room, nursing his now pink and grossly swollen hand. Next to him sat the traffic officer, still bleeding and in agony from the 'bite' the stinger had given him.

Bob's wrist had been injured earlier that year in training, and had only just healed. Car crashes, minor illness and injury seemed to beset him, and there was more to come!

Whatever the outcome, three people who definitely qualify as bullies in my book (and you know how I feel about bullies) had been run to ground. They had learned that, with the ARVs patrolling the Met, they no longer had it all their own way.

Now there was something for *them* to fear . . .

## The Saga of Twelve Hits

It was a particularly wet and uninteresting early turn. Keith and I had taken out the generally less-than-popular Volvo estate – its estate car image was too mundane and its performance a little too pedestrian by most of the relief's standards – and I had shanghaied Phil as our driver. So, you see, Phil's day had not started out perfectly.

However, mid-morning found us at breakfast in the canteen at Heathrow, already some four hours into our working day and halfway through our meal, when the call came out. Somewhere up in Muswell Hill a domestic had led to a phone call alleging that an armed man was at an address, and presented an immediate threat.

The remnants of breakfast were hastily consumed and we were soon back in the Volvo, hurtling down the M4 into London. Chiswick and Hammersmith flyovers were taken with gusto, down through Knightsbridge, bottlenecking at Harrods and on up to Hyde Park Corner, Piccadilly, across the top of Trafalgar Square then up Charing Cross Road. Right across the top of London's North East corner, in fact. Then up Highgate Hill to Finchley Road and off into Muswell Hill.

As we arrived in the now-protesting Volvo, Phil's infamous vocabulary had completely taken over, with him removing all the full stops and replacing them with 'Fuck'.

An RVP had been set up uncomfortably close to the target address and a sprinkling of locals, including the duty officer, had attended.

When we arrived, the girl who was the apparent informant/complainant had come out. She was a slim girl in her early 20s and had with her a small boy. Looking back on it now, perhaps she'd used the ruse of calling us to evict a boyfriend or some such from the flat and, having achieved her objective, lost interest. The amount of resource employed, and the danger she had caused mattered nothing, as she explained that she was not herself but her sister; that she had just come from the flat but she didn't have any keys; and that the man who wasn't her boyfriend might still be in there, but she couldn't confirm that because she hadn't been in the flat. That is, in her sister's flat, but she knew it well because she had lived there once. Confused? So was I.

Phil, in his inimitable style, explained that we would have to force our way in with this big, red, half-hundredweight key, if we had no other option. She threatened to sue us inside out and back to front it we damaged the door to the flat. However, we made the necessary preparations, laid on the resources and allowed for any changes in the scenario.

The local duty officer, whose 'advised' decision is the final word, was unhappy that the flat might contain some unknown horror and asked us to go in. So 'suited and booted', we made our way forwards, myself, Phil and Robin.

Phil, being a lightweight, is often hoisted into lofts which is a dangerous and unenviable task. The opposite end of the scale is MOE [method of entry], and I decided that this was to be Phil's moment. Guns in hand and Phil encumbered with the heavy enforcer, we moved towards the door, with the containment officers from other ARVs surrounding the building.

Tactically, we made our way in through the large, communal door, dripping with 1920s coloured glass and into the extensive hall. Several doors, all large and panelled and all locked, led off in differing directions. A wide staircase led up to the first floor where we knew our target flat looked out backwards from the house. We moved up the staircase, conscious of the unseen areas and then forwards to check the landing. We needed to ensure it was clear before we turned our attention to the door of the flat itself.

Outside the door, Phil lifted the enforcer un-enthusiastically, but I just smiled and gestured towards the door with a sweeping motion. There was a short pause and then Phil whispered, 'You're taking the piss, aren't you?' Gently he stood his MP5 against the wall, finally realising that, like it or not, he was MOE man for the day, and firmed up his grip on the enforcer. After an exchange of mutual nods, I shouted the challenge: 'Armed police. Come to the door.'

It elicited no response even when repeated.

I looked across at Phil, raising my eyebrows and a look of resignation spread across his face. There was the sound of him sucking in a huge lungful of air and, having taken the world's biggest preparatory backswing, he launched into an attack on the door that bordered on the lunatic.

Once, twice, three hits, four. This door was old, hardwood and tough. Not only did it have multiple locks, but poor old Phil was hitting it in the wrong place, where it could spring and absorb the impact.

Five, six, seven, eight. Phil was bright red going on purple; Robin and I were in tears. His consternation boiled over, sweat beading on his face, his body armour partially rotating around his chest. The radio mouthpiece had fallen from its perch on his lapel and swung pendulumlike at his feet.

He paused, allowing the ram to drop its oblique end on to the floorboards between his feet. The resounding thump lifted dust from the coconut mat. He looked back at us who, though still covering him with raised weapons, could not suppress our amusement. He exploded: 'Well you two have a fucking go then!'

I managed a moment's supervisory seriousness and said, 'No, you get on with it.'

Fury fuelled greater fury and in a tumult he relaunched his attack. Four hits later the unfortunate door capitulated.

The locks had maintained their virtue and remained firmly ensconced in the frame. The frame, on the other hand, did not have the same emotional or structural bond as the rest of the building. Door, frame, fixings, architrave, brick, plaster and sundries fell piecemeal into the flat. Forward progress was halted by a cloud of dust and debris, reminiscent of the demolition of an industrial chimney.

After a minute or two of waiting for the dust to settle, we cleared the tiny flat, checking under beds and in wardrobes for our alleged gunman. We did not find him.

On the way out, I said to Phil, 'Better stand the door up before we hand over to the locals.' Minutes later the door and frame were leaning against an accommodating wall. The door was relatively unscathed. 'There,' said Phil. 'She said, don't damage the door, and the door looks fucking fine.'

Several weeks later we undertook MOE training at Lippitts Hill. Phil (or Twelve Hits as we now refer to him) opened his particular door with one hit. I must say though, that the run up wouldn't have been out of place at Lord's.

## Back Doors, On the Roof, Upside Down, and Head Over Heels

It had me wondering for a while: why did they call him 'Back Doors'? You could come to many conclusions, some more regrettable than others, but you would be wrong! The nickname came from the use of a rather sneaky card-playing tactic.

You see, we had a problem: we just had too many Bobs. There was my good friend, the very experienced specialist firearms officer, Bobby Browne, now serving as ARV crew. There was Bobby 'Brackets', whom you will read of soon. His name first appeared on the duty roster, without a departmental number to identify him: just an empty pair of . . . brackets. There was posh Bob, a man of rather genteel speech; and there was Bobby 'G', always smiling and buoyant. He even managed a smile, albeit rather weakly, when he opened a raw and painful furrow across my very bare head with a round of plastic ammunition. Then of course, there was Lucky Bob. I often wondered how much chaos I could generate by posting as many of them together on cars as I could, but never tried it.

When I came to the department in 1991, Back Doors had been there while Fifty had done his thing, and throughout that initial course. Early on he had left to travel the world. Years later he worked his way back through the Met to return to SO19. He was posted to 'C' relief.

His face, too, was rarely without a smile, his presence never without warmth.

\* \* \*

'You could pay more for a bike in that place than some people would for a car,' commented Jake as they descended the steps from Olympia. Bobby Back Doors couldn't resist the opportunity. 'Down here in God's country, we don't mind paying more than the price of a Raleigh roadster for our cars, Jake!'

There was a long silence, as Jake considered his response. 'It's not true that all Scots are mean, and to prove it I'll buy you a drink,' he said, smiling through that dark moustache. They had spent several hours checking out all the latest in mountain biking, but now the inner man required reviving.

They were good friends. This kind of exchange was never going to upset the bond that the relief shared. In a pub in the Earl's Court Road, they sat enjoying the food and the ambience.

Jake wasn't going to buy just one round. Bob had bought a couple, and Jake responded. By the time the small group of women had entered the bar, both men were feeling unusually talkative.

A huddle had developed around a strange bohemian character. He seemed to be the centre of attention as, with a broad Glaswegian accent, he joked and told tales. He was perhaps fifty years old. His hair was long, in the fashion of the sixties. His clothes belonged to those days of peace and flowers, when thousands flocked to muddied fields to smoke joints and worship pop idols.

Slowly common ground was found between the two Scotsmen. They were so very different, and yet at once, so very alike. It was the Celtic bond. The humour and the banter rose as the 'hippie' told tales, and Jake played the straight man. Standing close by, Bob found himself surrounded by the women, drawn now to the entertainment the two men were providing.

As he turned, beside him was an attractive, slim, blonde woman, about the same age as he. Studying her empty glass, he introduced himself. Soon the glass was full. Now he knew her name, Carol, and that she smiled a lot. He liked that, he liked her. 'I would like to see you again,' he ventured, and once more she smiled.

On the bar were small pieces of paper, food-ordering slips, and a pen. She picked one up and wrote her phone number on it. 'And I would like to see you.' There was that smile again. As they left, numbers had been exchanged. The hippie knew where to contact Jake – it was too good a double act to waste. Back Doors had Carol's number. He folded the small piece of paper into the front of his diary.

The next tour of duty allowed the boys time to recover. A 4 p.m. start meant a lazy beginning to the day, and a leisurely journey to work. Jake was busy elsewhere. Tony ('Carrot'), a somewhat hard-nosed and fit man, was incensed. Today he would be 'maps and navs', confined to the rear of the car. In the front would be two Bobs.

I was the sergeant supervising from the north base, but it was fate and circumstance that dictated the postings. Bobby Brackets would be operator, and Back Doors would drive. For hours Tony fumed as each mention of the name 'Bob' met with a response spoken in duet. Wry smiles were exchanged in the front, as Trojan 573 patrolled central north London.

It was a spare day. That meant our cars supplemented the core relief, and that I was a spare sergeant. I could catch up with the paperwork. While I spent my time soul-searching over personnel files, annual reports on this man or that, Trojan 573 was, like the rest, out there taking calls. I laboured through my administrative backlog, as they dealt with a couple of fruitless robberies.

I sat transfixed by a computer screen. In the quiet of the sergeants' office high in the old building, I had allowed my mind to wander. Only the distant sound of traffic from the road far below intruded. Then the telephone pierced my thoughts.

'Sorry to disturb you, Sarge.' The worried sound of the base man's voice instantly alarmed me. 'An ARV's crashed in north London,' he went on. 'It's one of yours.'

Suddenly everything else fell away, unimportant. 'How bad?' It was all I wanted to know.

'On its roof down a railway embankment.' Then he paused, lowering his tone, adding that which I dreaded to hear. 'Apparently they're trapped.'

Second only to getting shot, car crashes were the greatest threat.

Earlier, Trojan 573 had drifted through Stoke Newington. A calm had descended on the crew after two frenetic runs to armed robberies, both frustrated by cancellation before their arrival. From the back seat Carrot chipped in. 'Where are we going for grub, Bob?' From the driver's seat came 'are you going to answer him Bob?' Then from Brackets: 'No, he's not talking to me, he's talking to you.' Carrot was no longer amused: 'OK, I'll just talk to myself. It's the only way to get any bloody sense in this car.'

The radio broke in. 'Trojan 521 or any Trojan unit . . .' There had been an armed robbery at an off-licence at the furthest end of Hendon's area. As the call was repeated it became obvious that all the other available units were already engaged. It was growing dark, and the commuter traffic was heavy. No one else, though, was available to deal, and Brackets volunteered them.

'Trojan 573, you are assigned,' said the voice of the operator, confirming their involvement. It was a bad time of day for such a long run.

Back Doors settled himself in to concentrate on a difficult high-speed drive. Brackets tucked all the loose gear into various pockets around him, wedging the logbook firmly between his knees. In the back Carrot put the spare kit into the footwells.

Bracing his left foot against the far side of the car, so that he was fixed, stable in one corner of the back seat, he turned the pages of the atlas until he found the right one. Calling out the route to Back Doors, he began to pray he would not be sick. On a long run, the rear of a Rover 827 can be a nauseating place to be. There would be no more piss-taking for a while now.

The back of the heavy car squatted down as Back Doors kicked down on the accelerator. Brackets hit the switches, the blue lights churned on the roof, tracking flashes through the surrounding shop windows. In the confines of Stoke Newington Church Street, the siren's wail amplified back from the tall, old buildings.

Over the radio, updates from the scene added an extra urgency. Possible sightings of suspects in a car. The ARV barrelled on, slowing for the red lights at Manor House. Back Doors had his eyes on the road ahead, but his ears were tuned to the man in the back seat as he called out the route. At the lights he threw the Rover left. Now with Finsbury Park on their right-hand side, they headed on towards The Nag's Head at Holloway.

With the stakes rising, Back Doors pushed the car ever harder, ducking back and forth, seizing every opportunity to overtake through the late rush-hour traffic. Then it was right and north through Kentish Town, until they reached the A1. When they had cleared the North Circular Road, and before the beginning of the M1, a small slip road allowed them to join the A41. As they entered Mill Hill, there came a further update. The suspect car had been seen near the Graham Park Estate.

At the end of the Broadway there is a small round-about. He threw the car left, treading hard on the accelerator as they entered Bunns Lane. Over the radio, anxious local units called for their attendance, fearful of armed confrontation. As the speed rose, Back Doors placed the car for the bends he knew awaited them. They passed another small roundabout to enter Graham Park Way. Ahead and to the left was the aircraft museum, and close by a local police station.

This was why so many unarmed officers were quickly in a dangerous situation, and why the ARV must urgently get closer. The road was very quiet, the locals having disappeared in a warren of side roads. Ahead a lone and aged Sierra laboured smokily.

The horns and blue lights had no effect, or perhaps the car lacked enough real power for the driver to get out of the way, but they would have to overtake. Back Doors pulled out to where his vision was clear past the car, and accelerated hard. The engine note rose as the Sierra fell behind them.

They passed a raised concrete bollard. Back Doors then brought the ARV over to the near side in preparation for the long sweeping right-hand bend that was the next challenge. In the passenger seat, Brackets was unconcerned. In the back, head in the map, Carrot was oblivious.

His attention, though, was caught forcefully as, in the front, the two Bobs spoke again in unison. This time there was no humour. Their voices were loud, harsh, tinged with fear, as they gave the classic alarm call: 'Oh, shit!'

The back of the car lurched first left, then right, as it 'fishtailed'. In the first split seconds Brackets turned, and caught Carrot's gaze. They smiled, expecting the strange motion to subside. Then suddenly the smiles fell away as their driver fought ever harder for control.

Carrot braced his left hand against the roof. There was a violent movement wide and right. The screeching tyres began to compete with the car's horns as it swung out and through 180 degrees. Brackets looked over his shoulder through the rear window. They were hurtling backwards towards a grass embankment, and several very substantial trees. Then there were two very loud bangs, like gunshots, close together.

Suddenly the world had gone crazy. The nearside wheels had hit the kerb, flipping the Rover on to its roof. The bangs were the tyres bursting. Strange smells, rending, booming, tortured metal. Fragments of flying glass by the hundred. The smell of freshly mown grass? The car's roof was cutting a swathe through it.

Carrot closed his eyes, waiting for the fear, and the movement, to end. Brackets cringed as the car, still travelling at considerable speed, rocketed through a narrow gap between two large trees. Still the horns blared as, for them all, the world went into slow motion.

Back Doors could see nothing. The roof beat a path across the grassy divide. As the rough ground struck it with hundreds of blows, it began to collapse. His head was forced down towards his chest, then crushed against the steering wheel. His own body weight pressed down on his neck while the car careered onwards. He couldn't speak, couldn't breathe. Soon he might suffocate.

A sound like thunder filled their ears, as the roof flexed and buckled. From outside a more remote sound, as shrubs, nettles and weeds were hacked down, cracking, snapping. Still the car slid on, horns blaring. Only Brackets managed to speak, suddenly finding religion: 'Jesus Christ!'

For nearly a hundred feet the horror continued, the damp grass providing a nice slippery surface, inviting them into the embrace of the waiting railway embankment.

Then another sound!

It was like both a thousand bedsprings, stretched to breaking, and the screech of a wounded animal. A tall chain-link fence marked the boundary of railway property. The car hurtled into it, its speed barely diminished, and it acted like a catch net, screaming in protest as it did so. Uprooted poles beat at the side of the car, but at last the motion fell magically, almost elastically, away.

And then the car stopped. Now only the sound of the horns rent the night, accompanied by a persistent 'peep'. The engine had cut. The rear offside door had flown open, the headlights were still on, and the alarm would not let them forget it. As the car rocked and creaked gently, Brackets spoke again. 'Turn that fucking noise off.' Barely able to breathe, Back Doors cut the ignition, and then the horns. Now only the radios still spoke, relaying messages to the rest of the Met with total normality.

From the back seat, Carrot spoke. 'Everyone all right?' Each of them ran his own injury check. Fingers and toes still move, look for blood . . .

From the passenger seat, the first shock reaction began to take effect, as Brackets felt his heart rate rising. He reacted with the only phrase that sprang to mind: 'Fucking hell, boys!'

In the back seat, Carrot smelled petrol escaping from the inverted tank, and the spectre of fire began to torment him. In the driver's seat, Back Doors was in more trouble than any of them. His habit of driving with the seat raised and close to the wheel was now threatening his life. Contained in a small space behind the steering wheel, his head was forced down on his chest by the collapsed roof. Now the car was stationary, there was no respite from the weight of his own body pressing down on his neck. In this position he could barely breathe, and he was panicking. The more he panicked, the less he could breathe, and it was getting worse.

From somewhere there came voices, as people ran to help, well-meaning members of the public. Carrot threw his body armour across a sea of broken glass and nettles and they dragged him out. He called for someone to get the fire brigade and ambulance, then turned to help his trapped mates.

Back Doors tore at his shirt collar and tie, desperate to clear an airway, and forced himself to be calm. In his mind he repeated the words, 'Breathe deep, breathe slow, keep control', fighting for his life with the fear that threatened to engulf him. In the passenger seat Brackets wrestled himself free of the seat belt, and, having used the radio to call for more help, turned to help his mate.

Back Doors indicated the knurled wheel that controlled the seat height. Understanding at once, Brackets struggled to turn it, creating more space between the damaged roof and the trapped man. When he had wrung every last rotation out of it, he wriggled himself around inside the crushed car, until he was able to force his legs under Back Doors' shoulders. Lifting him a little relieved the pressure on his neck, and he could breathe again.

They could not sustain this for long. Something must be done soon. Through the undergrowth raced local officers and a fire crew. Distant two-tone horns heralded the arrival of an ambulance, and traffic police cars.

While around them a huge build-up of resources was taking place, in and around the car the crew were oblivious. 'Can't find my tie!' Back Doors protested. Lying upside down in a crashed car, surrounded by mayhem, suddenly made small things seem important. Then, more significantly, 'My diary, I must find my diary!' as the thought of losing Carol's phone number triggered a panic. 'My phone, where's my phone?'

Brackets tried to calm him. 'Don't worry, they must all be here.'

Outside the car, Carrot weighed the options with the fire brigade and ambulance crews. Three ARVs sidled to a halt at the nearby kerb, anxious for their colleagues' welfare. A throng of local officers milled about near the scene, as the incident threatened to take on epic proportions.

As the first help arrived at the scene, I was punishing the car for not being fast enough, for not getting me to the scene instantly. My imagination ran riot, as it drew awful pictures in my mind. I visualised the most terrible injuries, then I cursed every living thing that got in my way. It did no good, though. The rest of the world didn't seem to understand.

Carrot was now having a three-way conversation. A second fire crew had arrived. They had brought cutting gear. Should they cut Back Doors out, or try to pull this big man through the narrow aperture the crushed passenger window had become? Through the shattered windscreen, ambulance and fire crew offered reassurance, and tried to assess the trapped man's injuries. All around, familiar blue and white cordon tape marked a boundary.

Metal tripods supported powerful arc lights. The whole scene took on an air of unreality, huge shadows contrasting the reflective markings of the overturned car, and the yellow fluorescent jackets of the rescuers, now appearing as giant marionettes, their outlines dancing across the trees.

As the fire crews argued, Back Doors' patience ran out. He turned to Brackets, still supporting his shoulders. 'Tell Tony I want to get out of this car *now*. If *you* can get out through what's left of that window, well then, so will I.'

Brackets called up to Carrot. 'He's coming out this way.' Around them an argument was raging, borne out of genuine concern. The fear was that Back Doors may have a neck injury, but within the car the matter had been decided.

A senior fire brigade officer spoke with Back Doors. 'Can you feel any injuries?'

He croaked an answer, his chin still perilously close to his chest. 'No, I think I'm OK.'

Then another question. 'Can you move all your fingers and toes?'

'Yes.'

The fireman looked across at the nearby ambulance crew, two men in their forties, who shrugged their shoulders. From behind them came a third, an older man, and a supervisor. 'It's your call,' he responded.

The leading fireman paused for a moment, and then spoke again. 'Cut the seat belt off, and lay out some sheeting.'

While Carrot hovered paternally nearby, Brackets prepared to move. 'When I take my leg away, you'll have all your weight on your neck again. Are you ready?' Back Doors grunted an acknowledgement. Young firemen stood by to drag them out, knowing that, once the movement had begun, it must be done smoothly and quickly.

There was a pause, then a fireman's hand reached in and tapped Brackets on the shoulder. They were ready. He extended his arms out of the window until willing hands gripped his. He and Back Doors exchanged eye contact, and then he pulled his leg away. The heavy man's weight descended fully, once more bearing on his neck.

'*Now!*' Brackets shouted loud. The combined strength of several men extracted him rapidly across the sea of plastic sheets, laid out to smooth his exit.

At once Carrot dived towards the narrow slit the window had become, as many hands reached into the car. From the other side firemen pushed and pulled, trying to turn the heavy man on to his side, so that he could breathe again. For anxious moments they all fought and cursed as Back Doors' breathing rasped and gurgled; they were unified by the urgency.

The blackness of unconsciousness threatened. He wriggled once more, and, with a thud, he fell on to his side. Now he could breathe. Carrot and Brackets were instantly half in the car, seizing at limbs and clothing. As his bulk threatened to jam him in the confines of the distorted window, many hands reached down to help.

He lay staring momentarily at a sky he had for moments thought he might not see again, his chest heaving, sucking in the good air he had been denied. His clothing snagged on the mangled window frame. He twisted it free, as the same willing hands pulled him clear. Suddenly he was standing.

The three men grinned, relieved, as Carrot slapped him on the back. 'Well done, Bobby boy,' he enthused, and Brackets moved to speak. Carrot wasn't having any more of that though. 'No, not you, you twat.'

Then Back Doors sank to his knees as the shock overpowered him, and he was placed on a stretcher. The ambulance crews were with them in seconds, insisting they should all be placed in neck collars. His 'stat' levels running low, the stretcher was lifted into a waiting ambulance. As Brackets and Carrot stepped up to join him, Back Doors protested one last time. 'My diary, I must have my diary, and my mobile phone.'

I had driven the Rover hard through the traffic, but this was late rush hour, and progress was difficult. As I passed through Finchley, around the North Circular Road, the radio beside me broke in. 'Trojan 500 from 99,' said the voice of the base man calling me.

I pulled into the kerb. Grabbing the handset I responded. 'Go ahead.' He spoke again. 'Go to Barnet

Hospital. Your crew is on the way there.' I had to ask, 'What about injuries?' There was a pause. 'I'm not sure, but I think they're OK, Sarge.'

I headed north, slower now, already feeling relieved. Their condition was still not confirmed, but my instinct told me it was good news. At the shiny new hospital, I arrived just behind them. The empty ambulance doors were still open.

A government promise was kept, and the boys were seen immediately. They weren't treated for several hours, but that's another matter.

I found them in a small annexe. Brackets and Carrot were walking wounded, still confined within the punishing neck collars, and sporting an array of cuts and scratches. Back Doors lay on a trolley in considerable discomfort from a ferocious device, apparently designed to immobilise his head.

While we raided the sympathetic but overworked staff's tea club, he again mourned the loss of his diary and his mobile phone. A short while later, and to his immense but misplaced relief, a local uniformed officer appeared carrying those very things. They had been recovered from within the devastation of the car. He opened the diary and shook it. The small slip of paper was missing. His expression was desolate.

I stayed with them until they were discharged in the early hours of the following day. We would not allow Back Doors, still wearing a neck brace, to go home to his empty house. He spent the next day and night with Carrot, his wife and very young daughter, Libby. Libby charmed the big man completely. 'When she grows up, she says she'll marry me,' he said.

The reason for the car's behaviour at the time was the subject of intense investigation, and several contributory factors were identified. ARVs are heavily laden vehicles, operating constantly near their maximum payload. Was it a combination of these factors, perhaps the 'sloshing' of the fuel-tank contents, an area of loose debris at the scene? Who knows? But driver error was not cited as the cause.

Whatever the current fashion for criticising police driving, please remember as you read this that those men, like so many of their colleagues everywhere and every day, were desperate to meet a perceived threat to life. Regularly they place the welfare of others above their own.

In researching this event, I went back to all three for their detailed recollections. Back Doors' response was to visit me at my home. We sat on my patio in the warm sunshine, and he told me about Libby, but I had cause to doubt she would ever be his bride.

You see, apart from the age gap, and Carrot's assertion that no daughter of his will ever marry a copper, there was another reason. That reason was sitting beside Bob on my patio as he related the story. Her name was Carol, and they are together still. Perhaps they always will be.

The small slip of paper had been lost for ever, but earlier that day Back Doors had tried unsuccessfully to phone Carol. So, when he pressed last dial on that mobile phone, the number was still there.

# **8** The Long Night

NIGHTS CAN BE THE MOST BORING and uneventful tours of duty, full of the mundane business of organising postings, checking equipment and other aspects of administration that are often the sergeant's lot. All of this while your head tries to stay awake in conflict with your body's demands for sleep. This night, though, was going to be different.

Instead of the usual handover from the late-turn sergeant – perhaps a smattering of information on any ongoing situations, or a deluge of managerial trivia – there was just the poor old, much-put-upon, base man, sweating over a console of blaring radios. Angry, incessantly ringing telephones accompanied the green flicker of the CAD screen, updating messages while its partner, the printer, spewed out a rainforest of paper he could not hope to keep pace with. The lack of both ARV and SFO vehicles in the yard should have told me what the returning relief's absence confirmed: busy, busy, very busy.

Before I would lie in my bed again, a great many hours would pass and even then sleep would not come easily, as the memories of that night danced about in my head. Memories that still often come to mind: terror, high emotion, gunfire, drugs and bombs. It would be a very long night indeed.

He was seated in the blackened surroundings of his small flat in Holloway, the walls still scorched by the fires he had apparently set there days before, and for which he was wanted for questioning.

Similarly, police wanted to question him regarding an allegation by the manager of the bar where he had worked that about £150 was missing. That was about the purchase price of the huge revolver that he was fondling. In his belt was a large, black-handled carving knife, not dissimilar to a couple of others lying on the floor nearby and fixing his gaze.

He had spent the night before in a small hotel in the West End, after returning from Ireland, where he had passed melancholy time with his puzzled family. They could not have known that this was his goodbye.

Who knows what thoughts were turning over in his head that night, as he mixed a cocktail of intense emotion with drink and prescribed medication? He had a good supply of the latter, keeping the identities of two doctors secret from each other, while getting 'scripts' from them both. That cocktail was taking his thoughts deeper and deeper lately, into the darkest recesses of his mind, where the demons of doubt and self-loathing came to preach to him. There they whispered of the secret wines of revenge, drunk to wash away this feeling of worthlessness.

He had telephoned his wife, now living far away in South America with his young son, and cancelled their visit. Plans that had long lain in his mind at times like this were suddenly taking shape. This time they would take notice. He would hurt them, make them listen and have control of it all. Just for a while.

I had changed into my uniform, upstairs in the over-crowded locker rooms that are the hallmark of the old Victorian building at Old Street.

I threw my kit into the bag where resided every odd piece of equipment I thought I might ever need. Chalk, pens, marking equipment, cordon tape or whatever. It went everywhere with me. I hooked the body armour over one shoulder and descended the echoing staircase. Down in the armoury, I could hear the familiar sounds of weapons being racked and cleared – the sure indication of an oncoming shift. The dull ring of a Glock pistol's action carrying a round into the breech greeted me as I went down the last few steps and 'Dunj' came into view. 'Dunj' was a 'handle' that had attached itself to Brian. With his thinning and fine fair hair above an equally wispy chin beard, he bore, as several of the relief had pointed out, an uncanny resemblance to a small cartoon character, the Dungeon Master.

'Hallo, Rog.' He smiled. 'Big siege on in south London. Some geezer's holding his whole family hostage, and the world and his wife are down there.' That accounted for the absence of the late turn and teams. 'Seems like a bit of overkill, though, to have two teams as well as the TSG.'

This was already more information than the poor breathless base-man could stop to give me.

'Has he offered to make you a cup of tea yet?' barked a sharp voice from within the armoury itself, beyond the loading bay where Dunj and I were conversing. The unmistakable tones of Lucky Bob, poised yet again to mock poor Brian.

'No, mate,' I replied. 'Men of your calibre are hard to find, Bob.'

'Well don't worry, Sarge, I'll do it.'

'Snivelling bastard,' Dunj muttered, just loud enough to be heard. 'And make one for me,' he said. 'I'm bloody parched.'

I took my Glock pistol off the rack, inserted the magazine and worked the action, loaded it at the sand-filled bay. Bob and Dunj took an MP5 carbine each. I was their supervisor. For me a pistol was enough, and there was only room in the safes for two carbines. They checked they were clear with the accompanying rack, rack, clack sound that is now so familiar to me. Then the three of us climbed the stairs to the base room, slamming the heavy, steel security door behind us. 'I must have a cup of tea,' Dunj said. 'I'm bloody dehydrated.'

In the base room chaos reigned, as crews rushed out to reinforce the hard-pressed late turn, now well over-due, while I struggled to find enough cars and crew. As the dust settled, I turned to Bob and Dunj. 'Well, boys, you've won tonight's star prize. The sergeant's riding with you.'

Bob quipped, 'Privilege, Sarge.'

Followed by Dunj with, 'Yes, but for who?' He grinned at me. 'Who's a lucky boy, then.'

'Cheeky bastard,' I countered.

The base man burst into the room waving a sheet of CAD message spilled out by the relentless printer. 'Trojan 500?' His eyes scanned the room.

'Yes, that's us,' Bob responded.

'Go to Kentish Town. Meet the late turn. There's an ambush to be done for the squad, a yardie hit man armed with a shotgun coming back to a flop.'

'No teams?' I ventured.

'None.'

'OK,' I said 'RVP at Kentish?'

'Yes,' he said. 'But listen out for the late turn because it's game on any time. The squad's up behind him somewhere and could call the hit if he goes on the plot. The late turn's sat up nearby.'

Bob grinned at me. 'He's been watching a rerun of *The Sweeney*, hasn't he?'

All of this meant that the flying squad were close to arresting an armed man. He was mobile and closing with an address. Arresting him in the street would be infinitely easier than allowing him back into the building. We were the only resource available.

We ran straight out into the yard, throwing the kit into an old Rover 827, and were out of the gate in moments. A late arrival for night duty slammed the steel gates behind us. We were over the traffic-calming hump into Old Street and across the front of the base as the first wail of the siren cut the air and the blue reflections began to circle above our heads – the first of many occasions this night when the Rover's wail would be heard.

Lucky Bob grabbed the handset and called out the message number to the operator at information room. 'MP from Trojan 500, reference your CAD message number 5863. Show us assigned.' We turned right towards the City and the car lifted its nose as Dunj kicked down: 'I could bloody murder a cup of tea.'

We read the information on the message the base man had given us, and I called the late-turn car, now hiding themselves away, not far from the address that our 'hit man' was due to return to.

A large and dreadlocked black man with the unlikely name of Ya Ya Pedro was our target. At that moment he was making his way, in a black cab, towards a Victorian terrace in a quiet north London street. The information the late turn crew were giving me over the mobile phone was grave enough to ensure that the gloves would definitely be off when this potentially violent man was arrested.

Dunj pushed the Rover on through the Angel at Islington, and the one-way system into King's Cross, his style of driving controlled but quick.

The dealers on the corners pivoted on their heels as we swept through, accompanied by microskirted prostitutes who scuttled along as if they suddenly had business elsewhere. They needn't have worried: we had other problems. The radio barked on a channel reserved for the Flying Squad, and one we were now monitoring. 'The suspect has left the club, now believed to be headed towards target address.' There would be little opportunity for briefing. We would have to go in cold and meet the late-turn car at the scene. Time was against us.

Dunj pushed the car to its limits as we approached Camden, the prospect of leaving the other car unsupported now paramount in our minds. Bob struggled to don his body armour in the front, while I wrestled my own over my head. I placed Dunj's as close to him as I could, as we forked towards Kentish Town, and bohemian crowds spilling from the Camden pubs jeered at our flashing, bellowing progress.

Bob contacted the other car, who directed us into a cobbled alleyway a short distance from the address. We swung in, silent now, and sidled up beside the other ARV. The late-turn crew briefed us rapidly; and now, properly prepared, we waited. While the following, unmarked, squad car commentated on their approach, I took the opportunity to survey the street outside the target address.

Not many parked cars. Tall houses with basements that descended to below the footway, leaving 'the servants' to stare out of subterranean windows at the ornate railings above. Half a dozen steps bridged the basement area, and led to a black-arched door. We would have to be quick or Ya Ya would be out of the cab and indoors before we could reach him.

There was no time to set up a rolling ambush and hit the cab on the move. We would have to take him stationary in the cab or on the footway itself. We set the cars up for a quick exit, knowing that we would have only seconds after the cab turned the corner to get him in the net.

The transmissions from the unmarked car tracked the cab's progress, as Bob traced his finger across the map. Gradually all conversation ceased. Then there were just the hushed tones of the two Rovers' engines, the bark of the radio, and the occasional update from Bob. Both he and Dunj were silhouetted by the glow of the map light, as the voice on the radio said, 'Approaching the junction now.' Dunj slipped our car into 'drive'. The swirl of smoke from the exhaust of the other ARV changed as it gave a gentle jolt, indicating that the driver had followed suit. Inside, kitted out in body armour, and with carbines across their chests, the crews tensed themselves. 'Turning in now,' came over the radio.

Over the back-to-back personal radios we all carried, I said, 'Stand by. Stand by.' Then, '*Go!*'

The front wheels scrambled for grip on the loose surface as the cars lurched forwards, throwing stones and debris up at the walls around us.

Dunj, as had been agreed, headed out first, driving directly at the startled cab driver, hitting the 'blues and twos' and blinding both him and Ya Ya with our headlights. The second ARV accelerated past us and cut off the rear, swinging in at an angle behind the cab.

The decision had been that we would offer him no opportunity to arm, and close immediately with the cab. Even so, he stepped out on the footway as the first challenges were given. 'Armed police. Ya Ya Pedro, stand still.' He had a large holdall in his right hand. 'Drop the bag on the floor now. *Now*,' Bob shouted at him. He had exited the car on the nearside, on to the footway ahead of me, and was facing Pedro. His left shoulder pressed hard against an accommodating lamp-post and his left eye closed, while the right one stared through the sights of the carbine. I moved left into a doorway and covered Pedro from the building line with my Glock, while Dunj covered from over the driver's door.

Bob took control of Pedro, giving clear, forceful commands. 'Now move away from the cab. That's it, now stop. Kneel down. Keep your hands away from your body.' Off to our right, the bright light of the torch mount of another carbine lit up Pedro from across the bonnet of the cab.

Bob, like all of us, had done this a hundred times before, and controlled Pedro, giving him no chance to reach inside the long overcoat he was wearing. Pedro's wild-eyed gaze pivoted left and right, unable to see beyond the beams of light blinding him. The long dreadlocks swung across his cheeks in unison. There was nowhere to go. Two choices for him: lose or lose badly. He chose the soft option.

Moments later the zipping sound of plasticuffs secured the suspect, now face down on the floor, while grinning squad officers came forward to read him his rights. Now it would be back to Kentish for notes and perhaps Dunj could have that cup of tea he had been pleading for.

I strode back to the car and peeled off the body armour, as the balding cab driver approached me. 'That was a bit out of order,' he said staring at me through thick-lensed glasses.

'Sorry,' I countered. 'But he's a very dangerous man.'

'Got no problem with that, Sarge,' he said. 'Shoot him if you like.' And then he grinned. 'But you scooped the bastard up before he'd paid.'

It was 11.10. We had only officially come on duty at 10.30 and would usually still be drinking tea, as Dunj had pointed out. This *was* going to be a long night.

Glad of a little calm, we rolled gently into the yard at Kentish Town and parked close to the canteen. I took the opportunity to straighten out my kit and then followed the boys up the steps. Bob had already begun to write his notes in a report book he had fetched from the front office, while Dunj had made it his whole mission in life to find some tea. He picked up a teapot lying on the table and swirled it around. 'Cold,' he growled. 'Bloody night duty's had theirs and gone.'

From somewhere on the table a hand-held PFX (a radio that allowed us to monitor the main channels) began to relate: 'Any Trojan unit, the vicinity of Ashley Road, Holloway, the sound of gunshots, information from the occupier of . . .' In the kitchen nearby, Dunj tipped several cups into the sink with a crash. 'Oh, for fuck's sake!' The notebooks were hastily scooped up as I grabbed the radio. 'MP from Trojan 500, show us assigned.'

We made our way back to the car, slumped into the seats and took off, wailing through the streets towards Holloway and the location given. The enthusiasm for this call could not, I have to say, be described as boundless, as such calls are as common as they are generally unfounded. Usually it's fireworks or a backfire from a passing car. Often at night, the exploding warning caps left on the railway lines by rail workers to warn of an approaching train give rise to such calls. So we weren't getting too excited. Yet.

On our arrival at Ashley Road, local officers redirected us to a road running parallel. We made two right turns until we came into Shaftesbury Road, a name that will remain with me for ever. At the junction with Trinder Road, which runs due south, another group of local officers gathered around a young inspector. He was a fresh-faced man in his middle twenties, with a forthright yet amenable manner. He told us that since the original call there had been several others up and down Shaftesbury Road, all complaining of the sound of gunshots, which seemingly originated from the back gardens. Since their arrival, his own officers had heard similar sounds in the distance, but no one, it seemed, could offer us anything more specific.

The only incident of note in the whole road of late had been an attempted arson days before at number 53. If I had known then that nearby were two women who could have added another dimension to all of this, my thinking would have changed altogether . . .

Late in the evening of 26 July 1994 the doorbell of number 55 had rung. The attractive, young, female occupant, who I shall call Clio, had answered the door to her neighbour, a slightly built man with an Irish accent. She knew he lived at 53 with his wife and child, but she had not seen *them* for a while, nor, come to that, *him* for perhaps a week or more. He had appeared agitated and sweating. He had stared at her intently and started to move towards her, when a second, older, woman appeared behind Clio. She was Clio's landlady and friend, Maria. He made his excuses and left, strangely flustered. The man's name was John O'Grady, and John O'Grady had a plan.

Quietly, we investigated the rear of 53 by using the alleyway between that and 55. It was divided into upper and lower flats and the gardens were split lengthways and shared 50/50. Looked at from the rear, the right-hand garden closest to 51 related to the downstairs occupier, John O'Grady, at number 53 and was reached via a patio door with a glazed surround. The door adjacent to O'Grady's bay window at the front gave access to the flat above, designated 55A.

The occupants of that flat, fortuitously, were away. O'Grady could enter by the rear patio door, or by a side door in the alleyway between him and 55. All of this was to prove to be very relevant later on.

In the garden at the back, not far from the patio door, we found a box that had contained an air pistol made to resemble a self-loading (or what is often called a semiautomatic) pistol. It was riddled with pellet holes, but did nothing to explain the gunshots or bangs, as they well might be.

Personally, I believe that O'Grady was watching all of this from the undergrowth nearby, engineering a situation according to his own dark plan. But I will never know for sure. In the absence of any further information, I agreed that we would, at the inspector's request, support him while he knocked on the door. Not risk-free, but we had to start somewhere. On the final approach he was, in fact, in close attendance, but it was Dunj who knocked on what appeared to be the front door.

There was no reply, instead the sound of a gunshot somewhere close by. Dunj turned to tell the inspector to take cover, but he had already run away. Smart cookie.

Now I had to make some kind of decision about how to progress the situation. We had nowhere near enough manpower to properly search the street, but I couldn't just ignore it. Equally, I could hardly call any more cars up here, based on the information I had. London-wide cover was already reduced from five cars to two because of the siege south of the river. In my heart at that time, I think I still believed that some crank was amusing himself at the expense of the Metropolitan Police.

I had this mental picture of a grinning Walter Mitty peering out from behind a set of curtains somewhere. I could not have been more wrong.

I decided that we would do a walk-down search of all the front gardens and call in the helicopter, India 99, to do an overhead search of the back, using their hi-tech aids of 'night sun' and thermal imaging. When we had established a link with them we set off along the street.

I placed Dunj on my right and Bob on my left, so that they could call me over for support when there were areas they could not clear alone. We checked our radios, then I called out to the helicopter, '99 from Trojan 500, are you ready?'

The reply came back, 'When you are, 500.'

'Bob?'

'Ready'

'Dunj?'

'Ready.'

I gave, 'Stand by. Stand by.' Then I looked at Dunj on my right and Bob on my left, and that feeling of personal responsibility rose up in me. 'OK, commence search.'

The helicopter loomed large above us and the sound of its rotors beating the air was suddenly very close. The brilliant white light of the night sun turned darkness into day, as it panned around us, scanning the rear gardens in parallel with our progress. The boys called out the house numbers as they cleared the gardens, weapons drawn.

I scooted back and forth between them in support, some gardens requiring us all. With infinite patience, 99 hovered above us, rattling roofs, no doubt drowning out the sound of televisions. Not a single resident emerged. Amazing. We called out the numbers and I controlled the progress until we had cleared all the way, virtually, to Hornsey Rise. A long way and hard work. We didn't find our man. But then, we didn't know he had a plan.

By now we were feeling drained. There were still the notes to do at Kentish Town and poor old Dunj was rasping with thirst. We regrouped in the middle of the road, content that we had exhausted our options while 99 hovered overhead. 'That's it,' I said. 'We've given this one our best shot. The rest of the Met needs us and I've had enough.'

Bob and Dunj smiled, heads nodding in agreement. Bob had just said, 'Back to Kentish then,' and Dunj had asked, 'Do I get to drink something now?' when somewhere to our north there was an earth-shattering bang.

A bright orange flash lit the sky, beyond Ashley Road where we had first attended, triggering the instinctive reaction in all of us. Go for cover behind nearby cars, handguns redrawn and eyes scanning all about. Above us, the helicopter circled noisily, dipped its nose and powered off in the direction of the blast. 'What the fuck was that?' Bob asked, echoing all of our thoughts.

Slowly we stood up. Sensing that, whatever it was, we were at least a safe distance from it, we holstered up. Bob then answered his own question. 'That'll be a bomb, then.'

Dunj stuffed his hands in his pockets and walked slowly away, shaking his head. He was muttering under his breath, and I could barely hear him, but it sounded suspiciously like, 'I don't fucking believe this.'

When Dunj had recovered his composure, we commenced a slow walk back down the street, eyes all about us, towards our start-point back at the RVP on Trinder Road. Standing by our abandoned car was the young inspector. I liked this man. He obviously had the kind of good sense that would allow him to become a much older inspector.

'I think we've done all we can for now, Guvnor,' I said. 'We've swept the whole road west of here, and 99 has done the back gardens. Nothing.' He smiled. 'Thanks, Skip. And by the way, the big bang is a terrorist car bomb outside a premises a few minutes from here.'

We agreed we would go back to Kentish for a debrief and to satisfy Dunj's now legendary thirst. I pulled off the body armour, and the rasping sound of peeling Velcro told me that Bob and Dunj were doing the same.

The reduction in weight on my shoulders came as a real relief, and for the first time for hours I began to relax.

Having packed the kit away we got back in the car. Dunj dropped into the driving seat like the proverbial sack of potatoes, his head rocking back against the restraint. He let out a long sigh. Bob shuffled the papers of the car's log as we got ready to roll, and Dunj started the engine. Then he turned around to speak to me.

Over his shoulder, I saw the young inspector run across to us and tap on the driver's window. Stopped in mid-flow, Dunj lowered the window.

Local officers leaped into their cars and tore off to some as yet undisclosed incident. The inspector breathlessly blurted out, 'Some of my units are chasing suspects from a stolen car. The suspects are Irish and there appears to be bomb-making materials on the back seat.' And as he ran to his car he called, 'Follow me!' over his shoulder. Dunj's face was aghast. Bob and I burst out laughing.

Once again the Rover was back on the blue and wailing its way through north London – this time, though, just a short distance to a long descending street, somewhere near Blackstock Road. We came to a halt not far from an old, white Vauxhall Cavalier, lying at an angle to the kerb with its doors wide open. It sat the other side of blue and white cordon tape, blocking the end of a street of Victorian or Georgian houses. The young inspector was marshalling his troops to either end of the scene, and speaking to his control room about the need for the expo, photographers, more manpower for cordons, and much else.

'There's a holdall in the back,' he went on as I approached him. 'My blokes say that in it are blocks of a brown substance wrapped in clingfilm, and some wires running about the floor of the car.' That was good enough for me. The old adage from my SPG days came back: 'If you can see it, it can see you.' And I voted with my feet.

'We'll be just around that corner, listening in on your PR link, Guvnor. If you need us to stop these suspects, call us in first and we will deal with them.' Maybe he wasn't going to make it to be an old inspector after all.

It's a reasonable supposition with Provisional IRA operatives that they will have some form of sidearm, however old, for personal defence. Nevertheless the matter was resolved when minutes later the suspects had succumbed, not to us, but to the tender mercies of a couple of large Metropolitan police German shepherd dogs. I think they would have preferred us.

They were Liverpudlian Irish and the 'explosive device' was a couple of blocks of cannabis resin. The wires were a particularly poorly assembled stereo system. However, the suspicion generated was well founded.

We were now united in the quest for refreshment. We had had neither food nor drink for several hours and it was after one o'clock in the morning. Somewhere up near Tally Ho corner, the might of the Met was dealing with a car-bomb attack on a Jewish centre, which accounted for the earlier blast. So much for the Irish connection.

None of this was of the slightest concern to Dunj right now, as he rescued the cups from the sink in the canteen that nestled in the corner of the yard back at Kentish Town. Bob and I were scribbling furiously in the uncompleted notebooks left over from the Ya Ya saga, clearing the decks before we located a takeaway somewhere nearby. Dunj's needs, however, were more pressing as he rummaged through the metal-fronted tea lockers.

'Don't these bastards keep any supplies?' he growled.

'No fees, no teas,' Bob cut in. 'If you were a paid-up member of their relief then you could have a drink.' He looked at me, grinned and went on. 'You know how it is, Dunj: fees plus keys equals teas.'

There followed the sound of more crashing cups and slamming locker doors, and a well-thought-out response: 'Bollocks!'

The three of us had pooled our change and, having made the best of a bad job, we were sharing a can of soft drink, at least placating Dunj for a while. As we scribbled away at the report books, moments after the words 'grub' and 'kebabs' had been uttered, my mobile phone began to ring.

'Sergeant Gray.'

'Reserve at Kentish Town here, Skipper. Sorry but I can't get you on the air and I understand you're supervising north as Trojan 500.'

'Yes, that's right.'

'Well we've been called back to Shaftesbury Road. Sound of gunshots.'

I looked up at the two men seated opposite me, who had already guessed what was going on, and were poised, pens still in hand. 'Yes, OK,' I said into the phone. 'We will deal.'

Bob raised his eyebrows and made to get up.

'No,' I said. 'We'll finish these notes first. This bloke's just pulling our pisser.' No panic. How wrong I was!

Quickly, we wrote out the last of the account of the earlier ambush, and strode out to the yard, stopping only to throw on the body armour yet again, and check out the comms. Once again the Rover's wail cut the air and the blue light drew lines along the exit into the street.

The flashing beams of the headlamps announced our arrival in the road outside, cutting a long, curving, brilliant arc as Dunj put the power down. The tyres bit with a 'chirrup' on the asphalt surface beyond the exist ramp 'I'm going to strangle this bastard if I get hold of him,' Lucky Bob commented. Some chance, I thought. I was beginning to believe we would be dancing to his tune all night.

As it happens we did, ending in a devastating finale.

We retraced our steps from earlier in the evening, through Ashley Road, a couple of rights and back into Trinder Road, turning off the noise as we did so. An RVP was at the same junction as before, with an ARV already parked there. Beside the driver's door a slim, dark figure was putting on body armour. It was Kevin 'Granny', silhouetted in our lights.

Walking away from us towards number 53 was Alan, whose general appearance and shock of grey hair had earned him the title 'Radovan' after a certain notorious figure in recent Yugoslav affairs, and to whom he bears more than a passing resemblance. Standing talking to the young inspector, again charged with the responsibility for this incident, was 'C' relief's version of a Mississippi gambler, Andy Pearce. It was for me a moment frozen in time. Seconds later the sounds of gunfire and breaking glass rent the air.

The muzzle flash and breaking glass came from the front bay window of 53. The whole scene electrified, as terrified male and female police officers dived behind cars and garden walls. The ARV crews went on to 'automatic' as their training kicked in, and they galvanised into action. A dozen things were happening at once.

Kevin and Alan went to cover, Dunj threw our car into a screeching curve, to get us in close, flanking a wall at the end of the terrace. With the car still rocking from the motion of braking, I could hear Bob opening the safe in the back, to extract the carbines. The doors flew open as Dunj threw me the keys. In a fraction of a second Bob was on the footway, handing him a carbine. Clack, clack. Both of them slapped the actions forwards, feeding a jacketed round into the throat of the breech. Condition one.

'Ready,' said Dunj, looking grimly at Bob.

'Ready.' Bob nodded to me, and they ran towards the scene.

Kevin had thrown the car keys to Andy, who was frantically dragging the carbines and body armour out of the other ARV. Having made the weapons ready, he ran, laden like a pack mule, to equip his mates, exposing himself to potential gunfire, rather than leave them vulnerable.

Two things were becoming clear. With all that was going on elsewhere in the Met tonight, this one was down to me. What was obvious was that this was bad. What would later become apparent was that it was going to get worse, much worse.

Several minds worked at once as we struggled to create order out of chaos. The urgency with which the crews had deployed left me with no one at control, a difficult situation because the Trojan control becomes the focal point for the collation of information from any number of sources. It is where the log of the incident is completed and briefings and planning originate. I would have to be the control, the tactical adviser and the negotiator all rolled into one. And that is too many hats!

Alan was calling back for ballistic shields, to get the unprotected local officers out of the proximity of the house. Again, Andy ran the gauntlet to fetch the kit. Bob and Dunj had worked their way along the far side of the road towards 53, taking cover in the front garden of the adjoining house, while they worked out how to get behind 53 without getting shot at.

Alan and Kevin were covering the front, while at the same time bringing out the unprotected local officers one by one, behind the shields Andy had supplied. The young inspector was with me again, now sensibly tucked in behind a wall, as his shocked officers trickled back to group up behind him.

'Give me your steadiest man,' I said. 'Someone with good local knowledge. I need him in that car as loggist and radio operator now.' I indicated the vacant Rover left by Kevin and his crew. I desperately needed thinking and planning time, and it was going to be hard to buy.

'500 from Dunj,' came the voice through my earpiece.

'Go ahead.'

'Can you blind the front window with the Dragon light while we get in?'

'Stand by.'

The inspector was obviously frustrated by my lack of deference to him, but he could see the pressure I was under. I ran to the back of the car and pulled out the 'Dragon' light, a powerful but short-lived beam.

At the same time I called to the PC, now in the front seat as radio operator. 'Tell the base I want more cars urgently. I want a paramedic ambulance and specialist dogs here now. Make sure they know it's "shots fired", and log everything.'

I ducked behind the parked cars opposite 53, well aware that the rest of the boys had heard what was about to happen.

Kevin, Andy and Alan were into the best containment points they could manage, but would use the distraction I was about to provide to best effect. I slipped behind the protection of a garden wall, and pointed the light towards the window.

'Dunj, Bob, stand by for light-up.'

'Received. Standing by.'

'Front containment?'

'Standing by.'

I hit the switch and a searing white light washed over the front of the house, illuminating the shattered right window and soot-stained remainder. Armed policemen scrambled from one place to another. Bob and Dunj, who by now had made contact with Clio and Maria in 55, slipped through the house and out to the back gardens. The information they would obtain from the women would prove crucial. I kept the light on for as short a time as possible. It's an effective tactic, but made me number-one target. I ducked down very low.

With hindsight, I suspect that in all probability O'Grady had run straight out of the back patio door. But then he had a plan, or I should say that, having missed out on Clio, he had devised another one.

While we continued to organise, the resources the control officer had requested for me screamed towards us at unthinkable speeds. The only other armed car available in the whole Met was desperately trying to break away from the conclusion of yet another job down south. On board was a new sergeant on the relief, a man destined to become my good friend, Ray, the Welsh wizard. With him were Harry the hawkish SFO man and Tony 'Prof', the studious one.

It was now 2.30 in the morning. On their way in, under the cover of the Dragon light, Bob and Dunj noticed that the glass from the freshly broken window was on the outside, suggesting it had been broken by something passing through it on the way out.

They had asked for a ballistic blanket to be brought to them and when, by a tortuous route around parked cars and across garden fences, this had been achieved, it was placed over the fence between 55 and 53. They covered the rear from there. Every move, every occurrence was to be logged by the PC in the Rover.

Bob was turning on the charm with the two women in 55 and slowly the events from the previous night took shape. Now I had a name, John O'Grady. What I wanted was to hear him answer to it.

The inspector was gleaning as much information as possible on our suspect and shortly a phone number emerged. Over the radio I announced that I was putting a phone call in.

What had been a hush became total silence, and distantly the sound of a telephone ringing drifted through the broken glass. From the rear Dunj's voice crackled through my earpiece confirming, 'Phone ringing inside.' Nobody answered.

In the silence created by the phone call, Dunj heard the sound of movement through undergrowth from across the gardens and beyond number 53. He waited to see what the cause might be, not daring to make a sound himself. The closer whoever it was got, the greater the control Dunj would have over them. The element of surprise would also be in his favour, but the closer proximity could increase his danger. Not daring to speak, even into his radio, he waited, knowing help was so close but unable to call for it. He chose his moment, then: 'Armed police, stand still.' His voice was audible even at the front of the house. Bob's voice followed, breathlessly over the radio, as he ran to aid him from the kitchen of 55. 'Contact. Contact.'

As Dunj threw in the challenge, he lit up the scene with his torch mount. The staring face of a white man, perhaps thirty years of age, confronted him. Just as Bob got there to give support, the man turned on his heels and disappeared. Seconds later the sound of a closing door. Nosy bastard, Dunj thought. The earpiece crackled again. 'Suspect appears to have been a nosy neighbour. Sorry, chaps. Stand down.'

I knew much more about O'Grady now from the locals, and, to a greater extent, from the two women at number 55. I knew about his depression, the wife and child who had left him, and the mysterious call at the women's door. This was adding a deeper dimension to it all.

ARMED RESPONSE

In the far distance, echoing through the still night air, was the sound of the approaching help. Still far away but busting a gut to get here. I did not have enough men. The west side beyond 53 towards the lower numbers was not easily accessible and still insecure. That was where the strange face had come and gone. O'Grady lived here. He knew those gardens and we did not. He could attack my men, the nosy neighbour or anyone else. Where was he? We believed he had a gun, but I did not then know about the knives, those silent killers in the night. I rang the phone again repeatedly. Nothing.

From the front I could hear Kevin's loud challenges. 'John O'Grady, come to the door.' Nothing.

Between us, the inspector and I marshalled our forces. He firmed up his cordons far away from the scene, while my mind wrestled with a dozen contingencies. A surrender plan. Which hospitals were available if there was a shooting? Which stations would we go back to? Who would be liaison officer? Safe routes in. Marshalling points for incoming vehicles like the dog section, the ambulance and no doubt, soon, the TSG.

My mobile rang. 'Base here, Sarge. The superintendent would like a sit-rep.' I looked at the young inspector, grinning at me with a local radio in his hand. 'Press are on to it,' he said. 'My guvnor wants an update.'

Beam me up, Scotty.

At the back of the houses, events were taking another sinister turn. From somewhere beyond 53, Dunj heard the sound of a door opening, and the crackling of foliage underfoot. He braced himself for the nosy neighbour. Both the torch mounts lit up the scene, as he choked back a scathing rebuke. Suddenly illuminated now were two heads. One was an attractive young woman, a blonde in a black dress. From directly ahead, Bob could see only her, while Dunj had a better angle.

Around her neck was the arm of a man who had tucked himself in close behind her. Unseen by either Bob or Dunj, he had a large revolver in his free hand. In his belt were two wicked-looking knives. In his mind was a plan. This was John O'Grady.

He had fired the first shots through the front window and then he probably ran straight back out of the patio door into the overgrown back gardens. Here, he had no doubt been ranging around earlier, firing shots in an apparent attempt to draw us in. His had been the face of the nosy neighbour. Sadly for him, we do not rush in where angels fear to tread.

Dunj could see O'Grady now, behind the wall of a garden backing on to 53, and had a favourable angle. Bob could see only the woman's face. One thing they both saw clearly was the look of terror spread across her features. Dunj later said, 'It was a look I've never seen the like of before or since.' Back at control, my earpiece crackled. 'Suspect out. Has taken a woman hostage. Stand by.'

Out in the garden, a drama began to be played out. Bob opened the dialogue: 'What's your name?' Misunderstanding the enquiry, the terrified woman responded, 'Angela Jackson.'

Bob directed the questions pointedly at the man. 'What's your name, mate?'

'You know who I am.'

'What are you doing?'

'I've got my neighbour.'

'Let the woman go. We don't want anyone to get hurt.'

'Don't patronise me, you son of a bitch.'

Then he dragged her back into the bushes and up the garden to the house. We cannot begin to imagine the terror she must have felt, being dragged away like that, from the only obvious hope of rescue to an ordeal she must surely have dreaded. At least now we knew where he was. But that was what he wanted; it was all part of his plan.

As all this was happening, messages and phone calls clouded my thinking. The hard-pressed local officer in the Rover tried valiantly to record it all, and I asked a nearby female officer to help him. I was aware that he was fighting to give me the space to think, while answers were required of me from any number of enquirers. To the uninformed onlooker I must have appeared to be losing my reason, as I paced about seemingly muttering to myself. In fact, masses of information was coming through the covert earpiece I wore, and the replies went back through a microphone secreted in my body armour, and operated by a small switch cupped in my left hand. This often made for entertaining face-to-face conversation.

It was now well after three in the morning. The boys had adjusted their positions now that it was clear exactly where O'Grady was.

Bob was closest, using a lean-to type of structure on the back of the houses for cover. He could look over the fence splitting the divided rear garden of 53, directly at the rear of 51. I found the time to speak to the base. 'I have a full hostage situation here. Can you get me an SFO team?'

'Don't think we can find one, Sarge.'

'What about Trojan 521?'

'They'll be with you as soon as possible.'

'Can you get me an armoured Land Rover up here?'

'I'll do my best, Sarge. And, oh yes, the guvnor covering the siege down south would like to speak to you, if you get a chance.'

I made that call. The inspector made it clear that I had his support and good wishes. That was all I was going to get for the time being. If there had been any more resources we would have had them. The box, as they say, was empty.

I thought about the woman shut in that darkened house with a man who had brought terror into her life, suddenly in the night, violating the sanctity of her home. Desperately, I wanted to know what was going on inside. What abuse was she suffering at his hands? And would our intervention precipitate her death? It would take only a microsecond for him to shoot her. Over and over I weighed these things in my mind. All this was on my shoulders; my stomach was an empty pit.

In the distance I could hear the sound of two-tones echoing for miles in the still night air, as Trojan 521 fought their way towards us.

Then, whispered in my ear from Bob at the back of 53, 'No lights. No movement.'

'You all right there?' I said.

'Busting for a piss.'

Such things become major problems as time ticks by. You can bet that, if you loosen your kit, that's the moment it all happens.

'Dunj from 500.'

'Go ahead.'

'Any movement?'

'No. All quiet.'

I began to think about how I could give them a break. After all, they had been in a state of tension for over three hours. The sudden bellow of two-tones, now relatively close, seemed to offer an answer.

'Stand by just a while, lads. I think the cavalry's arriving.'

That was not going to do anything to ease Bob's discomfort. Moments later I heard the earpiece crackling into life again. '500 from Bob.'

'Go ahead.'

'Movement. The back door of 51 is opening.'

The rear of 51 was accessed through a sort of wooden extension, which meant opening first the rear door of the house, and then crossing the extension, before opening the further door into the garden. This was what Bob was hearing.

Dunj's voice: 'He's out. He's got the woman in front of him like before.'

O'Grady came into the garden, holding the woman in front of him in the same manner, his left arm around her throat. Out in the street the challenges of 'Armed police – stand still' could be heard in the night. He was whispering in her ear so that he could not be heard, and he moved towards Bob. He was still one half of the divided garden away with Dunj covering him from the bottom, as the woman, obviously terrified, began to straddle the fence between 51 and 53. Later we would learn that he had already threatened to kill her.

Bob began to plead with him to let her go but the stranglehold on her neck was not released. He followed her across and, as he momentarily lost his balance, for the first time Bob saw the revolver. 'He's got a gun,' he called to Dunj.

O'Grady was only about the same height as his hostage, and used her as a shield with the revolver pointing into her left side as she struggled to cross the fence. The pleas for him to let her go went unheeded. His only words were, 'Don't shoot me, and I won't shoot you.' He backed towards the patio door of 53. 'If you shoot me, then I'll shoot her.' A couple more paces and he was in through the door, pulling the woman with him by the neck. The last thing the boys saw as she disappeared was that same mortally terrified face. For her the nightmare was renewed.

Trojan 521 swung in through Trinder Road and up to the RVP with all their lights and noise off, only the scuffing of the tyres announcing their arrival. Unlike in the movies, this time the cavalry were a little late. Nevertheless, Ray ran to my side like a lifeline to a drowning man. I shouted to Harry and Prof.

'I need you ready to go. *Now*.' I turned to Ray and said, 'He's taken a women hostage in the house, faced off the boys, and he's got a big revolver. He's already shown that he's prepared to fire it.' His usually smiling face was for once suddenly grave. 'Bloody hell,' he said.

It was now well after four in the morning. Soon new problems would arise. The press would get here. The first of the early risers would emerge from nearby houses and, if we were unlucky, appear in the midst of the containment. The young inspector would have to think about keeping his night duty on and calling out the early turn even earlier. My, they would love that! Not only that, but the hostage negotiators would arrive and ride roughshod over the fragile framework we were assembling around this incident. Vastly senior officers would consider it their duty to assume command, and no amount of briefing could give them the insight I now had, the insight that only living an incident can give. In my mind's eye I could see crowds, cordons and cameras, and I was beginning to feel tired.

It was certainly tiring for the two men isolated at the back of the house, unable to relax even for a moment. I sent Harry round using the access through 55, and I gave Prof the all-important task of getting to the vulnerable far side beyond 51, with instructions to inform me of his progress. I called Bob and Dunj and kept them informed of what was happening, while my adopted local PC scribbled frantically to record it all.

Inside 53, O'Grady was getting set to play out the final stages of his plan. I wanted to know what that might be and so I tried the direct approach: I phoned him. This time the phone was answered.

Harry had been driving 521 and had deployed with only a handgun and an extremely powerful halogen torch, pausing momentarily for the world's shortest briefing from me, while throwing his body armour over his head. Then he was gone. Prof, equipped with a handgun and an MP5 carbine fitted with a torch mount, was having a hard time getting round to the far side. He had found an access to the rear gardens and was fighting his way towards the scene. Later he would wryly comment that he 'had not been trained in jungle warfare'. Ray took the spare MP5 to Andy and checked on the front containment, before coming back to help at the control. The pressure eased for a moment.

No words were spoken when the phone was answered, but I knew at once that it was the woman. Instantly I could feel the abject terror in the trembling, halting breath on the other end of the line. I began. 'My name is Sergeant Gray. I am close by, just across the road from you now.'

'Yes?'

'You will be safe. Try hard not to panic and answer my questions if you can.'

No reply.

'Can you tell me where in the house you are?'

'No.'

'Can you speak freely?'

'No.'

'Is he near you?'

'Yes.'

'Has he got a gun?'

'Yes.'

'Is it real?'

'Yes.'

'Has he threatened you?'

'Yes.'

'Please ask him to talk to me.'

There was a pause, the sound of the phone being handled and muffled words. Then the phone went dead.

Inside the flat, I found out later, a conversation had taken place. The woman asked. 'Do you want to get shot?'

'Yes. I'm going to make them shoot me when it's light.'

'What're you trying to do, commit suicide?'

'Yes, but I haven't got the guts to do it myself.' He paused. 'If I start firing at the police, they'll have to shoot me.'

It was now well after four in the morning. It was rapidly becoming light. The plan was almost complete.

Bob had moved back to his original point behind the ballistic blanket in what came to be known as 'the rhubarb patch'. Prof was making his way through the undergrowth, torn between a gut-wrenching urge to get to where he could support his mates, and the need to be as quiet as he could. The two didn't equate.

At the control I wrestled with the prospect of having to storm the house, as the possibility of O'Grady shooting the woman was now an imminent threat. I desperately wanted someone to tell me they could at least see him. I needed the immediate means to deal with that contingency. Where in the house were they? I hated that moment of fear I had shared with Angela Jackson, and I could imagine the scene inside the house. At that moment I could have shot him without blinking an eyelid.

I tried to get Dunj to an observation point so we might know if things were deteriorating further, so that he could take a head shot if it looked as though O'Grady might kill the girl. I thought about getting the rear windows smashed as a diversion in a co-ordinated entry through the front door.

So many things. Not enough time. Not enough men. Me, Ray, Harry and two from outside, through the front door. Dunj to break the windows. I must prepare for it now or it will be too late.

'Ray, have you got the opening kit?' I asked, as I took the first faltering steps towards what would have been a fateful decision.

Out in the rear garden, things were happening. Harry emerged from the rear door of 55 to be met by Bob, who by now had a call of nature that must have reached screaming point. I had relayed the content of my telephone conversation to everyone and made sure it was in the incident log. Nevertheless, for all we knew, we might still be here for hours. Harry was going to give them each a break in turn. But that wasn't in the plan.

Then my earpiece crackled again, it was Dunj: 'Movement in the kitchen, suspect towards the rear door.'

Followed quickly by Harry: 'Suspect out in rear garden.' I frantically rang the phone in the house. She answered.

'Are you alone?'

'Yes.'

'Where is he now?'

'He's gone, he's gone out the back.'

'Get out. Get out now through the front door. Don't rush. Don't panic. Someone will meet you.'

'Yes.' And the phone clattered down.

I had pressed the switch cupped in my left hand while I spoke to her so that everyone would know what was happening. It was risking valuable air time at a crucial moment, but equally a calculated gamble that someone at the front would react as I hoped.

'500 from Alan at point 6. Will receive hostage.'

In the rear garden the pace of events suddenly slowed as John O'Grady walked deliberately out through the patio door, holding the revolver straight down by his right side. He was intent on confronting the armed officers deployed around him. Ahead of him, behind a low wall at the end of the garden, was good old Dunj, with an MP5 and torch mount lighting up the garden.

Off to O'Grady's right, across the other half of the divided garden of 53 was Bob, in cover behind the ballistic blanket draped over the fence.

He was also shining a torch mount across the scene. Coming from O'Grady's left, Prof was closing through the gardens but not yet close enough. Harry was at the back door of 55, safely in the cover that the brickwork offered, and able to see across to where O'Grady was pacing around the garden. The radio was alive with transmissions, as information was passed back and forth. Alan ran forwards from left to right across my vision as he prepared to snatch Angela from captivity. He dropped to his knee and raised the MP5 to cover her exit from the front door, when finally the perversity of the building became apparent, and she emerged from the alleyway at the side. Her face was a mask of fear. Repeatedly, she was screaming, 'He wants you to shoot him. He wants you to shoot him.'

Andy joined Alan, and they half carried the hysterical woman away. Local officers assumed responsibility for her then, delivering her into the arms of a waiting ambulance crew for sedation.

As the woman was being extracted, in the rear garden, O'Grady continued to circle, while Bob and Dunj entreated with him to drop the gun. Dunj challenged: 'Stand still. Armed police.'

'John, please put the gun down,' Bob pleaded.

'What will you do if I don't?'

He was perhaps twelve or fifteen feet away, calm and seemingly plotting where the armed officers were. His pace slowed almost to a standstill, and he turned away from them, lifting the gun in a long arc away from his body. Then he pointed it at the back of his own head and turned to face them.

Harry was relaying the events back through my earpiece, and to the rest of the containment officers. Alan and Andy had closed with the front of the house. On my hip the mobile phone rang. 'Sergeant Gray,' a voice said.

'Yes.'

'The team are released from the south London job and on way to you.'

'Thanks.'

In the gardens to the west, Prof was reduced to smashing his way through fences as he heard the pitch of the challenges rising, knowing that gunfire was the next step. The last but one fence was a larch lap panel that he judged would fall to a single blow, but instead it splintered as his hand went through, and it was trapped there. That may have saved his life.

O'Grady was facing the raised weapons, his gun still pointed at the back of his own head, but now with his finger on the trigger. The shouts were reaching a crescendo, audible in the street outside. Behind me a phone began to ring, and I could hear the young inspector.

'Yes, sir? I can't say.' Some distant senior was seeking an update. 'I don't think it would help. Maybe the TSG.'

I left him to it.

Bob and Dunj were desperately trying to negotiate with O'Grady. But he was unmoved. He said, 'Do you think this is a real gun?'

Bob replied, 'Yes I do. Put the gun down.'

'What will you do if I don't?' And then, 'What will you do if I shoot you?'

At the back, Harry was looking for a way to contribute, and he tried to dazzle O'Grady with his powerful torch and distract him. The brilliance affected them all, so much so that Bob cursed at him. 'Turn that fucking torch off.' The light went out.

Then O'Grady completed the final act of his plan, guaranteed at once to send a message across the world, and silence those whispering demons that came to torment him time and again. He brought the gun forwards over his head in one smooth and calculated movement, and pointed it directly at the carbines facing him.

Reacting in a way that both men had trained for a thousand times, they opened fire.

At the front of the house the young inspector was still on the phone, fending off more questions from a commander, huddled by a phone, still warm from his bed, the last of which was evidently, 'What's happening now?'

I had dumped everything as a sound like a burst of machine-gun fire split the air. Handgun drawn and Ray at my side, I ran forwards. I heard the inspector's reply. 'I think we're shooting somebody, sir.'

The machine-gun effect was six shots in rapid succession. Bob had fired a pair of shots, but O'Grady did not fall; instead he stood seemingly unaffected. For both of the officers now, a condition called 'perceptual distortion' took effect, where the body's senses and reactions are speeded up by the instinct to survive.

All else seems to be in slow motion. Even though Dunj also fired a pair, the threat was still there, seeming much closer than it actually was.

In their heads at that moment, perhaps thoughts of their families, pictures of the many horrors they had both seen before. All at once they combined into one threatening entity: John O'Grady trying to kill them, shot four times and still standing. All this compressed in a microsecond. A single thought: I don't want to die.

Bob fired another pair and O'Grady dropped below the false horizon of the carbine's sights.

Harry, having positioned himself to prevent a 'break-out' towards 55, watched the whole drama, ready to engage but aware that Prof was somewhere beyond the scene and perhaps in his line of fire. He had watched the deliberation with which O'Grady had adopted a textbook, single-handed firing position. Then the staccato rattle of gunfire before he dropped behind the waist-high fences. Now, perhaps he was dead. Or maybe not hit at all. Prof was at last able to pull his hand free, risking the resounding crack that moments earlier might have precipitated gunfire.

Ray and I crossed the road in classic 'cover and movement' as I shouted loudly over my shoulder, 'Medics up!' O'Grady was lying half inclined on his right side with his head against the far fence. He still had the gun. He was not dead.

Harry recovered from the shock waves of the gun-fire, which had reverberated round the brickwork that surrounded him, feeling at first as if the shots had been aimed at him.

The voice through his earpiece confirmed that the prone figure in the garden was motionless under the guns still pointing at it. He decided to approach while Ray and I were entering through the access between the two houses. We were just behind him as he crossed the garden. As I turned left round the rear corner of the house, I could see Bob and Dunj still with weapons half raised, across the divide of the gardens, and behind the cover that had been home to them for hours. As I turned again, the crouching shape of Harry's back presented itself as he tore open field dressings.

Facing him was O'Grady. Legs splayed, head slightly supported by the fence, he was staring blankly upwards. His face was calm, resigned perhaps. Nearby in the grass, where Harry had thrown it, was a large revolver.

Bob and Dunj seemed rooted to the spot, their faces pale and hollow with shock. You can train endlessly for the event but the aftermath you can only live through. There was really very little blood. Gouges marked a track through his hand and wrist, bearing witness to the gun raised in front of him, to threaten the men he had chosen to confront, but at first there was very little to indicate the gross injuries he had sustained.

As Harry fought to get the dressings in place, he pulled at the shirt where small blooded areas were appearing. Below them were neat holes in the flesh, one on the right just below his ribs and another high on his chest below the right shoulder. The shirt shifted. A further entry wound was visible to the left of centre in his stomach. Harry put his hand on O'Grady's back, to pass the long bandage around his body for me to secure it. His hand felt the leaden weight of a bullet head lying in the folds of the shirt. It had passed right through. The colossal bleeding was all internal.

O'Grady seemed to be looking straight into my eyes as he moved his right arm as if to prop himself up on the elbow. A sudden, thick rivulet of blood ran down from the hole in his right shoulder and for the first time he seemed to feel pain. He spoke, the heavy smell of alcohol wafting into my face. 'You've broken my fucking shoulder.' Then his eyes closed.

The paramedics were there in moments, throwing open equipment bags, grabbing syringes, lines and bags of saline. Fighting to get into his circulatory system, I brutally squeezed his forearms to bring the collapsing veins up enough to get the lines in that were his only hope of survival. All the while the pungent smell of lost body fluids and alcohol penetrated our senses. Ray, Alan and Andy cleared the house behind us.

Within perhaps a minute he was stretchered up and gone. Only the field dressing discarded by the medics, the fluttering blue and white cordon tape and the revolver bore witness.

Close examination of the scene in the growing brightness of this new day would reveal bullet holes in a wooden structure nearby. If fate had been cruel, Prof might not have been held in the embrace of that last fence, and strayed unknowingly into a field of fire, but that doesn't bear thinking about.

Visibly shaken, Bob and Dunj made their way out to the RVP. On the way through the house they encountered Clio and Maria. Seeing their obvious distress, Dunj, to his eternal credit, still had the presence of mind to call a female officer to comfort them.

The three of us stood by the Rover as the rest of the department began to arrive. Senior officers and SFO teams, hotfoot from a siege that ended peacefully. Too late, I thought. The Armed Response Vehicles had dealt, manfully.

Ray and the remainder of the crews involved that night filtered back to the cars. Familiar sounds resonated, peeling Velcro, carbines being cleared, somehow incongruous in the morning light. Bob and Dunj were standing with their backs to the end of a terraced house, drinking tea that had been contributed by some kind soul, to Dunj's huge relief.

I sat on the bonnet of the Rover facing the two men who had endured so much in the last few hours, and suppressed waves of emotion. After all, I was still their sergeant.

'You OK, boys? You've done right.'

Andy passed behind me, and looking over his left shoulder he smiled at me and said, 'I think you did really well.'

No one will ever understand how much that meant.

We returned to Holloway, where the complicated post-incident and evidencing procedures would last for many hours. Late in the day I listened again as the weapons were cleared and I placed mine back on the rack at Old Street. Everywhere were faces full of questions that few would venture to ask, and I wondered how the boys were feeling. In the base room lifts were offered but declined, and the three of us parted with looks that spoke volumes and thoughts that remained private.

As I drove home in the bright afternoon sunshine, I lived it all again. Over and over. I topped the flyover that empties on to the broad expanse of the M11. A voice on the radio began, 'Last night drama came to a north London street when a man armed with a revolver was shot by police.'

At home and unable to sleep, I welcomed the greeting my bull terrier gave me. He and I went for a long walk across the Essex hills. I was still not free from the tension. In the distance I could see Canary Wharf on the skyline, reminding me that it would all still be there for us the next time.

We went home, and I sat on the patio in the warm sunlight and drank a small glass of a good, Irish whiskey, then allowed it to carry me into a deep sleep. The end of a long night.

Excused that coming night's duty, I slept through to the following day, spending several hours at Old Street dealing with the aftermath. Then Bob, Dunj and I had our own debrief, quietly, in a pub near the base.

When I got home my wife told me that it had been on the news. After extensive surgery and over sixty pints of blood, O'Grady died that afternoon. Now his plan was complete.

I have never satisfied myself with any understanding of what drives a man to do such things and I know I never will. If I had any sympathy it was diluted by the faces of my men, forced to do his bidding, and it was washed away by the next poor individual I encountered who fought for life and lost.

Sometimes, though, I think an unseen hand weaves fate with irony. Within hours of O'Grady's demise, the man who sold him the gun and who has done the same many times before, died of natural causes.

# **9** For the Love of Mother

A ship sails and I stand watching till she fades on the horizon,
and someone at my side says, 'She is gone'.
Gone where? Gone from my sight,
that is all; she is just as large as when I last saw her.
The diminished size and total loss of sight is in me, not in her,
and just at the moment when someone at my side says 'she is gone',
there are others who are watching her coming,
and other voices take up a glad shout,
'There she comes!'

From the verse 'What is Dying' by Bishop Brent

ON 30 JANUARY 1972, when an end to the conflict in Ulster seemed further away than ever, a civil-rights march turned into a riot and British paratroopers opened fire in Londonderry's Bogside, killing thirteen men and youths and wounding a further seventeen. Opposition MPs described the killings as a 'Bloody Sunday' and a mass murder by the British Army. Major General Robert Ford, the army chief, said, 'There is absolutely no doubt that the Parachute Regiment Battalion had opened fire only after they were fired on.'

On 2 February, the British Embassy in Dublin was burned down by a crowd of about 30,000 people. The Republic's Foreign Secretary flew to Washington to win support for the demand that British troops be withdrawn from Ulster.

The IRA declared that its immediate policy was to kill as many British soldiers as possible.

On 22 February 1972, six civilians and an army priest were killed in an IRA bomb attack on the 16th Parachute Regiment headquarters at Aldershot at lunchtime. The IRA claimed responsibility for the blast, which they said was in revenge for the deaths of thirteen civilians in January's 'Bloody Sunday' battle. No warning was given before the fifty-pound bomb in a stolen car went off. Five of the dead women were domestic workers preparing food in the kitchens. Others were a gardener and a padre, Captain Garry Weston, holder of the MBE for brave service in Ulster. The army was now tightening security at all its bases, an end to open barracks like Aldershot.

A corporal, Tom Howard, at the scene of that explosion, was blown off his feet by the massive blast, which devastated the building and the surrounding area. Shards of flying, broken glass caused many horrifying injuries. He like others ran to the scene of the carnage.

'There were women in there. Safety didn't seem to matter, we had to get them out. There was blood everywhere. One woman's body could be seen. She worked in the kitchens and was the wife of one of the lads in the camp. I helped get the remains of another woman on to a ground sheet. Her husband is in Ulster at the moment.'

A report in the *Daily Mail* of Wednesday, 23 February, commented, 'Blast victim Mrs Thelma Bosley only returned to work at the officers' mess on Monday after being sick for a month. She had four children, one of them a lance corporal in the Parachute regiment.'

Thelma Bosley also had a fourteen-year-old son. He was Karl Anthony Bosley. He would grow up to be a soldier. A *para*.

The Provisional IRA, through a spokesman, issued a statement: 'Our intelligence reports were that no civilians frequented this part of the barracks. Any civilian casualties would be very much regretted as our target was the officers responsible for the Derry outrages.'

I can still remember what it was like to be a fourteen-year-old boy. The struggles of puberty, the developing personality. The security of a family at that difficult time. Especially the presence, the reassurance, the femininity of a mother.

* * *

It was a mild evening for so early in the year. This night duty had started with good-natured banter, mainstay of the character of 'C' relief. As usual, Barry OJ was there with the inevitable jibe about the state of the duties, the last-minute changes, product of barely sufficient manpower.

'So where do I appear in the lottery tonight, Sarge?' he asked. He was leaning on the old table spread with cups, and guarded by a huge steaming teapot. It occupied a space close to the door, and gave him a ready escape route. A mischievous smile was creeping on to his face, but he knew I considered small amounts of pain a useful management tool. 'If you think you can do better, then take promotion, or shut your gob,' I retorted.

He had started the bandwagon of typical coppers' humour from which no one was exempt. The pattern was familiar, first me then each other, and, if they were feeling exceptionally outrageous, Keith would be a target too. No matter, it was all taken in the spirit it was given. They were – no, *we* were – a good bunch. I liked them all.

'Post him base man, Sarge?' Lucky Bob was there as always, ready to deflate Barry's ego. There was little that Barry hated more than being tied to a radio console and a CAD screen for hours. He turned his attention to the big aluminium teapot, and began to pour.

I caught his eyes. 'That would be a way of sorting things out.' The grin turned to a weak smile.

'Tea, Sergeant?' Then he proffered a steaming mug in my direction. 'Always look after the sergeant, that's what I say.' He threw an icy glare towards the corner where Bob sat smiling wickedly.

Far away in the south base the pattern was being repeated, as Pete and Ray, my counterparts at the Lambeth base, suffered similarly. Among the crews were Tony, a.k.a. 'Carrot', big jovial Nicky Boy, and Darren, a fresh face. He was new to the relief and the challenges the role would bring. Before the night was out he would be tested as much as any of them with the heaviest issues a man can encounter. The threat of life or death, for them and for others.

In the yard, Keith and I manhandled the heavy door-opening gear into the back of the supervisory Volvo estate, as one by one the crews went out.

When all the gear, the body armour, radios, phones, maps and paraphernalia were in place, we tossed a coin. Keith would drive.

From the gate 'Shaky' Jake called my name in his inimitable Celtic tones, pointing at the huge steel gates. I gestured back to him. I would close them. In a moment he dropped into the back seat of the Rover ahead, the reflected track of its rear lights lingering for a moment in the glass of a building opposite.

Tonight, unwisely, I would leave the paperwork behind, gambling on some quiet time in the small hours. It was a poor gamble. I preferred distraction, colour, noise. Keith and I had become kindred spirits and he sensed my mood. 'Up West?' he said, smiling at me across the car as we swung right towards Bishops-gate.

I grinned, gesturing towards the grey buildings around us. 'Take me away from all this.'

The bond between us had grown strong over the years. He was a tall, slim man, whose soft features disguised a powerful will. Almost every day we would travel in from the edge of town together. This was our office, our very private meeting room. Many things were discussed and resolved on those journeys. The relief's day-to-day problems, the future of this man or that. What support, what advice, what sanction to be applied. In the cold mists at the crack of dawn, in the surrendering light before a night duty, summer, winter, light or dark, it went on.

As we passed through the City towards central London we spoke about home, each of us well known to the other's family.

Keith swung the heavy estate car right of the dividing island that led us into the mouth of the Strand. Almost like at a border post, the atmosphere changes, the abandoned blankets and street people in the doorways contrasting with the dark shiny limousines and stretch Cadillacs, double-parked at the entrance to the hotels.

Like the atmosphere the conversation changed as our more serious heads went on. The teeming crowds around the forecourt of Charing Cross station were busier than usual as cabs created chaos in our wake. Each seemed to be vying for custom.

As we drew up to the traffic lights at the edge of Trafalgar Square the traffic thinned. In the night air flashes from a myriad tourist cameras created a strobe-light effect across the junction. High above us Horatio Nelson presided, impervious to the scuttling ants of a later age that busied themselves with trivia at his feet. Now *there's* a man who knew what a gun fight was!

Keith swung the Volvo right into the bus lane at the further side, then across the top of the square and left into Charing Cross Road. Everywhere there seemed to be a throng of people, outside the theatres, the clubs. Then, as we entertained ourselves with the diverse spectacle that London's theatreland can provide, he turned left again. A group of drivers of many nationalities, some seated near their office, others leaning against cars, were smoking, drinking coffee from plastic cups. They looked uncomfortably on as he picked his way through a slalom of badly parked minicabs. Then suddenly we were in the cosmopolitan heart of Soho, Old Compton Street.

Groups of people spilled across the road from cafés, bars and drinking houses. From somewhere among a collection of coffee drinkers at pavement tables on our left, there were suddenly raised voices. Anger, the sound of breaking glass, as a table vomited empty cups and half-consumed glasses of lager into the road.

While some revellers fled, others, close by and unaffected, relished the free entertainment the two fighting drunks that spilled out of the door would provide for them.

The barrel-chested, bow-tied doormen stopped suddenly, freeze-framed in the door as the bright markings of the Volvo registered on their faces. Smiling, they waited for the 'Old Bill' to sort it out. This time it would be us. When you wear a uniform and carry a gun in London, life can get complicated: grappling with a fighting man takes on new dimensions, as you try to keep the gun out of the equation.

Keith was already braking as I shouted, 'Fight.' Two cursing, salivating young men fought across the top of a collapsing table, as its occupants recoiled and faded into the crowd.

'She's not your fucking property. You can't tell her who to speak to,' screamed the ruddy-faced young Irishman, whose sweater was twisted and stretched around him now like a misshapen woollen gown. At the bar a barely clad, over-made-up girl, swung a crossed leg in apparent amusement at the two men in contest for her favours.

The hard-faced man who seemed to be winning the exchange had pinned the Irish boy across the table, and against the glass frontage of the bar. His clenched fists bunched handfuls of wool about the face of the other man like a great knitted beard. 'I bought the drinks, I get the goods.' Nice people.

In a moment we were out. I dragged the hard-faced man off and he fell to the floor. The Irishman was at

FOR THE LOVE OF MOTHER

Keith's mercy, twisted in an arm lock, bending him forwards till his face pressed down on the beer-stained plastic of the same table.

I dropped my knee into the man's neck, pinning his face half turned to the footway, his left cheek flattened against the cold dirty paving. The girl at the bar drew heavily on a cigarette, a smug half-smile on her face. In moments the locals were there, the van doors opened and the fighting men gone. I turned to a smiling, rotund young sergeant, who was evidently supervising a 'rowdyism' patrol of several young constables.

The prospect of being confined to a charge room while a library of forms were completed was looming. 'Do you need us back at CD?' I asked. (CD is the station code for West End Central.) I cast a sideways glance at the sergeant, as Keith broke into a timely conversation on the mobile.

'Yes', he was saying, 'this is the duty officer. Anything happening down south?'

'Nah!' said the sergeant to me. 'You got other fish to fry. And anyway, there are enough probationers in this van for a dozen drunks.'

The sergeant had understood me perfectly. The last thing we wanted on a busy night was to be dealing with trivia, and have 'the wheel come off' somewhere far away, to be needed to advise, organise and brief, when we were stuck in the quagmire of a charge room. As we left, the doorman ruefully eyed the handguns at our hips.

We exited Old Compton Street, where the poker-faced models stare blankly from the Anne Summers window, dressed in peephole this and open-crotch that. Signs that the night was to be frenetic began to show.

Keith grinned at me. 'I told my wife that this big, ugly mean old sergeant would protect me, but I reckon I got the biggest one out of those two.' I paused for thought.

'You get paid more money than me. You're younger than me. It should be the other way around. Anyway, he was a pussy,' I replied.

Suddenly the radio barked again. 'Any unit Charley Delta section, the Hippodrome, Charing Cross Road, disturbance at the door.' We were moments away.

At the railings in front of the Hippodrome the crew of Trojan 521 had just arrived. As we rolled to a stop, the car nose to nose with theirs, they vaulted over to confront the group of short-haired young men now involved in an escalating exchange with the huge, suited doormen. One man with a tattoo of a regimental insignia on his forearm was jabbing at the lapel of a giant, shaven-headed bouncer. The bouncer was flanked by two equally big men, hands clasped behind their backs, at pains now to be the innocents, for our benefit. West End doormen know how little time it takes the Old Bill to arrive up there, and that the blade has two edges.

Martin, a softly spoken young Scotsman with a chin beard, placed himself between the opposing factions, quickly followed by the fresh-faced, fair-haired and usually smiling Robin. Bobby Brackets stood off to observe and intercept. Keith and I ranged around the far side of the group now largely blocking the entrance.

'He won't let us in, says we're not dressed proper.' The slurred voice declared in broad Liverpudlian tones. 'But I reckon he don't like my fucking accent any more than I like his face.'

Soldiers. Young, off duty, headstrong soldiers. And this one had a chip on his shoulder. The thing is, I don't like to nick soldiers.

I always reckoned they deserved one chance more than anyone else, that society owed them the odd extra favour. So I stuck my oar in.

'Do yourself a favour, son. You're not dressed for it. You've had a good drink. Leave it.' But it wasn't going to be that easy.

'I know the fucking law. You can't nick me for nothing. You're on their side.' As he gestured up the steps, the three other soldiers were growing anxious. Aggrieved as they were, this was not what they wanted.

I looked at the older, seemingly quieter, man of the group and stepped clear to appeal to him, as Keith placated the others. Young and stroppy, Mr Tattoo was having none of it. Thrusting out his chest, he took a half-step up towards the bouncers, clenching and unclenching his fists. Martin's Asp – his extending steel baton – crackled as it flicked out as a warning, a statement of intent. If the soldiers started to fight, we would not lose. A huge, fat doorman grinned.

I wanted a peaceful resolution. But Martin, concerned as always for his rather senior sergeant, was right. A show of force was needed, and it was my back he was watching. 'Get your mate out of here,' I said. 'You're all squaddies. We don't want to nick you. Get him out of here.'

Behind me two sets of men of uniform, one in and one out of 'the cloth', were getting eyeball to eyeball as young men do. The older soldier saw it too. Suddenly I realised that he had power in the group. 'Leave it, Charley.' He dragged the aggressive one away like pulling a moth from a flame, and cursing they melted into the crowds of Leicester Square.

Maybe we lost a bit of face, but it was better that way. The doormen were right: Mr Tattoo would have been a problem in the club; but their smug grins were an abhorrence. After all, tomorrow the soldiers would be sober and different people. The fat doorman nodded at us. Keith and I blanked him completely. We returned to the Volvo as local cars arrived too late. A brief word, and we left. Soon we were circuiting central London again.

As we rolled through Whitehall into Victoria Street, we heard Trojan 521 take another call over the radio. 'Trojan 521 from MP. Oxford Street, towards Hanover Square, a black BMW 5 series, the occupants believed concerned in an armed robbery of a service station.'

'MP from Trojan 521. On way.' And then, distantly, 'MP from Trojan 552. Running from Lambeth.' The south-base car was well placed to help.

Minutes later the armed occupants of that BMW learned the meaning of submission, as a white police car with a yellow spot on the roof swept across its bows. Another quartered it from the rear, as from behind lethal carbines the voice came cold and clear. 'You in the car, show us your hands.' You know what they say: If you can't stand the heat, don't go into the kitchen.

As 552 left their colleagues in 521 with the paper-work and headed back south, perhaps fifteen minutes had passed, and we were in the Haymarket, making a final run-through before heading west, when the radio broke through again. 'Trojan 552 or any Trojan unit, Streatham Common and now towards Greyhound Lane, a male, late thirties, stocky build, dressed in camouflage gear and beret. The male is in possession of a handgun and grenades, accosting passers-by.'

Immediately the response, 'MP from Trojan 552. On way.' I said, 'Yes, and pigs might fly.' Keith grunted in agreement.

As we got ourselves assigned and headed south we were never likely to be as wrong again. A thousand calls that have no real substance can make you think that way. Then something happens to remind you that such scepticism is an expensive luxury. This was to be such a call.

*   *   *

As I was striving to save four drunken squaddies from their own foolishness, a soul mate, an ex-para was boiling over, reliving the agonies of another age. The pain of a youthful loss of his mother. The years without her. The knowledge, the intimate knowledge, of the carnage wreaked by atrocity was always in his mind. Never a day went by when he didn't picture her torn and broken body. Nobody else cared. Nobody else remembered. But they would. Incensed that twenty-five years on the carnage of Bloody Sunday was remembered, commemorated almost, while his and his family's agony was ignored, he was driven to act. Dressed in camouflage clothing, proudly wearing his red beret, he set out to die. Publicly. In his belt a pistol. In his hands, grenades.

Trojan 552, crewed by Carrot, Nicky Boy and Darren, had a head start on us. They were on the way back down south as the call came out, but other unarmed local officers were closer, much closer.

Peter Le Shirley piloted the local area car towards the point where Streatham Common crosses the 'T' of Greyhound Lane, and turned right toward Streatham Vale. Neither he nor the young female radio operator held a trace of our scepticism. As they approached the ambling figure of the stocky man walking away from them, every sense was prickling.

The speed dropped to a walking pace as they matched his progress. Peter watched him through the driver's window as he climbed the small hill leading to Streatham Common Railway Station. Clearly now the beret and the uniform could be seen. Another reason for caution, for fear. At the top of the hill the figure reached into his belt, drew a pistol, then, strangely, threw it over the bridge. When he seemed satisfied his actions had been seen, he walked on. A few yards further he turned and faced them, grenades in his hands.

The girl's voice on the radio was calm, controlled. A few words and my complacency was shattered. The radio signals broke a little but the meaning was clear. 'MP from Lima 5 [call sign of the local car]. Man in combat gear, gun, appears to have hand grenades.'

We were just entering the one-way system at the Elephant and Castle, when, with uncharacteristic violence, Keith threw the Volvo into the curve with such force that the back broke away in a screech of protesting tyres. At a junction far ahead of us 552 dipped its nose under heavy braking then took off again, a blaring, raucous light show.

Clear of the Elephant, Keith stamped on the accelerator and the car's automatic gearbox kicked down, the engine noise rose, conspiring with the horns to overpower the radio transmissions.

Now barely audible came the words, 'Pulled the pin with his teeth . . . making to throw the grenade.' This was suburban south London. We were doing ninety miles per hour.

Tracking his progress in Lima 5, Peter Le Shirley was mindful to keep thirty or forty yards back, as Karl Anthony Bosley turned abruptly several times to confront them. He would pause in unspoken challenge, sinister shapes in his hands. Behind him more local units blocked roads while aid from all around was scrambled to form cordons, to contain this threat, so different from anything else they had encountered.

Cars, buses, people were still driving towards them. Ordinary people blissfully unaware that anything was wrong. But they would notice. Karl intended they would. In the car Peter fretted. They did not have control. They needed help.

Ahead lay a parade of shops, to the left beyond a small crossroads, and beyond that again, an insignificant bridge across the stream grandly called the River Graveny.

Karl Bosley had been a soldier. The soldier was about to make his stand.

As Trojan 552 descended the hill, howling past Streatham Police Station, Darren, maps man that day, was passing out body armour and readying the weapons. The route had been read and Nicky Boy knew exactly where he was going.

As they crossed the lights at the bottom of the hill, they too heard the WPC's voice over the radio. The threat of the grenade.

As Peter Le Shirley watched the soldier pulling the pin, preparing to throw the grenade, the instinct to escape was overpowering. Too late to go back. No time to stop, to select reverse. But the voice in his head: Go. Get away. He stamped on the accelerator as the man's arm drew back. Within moments he was behind them.

He threw the car across the road, blocking it to people, to traffic, as distantly more sirens echoed into the night. From where he now stood, ushering people away, redirecting police aid as it arrived, he could see beyond Karl Bosley and up the hill towards Streatham. The alternating glare of headlights masked the glittering blue strobe on the roof of a fast-approaching police car. Help was arriving. It was the ARV. Over the radio came Carrot's voice. 'MP from Trojan 552, on scene. Please show us time of arrival.'

On the bridge Bosley sat on top of the parapet, the pins pulled from both grenades, and, with his elbows casually resting on his knees, he waited for Nick, Tony and Darren to approach.

We were still far off, but travelling at breakneck speed and closing fast. In central London, another ARV crew, having gained early release from yet another deployment, were setting new records as they too hurtled towards the scene.

The ARV crew were impressed: local officers had treated the situation with all the respect it deserved, and it showed. As 552 turned into Greyhound Lane, successive cordons of uniformed police officers lifted blue and white tape, directing the now cautiously approaching car towards the bridge. The last tape was strung at the top of a gentle downward slope that ran to the little bridge.

Beyond the parade of shops, across the width of the road, the solitary figure sat hunched and waiting. At the bridge the three armed officers would face a dilemma not covered in any training scenario. Shoot a man with a gun and it's over. Shoot a man with primed grenades and they go off anyway. Maybe you die as well.

In the far distance, the cordon position set up by Lima 5 set a further limit. But still there were houses that Karl Bosley was free to attack, people who might at any moment appear. The crew must close with him, make contact and negotiate. They had to keep him on that bridge.

At the car Darren and Carrot checked their MP5s, striking the action forwards with a familiar rack, rack, clack. A round in the breech. All that was left then was to flick the safety catch off, a controlled pull of the trigger, a sudden jolt to the shoulder. The end of a life. As Nick waited to deploy the car, to monitor the radio, the two armed officers melted into the safety of the shadows.

Then, with Darren leading, they moved from point of cover to point of cover, ever closer to the static figure. Across the front of the shops, screened by empty cars, clumsily parked vans, ever closer. Quietly cursing at every sound, the gravel crunching underfoot. The metallic rattle of the gun clips, the rustle of nylon clothing. In the still night air a breath could be heard.

Karl Bosley did not move. Still he was waiting. The bridge was to be his stage. When all the players were there, the second act would begin.

Behind the crew, Nicky Boy had quietly slipped the car into drive and allowed it to trickle forwards, tracking the walking men. Over the back-to-back radio, Darren whispered their progress. Hushed, unlit, just a quiet ticking from the engine, a wisp of steam from the exhaust, waiting for whatever the man with the grenades would do next. The muffled sound of the radio, the rustle of tyre rubber on the road, the occasional hiss from the brakes as its whispering progress was checked.

Silently, in the cover of parked cars, the officers on foot crossed the bridge. As Darren settled in on the far side, Tony tucked himself in behind a car on the approach side, putting their man in a potential crossfire. Over the radio: 'Nicky, from Darren. Contained on the far aspect.'

'Received. Tony, how are you fixed?'

'Nicky from Tony. Contained on the approach.'

Then, as the moment to confront came, Nicky Boy said, 'On my move, come up to cover.'

From Tony, 'Received.'

Then Darren, 'Received.'

'Stand by. Stand by. *Go*.' Nicky stamped on the accelerator, protesting tyres dragged the heavy car forwards.

He swung the wheel right, hitting the headlights at the same time, dazzling the man with the grenades. In unison the carbines rose up and arced forwards to threaten him.

Alien sounds rent the night: the screech of the tyres, the sudden calls of 'Armed police. Stand still.' Karl Bosley was unmoved, blinking in the glare of the headlights, still gripping the grenades. He knew the real play was still his although he risked a terrible price.

Nick threw open the car door, relying on the headlights to blind Bosley long enough to give himself a moment to deploy. Standing upright beside the car in whatever minimal protection the door afforded, he was suddenly The Man, the voice that Karl Bosley would hear, the first line of the enemy.

As Nick levelled the handgun at the threat, fumbling for the radio handset with the other, the headlights lit up the man as a clear target. To his left and from behind him were Tony and Darren. The same thoughts occupied both of them. Bring the lethal concentric circles of the gun sights together. Selector lever to fire. Move your head a little. Put the single pole of the foresight in the centre of his chest. Control the breathing. Steady.

On the radio, a whispered voice through Nick's earpiece. 'From Tony. I've got him.'

Then Darren. 'Likewise. Confirmed.'

At the same moment Karl Bosley moved. He jumped down from the wall and began to approach Tony, step by step, closing the gap, using the width of the road like a stage, taunting them.

'Go on, then,' he said. 'Slot me.' With his life hanging by a thread, this anguished man defied the three of them to kill him. Tony gave the classic challenge: 'Stop. Armed police.' But Karl Bosley came forwards, his hands held wide from his body, in them, clearly visible, the grenades. With the pins removed, only his grip restrained the clips. If they were released, the grenades would detonate.

So many questions without answers. Would he stop? Would he throw the grenades? If they shot him, his grip would be released. Would they still be killed or injured? Decisions to make, to weigh in less than a breath. Living or dying. For him. For them.

As the distance closed between them, Tony had made up his mind. He'd drawn an imaginary line his adversary would not cross. Then another challenge. 'Armed police. Stop. *Now*.' His finger tightened on the trigger. The uniformed figure closed with him, grenades in hand. 'Go on, then, slot me. Go on, slot me.'

Too late now. In Tony's mind it was already happening. Pull steady. Sight picture. Inhale deep, exhale slowly. Keep pulling. Wait for the bang. And then the uniformed figure stopped.

Fate. A microsecond. Perhaps God Almighty stopped him there, but Karl Bosley was to live at least a little longer. Feet apart he dominated the centre of the road. 'Go on, slot me. I got two grenades here. You got an MP5. Go on, slot me.' The conviction in Tony's mind that he would shoot the man if he came even one step further had washed over him. He felt calm, methodical about that decision. And yet the soldier's accurate weapon recognition was disturbing, somehow unsettling.

Darren had moved around the Transit van he was using for cover, the sights of his MP5 now fixed on the centre of the threat, aware of the gravity for him, for Tony, and for so many other people. Yet he did not fire. Much later he would reflect on why. Karl Bosley was taking them to the edge of their restraint, provoking them to shoot him, daring them to. Yet he seemed to know where that edge was, to be prepared to trip along it, to risk tripping over it, but not to leap over it, to take his own life.

What he needed was to unleash his own anger, a supercharge of emotion to carry him through the gates of life into the black oblivion of death. Then they would all know the depth of his agony. But to call up his own personal demon he needed an enemy to hate, to abuse, to torment, to confront. Decades of pain, anger and hurt unimaginable, hidden behind the face of a professional soldier. Now they sought release, even at the ultimate price.

All he had was Nicky, Carrot and Darren, three policemen in uniform. Very soon he would have Keith and me. But the guns changed everything. As we drove towards them, Nick's voice broke in on the car's radio, the fear and the strain almost palpable in its tone. He was normally so jovial, so calm. His situation was dire. So many considerations, things to do, risks to calculate. Yet his mind and body were somehow trapped, riveted to the spot by this awful, and now worsening threat.

'They're phosphorous grenades.' The ex-soldier confronting them identified his weapons as sticking, burning, incandescent death.

Anyone within fifteen metres of detonation would have been killed. A searing light, white smoke would accompany clinging, crackling, flesh-consuming detonation.

Through the sights of his pistol Nick covered the uniformed figure that now seemed so close. Later he would relate that, brightly illuminated in the headlights, Bosley seemed to physically grow as Nick's perceptions were warped by fear and adrenaline.

His right hand shook, the gun sight dancing across the camouflage coloured shape, as with his left he struggled to retrieve the microphone from the car, to satisfy his need to call for help. To speak to someone, to tell them of the nightmare he was living. His fingers gratefully clutched the smooth shape of the microphone as his stomach contorted in unison with a silent prayer. There were two fixed radios in the car, two microphones. Please God, let it be the right one.

If Bosley moved on him he would have to shoot or run. If he ran he must take the car keys. He mustn't leave him an escape vehicle. Over the radio he must tell them exactly where they were, the threat.

Need the duty officer. Military advice, expo. So many things, with the threat of death so close. It's too much, can't think. For him the threat was at the end of a short mental tunnel, where all other sounds, all other movements, were excluded. All he could see, all he could hear, was Karl Bosley. Catching his breath, he spoke into the microphone.

'MP from Trojan 552. On scene with your man with grenades. Require urgent armed assistance. TSG and expo.'

To his horror the reply came back. 'Sorry, Trojan 552. Can you give me the CAD reference number? I have no idea which call you are referring to.'

Nick exploded into the radio. 'I am actually standing here with the mike in one hand and a gun in the other, covering a man who is threatening me with two fucking hand grenades. *You* find the bastard number.'

There was a short pause. 'Received.'

As Keith and I drew ever closer, the boys were covering the contingencies, working out tactics, identifying escape routes. They must keep him on the bridge at all costs, where there were no houses and no people. There was somewhere to throw the grenades where there was hope no harm would be done.

But what if he threw a grenade at them? They had made their plans, quietly whispering through the earpieces of the back-to-back radios. They had decided that the intended victim would seek best cover, while the others would neutralise the threat. Shoot him. Probably kill him. There would be not the slightest hesitation. As the minutes ticked away an uneasy stand-off was achieved, punctuated with occasional threats. He dared the armed officers to shoot, defying them to. They may not hesitate, but they would be the consummate professionals.

In Islington, far across London, Trojan 561, with the young, dark-haired and amenable Nick Bell driving, smiling Stevey 'A' operating, and 'Gorgeous George', king of the hair gel, as 'maps', were broadsiding junctions, lifting off over bridges, while they listened to the drama being played out over the radio. Voices, sounds, every one a small, tormenting demon, taunting them with the thought that they would be too late, that their mates would die, whispering a siren song: Faster, faster, *go faster*.

Keith and I were on the last leg of our journey, our ears assailed by the screeching siren, the blaring radio.

At the scene voices were subdued, communication a soft murmur through the shell of an earpiece. During a lull in the soldier's threats and goading, Darren's mind focused on the power of the grenades. 'Carrot from Darren.'

Tony responded to the tiny voice at his ear. 'Go ahead.'

'Look, mate, you were a soldier. All I ever did was sell stereo systems from a Comet warehouse.' Darren whispered. 'So what do you know about these phosphorous grenades?'

There was a long pause, then in a subdued voice Tony answered. 'I'm not sure, but I'll tell you this: they're definitely fucking dangerous.'

Forced to settle for that somewhat prosaic description, Darren imagined, as we all did, that the effect would be agonising death by burning. Then his mind wandered to the houses nearby, innocent faces, children, his unarmed colleagues. His resolve hardened. There was no way this man would leave the bridge armed. Then he pondered the man's motives. He had not quite delivered himself into death, yet he was close enough for it to happen in a moment. Not ready yet, he concluded. But he really *is* prepared to die, and *is* working towards it.

While Tony worked away to gain some kind of rapport, to maintain a dialogue, Darren settled in, readjusting his sights on the target. Whatever, if Bosley's arm went back, it would not come forwards to throw.

Karl Bosley watched him, becoming angry, excited. 'You got an MP5 there. You could put it right between my eyes.' He pointed at the bridge of his own nose. 'Go on, put it there. With an MP5, it'd be no problem from that range.'

Slowly, painfully, the truth began to emerge. Now they knew his real identity, that he had a family. Darren responded: 'Karl, if I shoot you, well, I've got two kids myself. To your kids I'd be the bloke who killed their father.' For a few moments the man in camouflage fell silent.

Keith and I were coming down Greyhound Lane as Trojan 561 rounded a bend at speed, not far behind us. The rear of their car slewed sideways, clipping a kerb, buckling a wheel. Later, bureaucrats would criticise the driver for limping on for the last few hundred yards.

As we drew close Bosley was pacing back and forth within confines he seemed to clearly understand. 'Nobody remembers! Bloody Sunday. January the thirtieth, 1972, the bastards all remember that. But not Aldershot! No, that doesn't matter.'

Suddenly the danger, momentarily eased by the dialogue, was back on a knife edge. His face contorted in anger and in grief. Then the challenges began again. 'Go on, slot me. I don't care.'

Tony desperately worked to communicate with him, to calm this man caught again in an upward spiral of emotion. 'Karl, please. Don't do this.' The pace of his footfalls became feverish with emotion.

'Why are you so angry? What can we do? How can we help?' Like a lanced infection now, the poisoned emotion poured out. 'My mother. They killed my mother. She was a cook in the sergeants' mess, not a soldier. She didn't hurt anyone and they killed her. Now no bastard even remembers!' The hard military edge in his voice tailed off. The three policemen's hearts sank. Now the last thing in the world they wanted was to have to shoot this man. But he could still force their hand.

The pacing slowed but did not stop as he told them that he had a wife and two children. Something Darren had gambled on.

'What's your name?' He asked as he rounded on Tony, suddenly the soldier again, brash and forceful. 'Tony,' came the reply. 'And that's Darren.' There was a pause and Bosley grinned mockingly. 'Oh, my God, I'm going to be shot by *Tony and Darren*.' Then he turned and sat down, slumped against the parapet wall.

As Keith and I arrived, that was where he was. I remember him still. Looking across the roof of a parked police car, the stocky figure of a man in camouflage, seated on the footway with his back, significantly, against the wall. On his head sat a red beret, from which the occasional glint of a cap badge could be seen by the light of the street lamps. In his hands were the grenades, clips still retained within tiring grip. Between his feet lay the pins.

Below the beret, below the badge he wore with such pride, another glint, seen first by Tony, then by us. From within the soldier the bereaved young boy was emerging – Karl Bosley was crying. Perhaps quietly within ourselves, though few would ever admit it, so were we.

Tony picked up the conversation again as Keith and I prepared to become a negotiating cell, one to speak, one to frame new questions.

'Karl,' Tony said. 'Throw the grenades over the bridge into the stream where they can't hurt anyone.'

The soldier returned to his face 'What if I do that? No. You know I can't do that.' Tony began to plead with him. 'Just lob them into the stream where they can't hurt anyone. Please, Karl. Get rid of them.' But the soldier just smiled, dropping his head forwards, staring between his feet to where the pins lay. Ever more loosely he held the grenades still in his hands.

From a house nearby, the inquisitive face of a man appeared. The night was cold. Seated there on the footway, I reasoned Bosley must be feeling it. I caught the man's attention. Minutes later, a cup of hot tea stood on the roof of the ARV, seductive wisps of steam dispersing in the night air. I called towards the seated figure.

'Karl, you must be freezing your nuts off over there. Call it a day. You've made your point. Knock it off and have the tea.' He raised his eyes towards me, his vision still limited by the car's headlights. 'I've got a better idea,' he said. 'You bring it over here.'

Tony and I exchanged glances. 'Don't look at me,' Tony said, a half-grin on his face. Then he picked up the cup and downed the tea. 'Shame to waste it.'

The cold was beginning to hurt Bosley, though. He shifted uncomfortably on the freezing paving. Then he began to move, the tension rising as Darren and Tony brought their guns sharply to aim.

With practised hands, he wedged the grenades beneath his knees against the paving, still retaining the clips, and began to wring some warmth back into his freezing fingers. Slowly the tension ebbed again. What was apparent was that he knew more than enough about weapons.

Trojan 561 had limped in and its crew deployed on foot. While the driver stayed in support, Stevey 'A' and Gorgeous George ran the better part of a mile, fully kitted, to cross the river one bridge further down and come up on the far side of the scene. Hot and sweating, they were not amused. At the RVP Pete and Ray, my opposite numbers operating south, had arrived hotfoot from yet another job and moved up in support.

Keith, schooled in negotiation, began to build a rapport. 'What's it all about, Karl? Tell me what it's about and we can sort it out.' But Bosley was slow to trust. I framed questions, made suggestions, searching for a way to reach him, to bring this to an end, to save lives.

For long minutes we probed, question after question, making no inroads, no headway. Then we returned to that which in truth we already knew. It was an emotive subject, a risk to generate emotion. But a breakthrough was required.

'Are you married?' Keith tentatively enquired. 'Have you got a wife and kids?'

The cracks in the soldier's hardened façade began to show. 'Yes.'

'Where do they live?'

'Near here. Close.' Came the reply.

This was the lifeline we sought, the door to his soul. Now it was open, Keith intended it should stay that way. 'Don't do anything stupid. It will all be so different in the morning. You've got a wife and kids at home. Just think about it.'

In the following anxious negotiations, the sentence would be repeated over and over again. To remind a man who thought he had nothing left that he really had so much. To step back from the abyss, to choose life. Keith gestured towards the grenades. 'What have you got there?' He was met with sullen silence, then Bosley lifted his head towards the still-aimed carbines. 'Yes that's it. Just line me up there.' He pointed to the middle of his chest, and then, 'And one through the head.'

The tone of Keith's voice changed, softened. 'We don't want to shoot you, Karl.' The man looked up again, a watery smile on his face. Holding his coat open, inviting the rounds that could smash bone, fragment his

organs, he said, 'No, just line me up and there you go.'
Beneath his legs the grenades waited. A relaxation, a
release in the tension of the clips, and they would
detonate. Reaching down with revived hands, he
retrieved the grenades.

He looked up at us. He was hemmed in on three sides.
To my right stood Nicky Boy, still covering over the car
door. To my left beyond Keith and the car we sheltered
behind was Tony. Beyond him again and completing the
half-circle was young Darren, all of us using various cars
for cover. Behind Karl Bosley and the parapet at his back,
was a thirty-foot fall into cold dirty water.

Keith began again. 'Karl, please. What's it all about?
Please tell us. We can't help if you won't tell us.' Again
and again he pleaded with the hunched figure, until the
soldier's face began to fall away and the injured boy
emerged once again. 'My mother. My mother.' There
was almost a sob in the voice.

Keith broke in. 'What about your mother?' The glint
at the corner of the eyes was there again, the voice was
changed, suddenly tired with the weight of an age of
grief, quavering 'The IRA killed her. Fucking IRA.' The
voice tailed off.

Make-or-break time. Get it wrong now and we would
lose him. Tucked in behind the car, Keith and I stared
at each other anxiously, weighing the next move, the
next question.

On the other side of our car, his back in every way
still against the wall, the distraught man drew near his
crossroads. Do it or give it up. Live or die.

'About your mother,' Keith began again. Then he
faltered. The pressure had wiped her name from his
mind, and in a second Karl the soldier and his anger
were back.

'You're not listening. *You're not listening*,' Bosley
exploded. His voice rose hard. The knuckles, gripping

the grenades, flexed white, then pink, in the cold air, as he tensed and released in sudden fury.

'No. No, Karl. We *are* listening. Please, Karl. I'm just a little cold and tired. Please, Karl. Calm down.' Keith was desperate to retrench.

'Aldershot, 1972. Aldershot, 1972.' The soldier and the boy in him spoke at once. Carrot whispered in the night air, his breath a mist, 'Yes, that's right. Aldershot. They killed a load of civvies. I've read about it.'

Suddenly the figure against the wall looked smaller. 'They won't help me.'

'Who won't help you?'

'No one will do anything about it. No one will do anything.' The pain, the hurt, was palpable.

Desperate to find a way through, Keith spoke again, a question that was almost a plea. 'How can we get out of this? How can we sort this one out?' But there was no reply, just a terrible sad look, hopeless, lost.

'Phone my brother.' Suddenly the hope of a breakthrough. 'Phone my brother.'

'Give me the number, Karl,' I called. Feverishly, as he spoke, I wrote it down.

Keith placated him. 'The sergeant is going to phone your brother now. OK?'

'Let me speak to my brother and I'll call it a day.' The first real hope of resolution.

The voice on the phone was sound, solid, surprised but unfazed by what I told him. 'Bloody fool. Tell him I said to give up.' He gave his name.

I called across the roof of the car. 'Karl, your brother told me you should give it up now. It won't help.' And I quoted his brother's first name. 'But I can't come over there with the phone. You know that. You're a soldier.'

His features softened. Then with a stroke of genius, Keith said the right thing at the right time. 'Karl, we're all the same. We're the police. You're the army. Why are we fighting each other? It's the IRA that are out of order here. Why are *we* doing this?'

Resignation began to cross Bosley's face. Keith began again: 'We can tell this story, but let's not do it with you or anyone else getting hurt.'

I picked up the thread: 'Karl, don't make this any worse. If anyone else gets killed, then they've achieved even more. Don't give them what they want. They've had enough already.' He held my gaze for a moment. 'It's enough now, Karl. End it now.'

There was a pause, then he lifted the grenades in front of him. With a dexterity that could only be practised, he held both of them in one hand. Keith winced. 'Be careful what you're doing there. Take your time.'

The soldier looked up nonchalantly, his expression tinged with a hint of pride. 'Oh, don't worry, I know what I'm doing.' And he slipped the pin back into the first grenade.

There was a long empty pause while he glanced around, seeking every eye, asking attendance as the final act of surrender was performed. For what seemed like an age he sat staring at the remaining grenade, the last vestige of his power, the means of his protest. Then, in a moment, he deftly replaced the pin, and laid the grenades down. It was over.

While Pete covered from where the exhausted, cold Nicky Boy had been for so long, Ray, my little Welsh buddy, took his surrender at nominal gunpoint.

He called to the soldier, 'Walk forward, keep your hands away from your body.' Slowly, with measured steps, Karl Bosley complied. Behind him, the grenades lay green and menacing, near the parapet wall.

Ray began again. 'Stop,' and the militaristic figure halted. 'Now kneel down.'

Bosley raised his eyes, a hardness glinting there as he spoke. 'I will *not* kneel,' he declared, seeking to retain a last vestige of pride.

Ray smiled gently. 'OK, mate.' His soft Welsh tones were suddenly filled with sympathy. Ray had once been a soldier.

Carrot slipped the handcuffs over Bosley's hands, now linked behind his back as he leaned forwards against the side of our car. Somehow though, he was humbled. Beaten. Not just by the events of that night, but by much, much more.

Always at the end of an incident there is a feeling of relief and this one was, in that respect, no different. At no other time, though, have I felt such empathy for the offender, such a feeling of sadness. As I watched him being placed in the van, I reflected that he had been a victim before, in fact for all his adult life.

Now that same crime against humanity was making him a victim again. In law he had offended. But life is not so simple.

There is a terrible irony that, in references to the event, the word 'terrorism' has been attached to the name of a man who, far from being a perpetrator of such, was its victim. I believe that the principal reason my officers were restrained from shooting him was that in all of his behaviour Karl Bosley only ever really meant to hurt himself. And they sensed that. When young Darren questioned himself, that was the conclusion he arrived at. Perhaps that tacit respect I have for men of uniform is in them also.

One thing in this narrative pleases me greatly. Keith made Karl a promise: 'We can tell this story, but let's not do it with you or anyone else getting hurt.'

Now I am satisfied. I have kept that promise.

# **10** Bullseye

THE CROWD WAS BAYING FOR BLOOD as the two combatants were readied for the next exchange. Their seconds, or handlers, cleaned them up, perhaps offering them a little water. A sour-faced little man was taking money for side bets on the victor from among the many reddened, excited spectators who thronged the wooden stands around the pit.

They had been fighting for hours. Those were the rules. They would fight until one either failed to come out, or died. Both were covered in blood from their opponent's or their own untreated wounds. As the handlers urged them on with threats and curses, they screamed and bayed at each other, the sounds taking the crowd to new depths of hysterical, perverse bloodlust.

The stakes went up with each new exchange as individual gamblers slapped spittle-soaked palms on a new wager. Then at a signal they released them to tear into each other once again, streams of blood-flecked saliva leaving staccato lines across the sawdust floor and up the pit walls.

These were not the fists of bare-knuckle fighters, but the savage fangs of dogs bred for combat. The terrible, screaming, throaty growls descended into pain as one dog began to lose. To die. The crowd reached fever pitch. Money to be won. Money to be lost.

The dogs, though, would always lose. The victor on one day, scarred and wounded, would lose on another.

If he lived to grow old he would be deemed useless, to meet perhaps an even more distressing fate. This was dog fighting maybe a century and a half ago in England. In the last decade certain revolting men have sought to engineer its resurgence. The pursuit of that end led to the importing of a dog born of ongoing breeding development, from places where such 'sports' continue: an athletic, ruthless animal, wishing only to please the master and knowing only one way to do it: to fight and win. The American pit bull terrier.

With over fifty pounds of muscle in such a compact package, the *English* bull terrier is bound to be seen as formidable. If you add a set of teeth that appear scaled down from a shark, a tenacious nature and a warrior history that goes back centuries, it would be optimistic to expect anything more than an aggressive, dangerous killer. But it's not so.

Actually, Casey is a pushover. That's because nobody has ever taught him aggression. He sleeps on a duvet, eats like a horse and is my great companion. I trust him implicitly. He is loving, gentle and extremely stubborn. Children love him and have been seen climbing all over him, a situation he revels in. My favourite recollection is the look of joy on the face of a boy with cerebral palsy, his arms round Casey's neck.

How is it, then, that such a terrible reputation has attached itself to certain 'dangerous dogs'? Any dog, as we know, can be dangerous to a greater or lesser extent; and it's true to say that a dog of the English bull terrier's capability is, if aggressive, a huge threat.

Sadly, human intervention is the key. This was the factor that created the breed in the first place, when there was money to be made in the bear-baiting and dog-fighting pits. We watch, aghast now, at the continuation of such cruelty depicted through documentaries on our TV screens, distancing ourselves with the thoughts that this is some far-flung country or at worst the pursuit of a minority group in our own.

We have a saying often used to describe goods or services that are lacking, that they 'don't come up to scratch'. Across the centre of the bloodstained pits in which such dogs fought, a line was drawn. It was called the scratch line. If one of the opposing dogs failed to join combat, to rush out and tear at his opponent, he was deemed a coward, a failure and worthless. He had not come up to scratch.

I find it a sobering thought that this revolting 'sport', where animals were deliberately scarred and mutilated, their ears carved to points and false battle injuries inflicted to make a dog appear more formidable, is woven into our language.

In the intervening years bull terriers have been on the whole bred and refined into the characterful animals beloved by so many people.

Sadly, running parallel, the fighting dog remained and has surfaced to stain the character of many totally benign and loving animals. That in itself is a tragedy.

I once attended a house in Stoke Newington, north London, where such pit bull terrier had attacked a neighbour's dog with such ferocity that the possibility I would be asked to shoot the dog was real. At the scene the carnage and chaos wreaked was incredible. The dog had leaped a wall, perhaps six feet in height, to attack the large mongrel occupying the adjoining garden, and then followed the fleeing mongrel indoors. In company with dog handlers, I approached the house, the occupiers of which had all fled. Through the letterbox I could see the animal covered in blood and saliva. On his face there was not a trace of aggression, and his tail wagged enthusiastically. When the door was eventually opened he greeted us like long-lost friends. Such is the Jekyll-and-Hyde nature of these animals.

But inside the house I found the dying mongrel similarly covered in blood and saliva. It lay on the kitchen floor unable to move, paralysed by injury, exhaustion and shock. The room was wrecked. The pit bull was unmoved by it all. He was ready to play or be friends. He was what he was bred to be, the consummate, dispassionate killer. Shortly afterwards, at the hands of a vet, he was summarily put to death.

In 1991 a series of incidents followed by wide media coverage focused public attention forcefully on the issue. Parliamentary debate followed with unusual haste. The legislation became law that same year as, the Dangerous Dogs Act, 1991. The main provisions of the Act were that no person could breed from, sell, exchange, advertise or even give such an animal away; it must be muzzled whenever in a public place and kept on a lead; abandoning or allowing a dog of the type to stray constituted an offence.

A six-month term of imprisonment and/or a fine could be imposed. A form of bounty, a payment in lieu of destruction, was payable as an inducement to owners of such animals provided they were destroyed before the due date.

Those who chose to keep their pit bulls were required

- to have them neutered
- to have them tattooed with an identifying mark
- to have a microchip inserted
- to have proper third-party insurance against the dog's actions.

As you read what follows, remember those provisions. They had all been met, except this one: no one under sixteen was to supervise the animal.

\* \* \*

There was already fear of this south London address. There had been reason for the police to call before, and though Bullseye, the pit bull terrier, was properly tattooed, insured and licensed it remained a threat. In the autumn of the previous year, a warrant to arrest a man for motoring offences (for which he had refused to attend court) was to be executed. It was considered a dangerous undertaking – Bullseye would be there. The local officers were so afraid that they enlisted the aid of dog handlers specially trained in dealing with dangerous dogs. So serious was the threat that in support of them, on standby not far away, was an Armed Response Vehicle.

The dog handlers, with the benefit of past experience, were equipped with 'dog catchers', long, hollow, steel poles through which a flex could be pulled creating a loop to catch the dog around the head. Also, there was a $CO_2$ fire extinguisher to discharge in its face if it got too close. As they approached the house the front door had been left invitingly open.

At the sight of a uniform, the muscular dog launched an attack. The officers just managed to pull the door closed in time, and the dog savaged the other side.

After a while it became apparent the dog had gone back upstairs, so they gingerly opened the door again, to call on the man inside to surrender himself. There were voices, then the dog reappeared, snarling, growling. It attacked the poles presented as the only barrier between the officers and appalling injury. Frantically they struggled with the dog, appealing to the owners to call it off. The only response was, 'Go on, get him, Bullseye.'

Retreating again into the street, the local police officers, along with the dog handlers, closed the door. A man appeared at an upstairs window with a large knife and a baton-type weapon, threatening the officers. Only the intervention of armed officers brought about a peaceful resolution on that occasion. But Bullseye had learned who the 'enemy' was.

It was a mild Sunday afternoon, one of those days that provide a taste of summer to come, but still have the crispness of late winter nipping at their heels. Keith the inspector had taken the day off. Similarly Ray was missing, playing golf somewhere – his way of relaxing. If they were together Ray would inevitably lose the game. That left Pete and me with the whole of London as our responsibility. I was operating mostly north with Pete overseeing south. I took the opportunity to do a little extra shooting. It was after all a Sunday late turn. How could I be so naïve?

Down on the range with the targets in place and the weapons ready I stood on the firing line, feeding round after nine-millimetre round into the magazine of the carbine. The instructor gave the first range orders: 'Muffs and glasses, and with a magazine of twenty-five rounds . . . load.' Behind the thick glass of his office, barely audible, a phone rang. He tapped me on the shoulder, saying, 'Stand by, Sarge.' I had fired not one shot as he then beckoned me to the telephone.

'Base here, Sarge.' It was Bobby 'Brackets'. 'Sorry to interrupt, but, as you're duty officer, it's a need-to-know situation. Just had Pete on the phone. He's shot a dog.'

I thought at first it was a wind-up, that the relief's sense of humour was trying to test me on this quiet morning. I was wrong. I looked at the instructor with consternation. Stepping back on to the range, I opened the breech of the carbine and, ensuring it was clear of any live rounds, handed it, together with the charged magazine, to the instructor. 'Mind clearing up, old mate?' I said. 'I'm needed down south.'

\* \* \*

The bus driver had completed his shift. He was enjoying his walk home as Sunday lunch beckoned. Work was over and it was Mother's Day. He would do all the right things for his own mum, and for the mother of his children. Just a decent working man from a West Indian background, making his way through the side roads on this beautiful, clear, early-spring day. But someone was going to spoil that, first for him and then for many others.

There was a sharp crack from somewhere over to his right as he passed the DSS building. Next to him, at head height, in a thick reinforced-glass window, an impact. A ragged hole appeared with spidery fractures around it. A puff of powdered glass blew in the light breeze. The startled man had been shot at. In a house across the road, at the top bedroom, a window was hurriedly closed. There was no other movement.

Pete begrudged doing this late turn, but that was quite understandable. Anyone would rather be at home on a warm sunny day. However, at Lambeth the numbers available to crew the cars were barely adequate. There were only two PCs for Trojan 561: Mike the 'headmaster' and Gorgeous George. Pete would be third man, while acting as supervisor. That bit was fine by him, a chance to mix with the boys, some company for the day. Maybe this late turn would pass more enjoyably than he'd thought. But life can be perverse.

The day became busier and busier as they ran from call to call, none of which proved to have much substance. Finally, a call drew them to the Peckham area, where (at its fruitless conclusion) they were still on the local radio link when the call from the distressed West Indian man came in. In support of local units 561 went to the scene. Mike was driving with Pete as operator. Gorgeous was 'maps' in the back. Outside the DSS building the black man told his story. He indicated an end-of-terrace house as the source. On the steps below the damaged window they recovered the spent pellet. It was later discovered that the shot was from a high-powered air rifle.

I personally have two particular experiences of such weapons. Between my eyes I carry the scar from a .22 Webley. The bone below the surgical incision made in its removal is a permanent lump. A young boy, the son of my neighbour, was accidentally hit in the shoulder, also by a .22 pellet, fired from a distance of thirty or forty feet. Penetration was to the bone, requiring full surgical intervention to remove it. Such an injury to the head or possibly elsewhere could easily kill. They are not to be underestimated.

Thoughts were of the danger from the air weapon, of the ballistic protection the ARV carried, or the remote possibility of some other gun in the house. The local inspector, in a telephone conversation with Pete, decided, perhaps unwisely, that *his* officers would approach the house. The ARV crew would remain nearby. They did not wish to overreact to an air-rifle incident. They unfortunately had no idea of Bullseye's record. Programmed in his mind. Love the children, please the master, kill the enemy.

Local knowledge was sadly lacking as the two young uniformed officers approached the address. Pete, being the only supervisor present, had briefed them that, although they would have to make the enquiry, he and his crew would be close by. He, like them, knew nothing of Bullseye.

The houses all faced inwards on four sides of a large paved square area that was now loosely populated by residents enjoying this warm day. One of those was the mother of the children with whom Bullseye now played. As the officers appeared she scurried across to them. 'My kids have let their mate in the house. He's let an airgun off.' As she spoke, her children inside the house became aware of the police presence outside. Her young daughter moved towards the door, which stood ajar, suddenly fearful of blame. Bullseye had noticed too.

The woman walked ahead with the two unarmed officers. Pete, Mike and George trailed behind, their instincts strangely alerted by a scuffling at the door. Then the door opened just a fraction more, and the broad, brindle head of the dog emerged beside the little girl's legs. Her hands clawed at the collar, but he was gone. For him it was simple: he could see the uniform. He knew what he was required to do. No one would stop him. No one.

The woman ran forwards, clawing, as the child had done, at the dog's collar. But he passed her as if she were not there. Perhaps at other times she could strike or chastise him, take a bone from his jaws. But right now generations of ancestral combat focused his intent.

The nearest police officer was big rugby-playing Steve, now stationed at Peckham. He had in the past confronted violent men, and been subjected to gunfire in a terrible armed robbery in Putney. Now, though, terror etched itself on his face, as within a split second the dog launched itself through the air and clamped its immensely powerful jaws around his forearm. Then, having secured its hold, it began the next part of the killing process, to rip the flesh from the bone.

Suspended by fear at arm's length it began to tug and tear as the man spun around, propelled at first by the impact and then by his own momentum. The dog was hanging from his arm by its teeth. His cries rose, first with terror, then agony, as ruptured tissue and torn nerves sent messages to a shocked brain.

In that moment Pete could see that, unless the dog were supported, the combination of weight and teeth would literally tear the flesh from the arm. Nearby, the woman screamed. The children cried. Terrible sounds matched only by the savage snarls of the dog, the agonised cries of the man.

Pete ran forwards, grabbing the body of the dog to support it, hindered by the injured officer, still turning, screaming, 'Get this fucking dog off me!' They rotated anticlockwise, Pete holding the dog's body with his left arm, trying vainly to prise the jaws apart with his right hand. But Bullseye wasn't having any of it. He knew what he was supposed to do. Generation after generation of fighting dog stood behind him. No fear. No pain. Not until death. He tugged and tore.

Only too aware that it was beyond his power alone, Pete called to George. 'Asp it. Asp it.' From the pouch at his back, George pulled an extending steel baton, flicked it out and struck the dog several times with all his strength. Nothing. They say you can cut a fighting dog in full combat and he still won't let go. The last blow was to the head, and a good proportion was absorbed by Pete's right hand. George will never be allowed to forget that.

The second local officer waded in now, with a long acrylic baton, striking the animal several times around the body. It registered no effect. Then he kicked it, but the dog continued to tear at the man's arm. His screams rose to match his spiralling agony. From beyond the other side of the house, Mike ran towards those sounds.

The gravity of the injury was uppermost in their minds. He would be maimed, perhaps for life. The dog *must* be stopped. They would have to shoot it. Pete was the sergeant. His decision. His responsibility. The situation was nightmarish. There are considerations few would be aware of. For example, the round would certainly pass right through the animal at this range. Innocent people were all around.

The target was both moving with its own efforts, and rotating with the terrified man, who by the most exact definition was less than an arm's length away. Time for thought was denied Pete, however, as he could not allow the injury to worsen, and an already angry crowd grew more excited. He drew his Glock.

All around them people were spilling from the houses, women, children, a truly awful dilemma. But he must act. There was no time and the stakes were too high. A man was set to lose his arm. With the gun pressed against the dog's left shoulder, angled down towards the ground, he fired.

The sound was muffled as the full force spent itself into the animal's body. The second local officer recoiled with pain as something tore into his shin. Unbelievably at first, the dog would not let go. That terrible heritage showed itself as Bullseye continued to thrash, still ripping at the flesh. Pete began to despair. These dogs were bred to fight until death. Bullseye wasn't dead. So he would fight.

To Pete's sudden and incredible relief, the dog let go. Grasping the dog's collar with his left hand, he held it hard against the ground. The injured police officer was rapidly going into shock, his arm torn and bloodied, staccato teeth marks and torn tracts of flesh from wrist to elbow. To Pete's complete horror the dog moved, he had it pinned it to the floor with hand and knees, but still it began to scramble to get up.

Bullseye turned his head to find a new target, to bite, to tear. To the dog it was a simple choice. He could fight. He *would* fight. Pete would be next. For Pete now there was no other way. With a crowd gathering, in front of the children with whom the dog had been playing, he would have to end this terrible incident, remove this mortal threat.

He placed the gun against the back of Bullseye's head and fired. The combat was finally over. Beneath the dead dog a grotesque pool of thick blood began to spread. Although he was not aware at first, Pete's face, shirt and clothing were spattered with blood. As he stood up a sea of hostile, horrified faces greeted him. Shocked and bloodied as he was, he had to 'put his sergeant's head on' – he was still the only supervising officer there.

The mood of the crowd was turning to aggression as calls for more police assistance went up over the radio. The injured officer, close to fainting, was led away. The woman owner fought hysterically with an unarmed officer to get to where Pete and the dog were. At the door of her house, four or five children between the ages of four and thirteen had gathered. They became the focus of attention as their combined, anguished cries filled the square. Pete's heart sank as the full impact of what he had been compelled to do etched itself on their desolate faces, echoed in their cries.

That memory will remain with him. So much pain. Truly, though, I suspect the person who should carry the blame, whose conscience ought to be most moved, was not there. What Bullseye had learned best, someone had taught him.

Through his own distress Pete still remained the professional. Doing his best to spare the children, he directed them away from the windows and covered the dog up. Further police units were arriving, just in time to head off what was fast becoming a potential riot. Accusing fingers began to point at him, and his hand was now swelling from the misplaced blow. Pete retreated to the respite of his car. Now the pain and the shock were taking their toll.

A short while afterwards the thunderous beating of helicopter rotors announced the arrival of the Helicopter Emergency Medical Service (HEMS). It hovered over the square, but was prevented from landing by the angry throng still present and flew off. Moments later an area car screamed off on 'blues and twos' with three local officers on board, just before local supervisors arrived.

Pete was taken to the local station, where I saw him in the canteen, nursing his sore hand but having regained his usual composure. The car that sped away had contained the injured officers, Steve with his terribly injured arm, and one who was convinced he had been shot in the leg. On my way to the scene I had been told that a local officer had been hit, which would have meant big problems for me as duty officer, and Pete as the shooter.

The information that a police officer had been shot began to circulate on rumour control, to Pete's huge concern. As laughter resounded from the front of the queue, he heard the truth of the matter. A small fragment of paving thrown up by the first bullet had struck the shin of that other officer. It had caused a barely visible mark. Standing there spattered with the dog's blood and body fluids, awaiting a change of clothes, Pete was relieved, but definitely not amused.

After the incident the Met received a letter of complaint on behalf of the woman dog owner from Harriet Harman, MP for Camberwell and Peckham. It alleged abuse of authority and criminal damage. Quite properly the alleged criminal and disciplinary matters were investigated, and found to have no substance.

Several other letters were received complaining of brutality by the police. Grossly misrepresented accounts appeared in certain publications. The fact that photographs taken at the time show the scene as several yards from the house did not prevent an account of home invasion and canine execution being printed for public consumption.

The injured officer required emergency micro-surgery. A year later he had still not regained the use of two fingers and had inhibited use of the hand and arm. He is severely scarred and his career and future are in jeopardy. Apart from the various canine-defence organisations' correspondence, two unsigned notes were received. One read,

> May the memory of Bullseye and all he meant to his family haunt you forever. You deserve the same fate as they say . . . an eye for an eye a tooth for a tooth.

And the second note said,

> **Bullseye a martyr**
> The lord says any one who harms one hair on the head of one of my innocent creatures better that he had never been born for he shall be flung into the pit where all loathsome things reside.
> ETERNAL DAMNATION.

It is the children who deserve all our sympathy for the memories they will carry. It's in Pete's mind also – he must bear that sadness in his memory for ever. If there is any damnation it should be upon any and all men who ever bade a dog to fight for sport or wager. And it should be upon whoever taught Bullseye to hate.

Because I know it doesn't have to be so.

# **11** The Putney Incident

ARMED ROBBERIES ARE THE COMMON CURRENCY of ARV work. Several times every day the cars will run to them, make the required effort to be there should the worst happen. It's not very likely and the crews know that. Nevertheless they try flat out to be there until the inevitable cancellation is given.

The pattern of armed robbery is repeated over and over so that blueprint for the next aspiring robber is clear, until they can operate smoothly.

Always a number of 'jobs' on the drawing board. Plots will have been walked dozens of times, watched, visited, photographed even; some money will have been changed, some questions asked, goods looked at – everything sussed out. By the time the alarm is sounded on the day they will be halfway home.

When there is enough info, the jobs will be tabled, scrutinised. Someone with influence will give it 'the nod'. Cars to be supplied for getaway. Drivers, the fence, the 'armourer' for the guns. He's the faceless evil bastard who sells or hires terror and death for cash. It's a mini-industry. Anything can be obtained from an ancient pistol bordering on the antique to a machine gun – and much else in between.

This time, though, there was a man with something different: a self-loading shotgun. Not the Remington, with its pump action so beloved for the sound of the next round being fed into the breech. No, something much worse. A little Italian gem that fed a new cartridge with every shot, using the force from the last discharge, bang, bang, bang, until it was empty. Just keep pulling that trigger. Sophisticated, lethal and not easy to obtain. A polished and decorated weapon, it was a sin to saw it down.

On this hot August day a long heavy coat was ridiculous, but he needed it to conceal that gun hanging from a sling on his shoulder, to conceal the 'bum bag' filled with ammunition around his waist. While his partner in this little expedition had a revolver and a ridiculous deerstalker hat, the man in the long coat had enough fire power for a serious exchange. Strapped to his ankle, hidden, was a dagger.

One question I shall always ponder is: which was he really seeking, monetary gain, the thrill of the crime, *or the thrill of a gunfight*?

Tuesday, 2 August 1994, would be a day that 'C' relief, I, the department and so many people would never forget, a day when more bravery awards and more commendations would be won than at any time in recent police history.

It would be a day when fate would conspire in a way never to be repeated and men's lives, their characters, their fears would be changed for ever.

Central to all of this was the man in the long coat. He enjoyed some notoriety in the criminal world, and revelled in his nickname. In prison and among a certain fraternity he was known as The Soldier.

## Part 1 – Another Kind of Soldier, Another Kind of Bridge

Past experience should have warned me not to become complacent, but I thought the events of a few days prior should have fulfilled 'C' relief's quota of violence for at least a while. Only days earlier John O'Grady had died at the guns of Lucky Bob and Dunj. Whenever such things happened, a world of paperwork would inevitably fall fluttering about my ears.

Barry Oldroyd-Jones – 'OJ' – was due to have a drink that night with Bob to talk through the O'Grady incident again. It sometimes helps, but there were other things happening for Barry.

His mother, not a particularly well woman, and his father were up from Wales. It was going to be a big day. They were booked to see *The Phantom of the Opera* that evening.

Before that Barry, with Barney as his operator, were to meet them, show them the car, the guns, the equipment. This was all new to them, and to an extent also to Barry, then a relative newcomer to the department and to the relief.

The two men were really almost opposites. Barry was fanatically fit with an intense social life and a permanently full calendar. Everything had to be done 'yesterday'; even his speech, as I often quipped, was in fast forward. Slim and dark haired, he highlighted Barney's bulk.

Barney the unshakable, the hotelier in waiting, qualified chef, territorial soldier, barrack-room lawyer. Rarely have I encountered a more awkward, dogmatic individual, which is the root of his greatest virtue. He is immovable, and he hates to run, particularly away. In fact the one thing you always knew about Barney was that he never would.

Though the ARVs had been in existence since 1991 the battle for status and equipment still went on. This was a spare day. What that meant was that in addition to the early, late and night shifts, extra patrols starting at 8 a.m. and 4 p.m. were fielded, equipped with whatever gear and cars there were remaining. If that sounds 'Heath Robinson', it's because then it still was.

Barney emerged from the small enclosure at one end of the parade room where the radios resided, wearing his complaining head. 'No fucking back-to-backs, Sarge. We shouldn't go out without them, you know.'

I knew this was coming. 'What would you suggest, Barney? Perhaps you'd like to go upstairs and complain.'

There was a short pause before he began again. 'No, you're my line manager: you should go and argue our case.'

This was like a script we had read a hundred times. 'So, I present the same arguments, get the same answers, no money, still waiting, and then you go out anyway.'

'Yes, but it's not right,' he went on.

'I know,' I acknowledged, because he was right. But finance was the master.

Barry coughed as he walked past, his eyes downcast on his way to the armoury. In his hands were a small portable 'main set' and a mobile phone. The absence of enough short-distance back-to-back radios was a sin that might deny my men communications at a crucial moment. Today it was to prove almost a mortal one.

As I sat down at the desk to fill out the duties, distantly I could hear the racking sound of weapons being checked and cleared, and the unmistakable drone of Barney's further grumbling. Downstairs in the armoury Mark Bradberry, another sergeant and my partner for the day, was on the receiving end. Shorter and darker than I, and about ten years my junior, he is something of an academic, and from a public-school background. Notable for his calm manner, he had a deep-brown voice that would not be out of place commentating sheepdog trials.

Through the door walked Jake with a grin on his face. In his broad Scot's accent he began, 'Barney's on form.'

'What now?' I enquired.

'We're low on ammunition,' he went on. 'We can only go out with single magazines for the MP5s.'

Poor old Mark, but Barney was correct: it was all very wrong.

It was a quiet day on the Putney and Wandsworth section. The warm sunshine had lulled them all, the uniformed officers patrolling the area, into a sense of peaceful wellbeing.

Mark Williams was driving the Rover area car, call sign Whisky Two, with a female officer as his radio operator. Several calls had come and gone without the slightest hint of real trouble. He nosed the brightly marked Rover along Putney Embankment West past the imposing presence of the Star and Garter, the huge pub that sandwiched the road against the edge of the river. Out in the mainstream, small boats bobbed at anchor beyond the jetty reaching out to them.

As they drove on he slowed the car. Practising rowing crews carried out their craft shoulder high from storage on the shore side, across his path and down to the river, or made them ready at the base of the launching slopes below the towering plane trees. In midstream, river buses were ploughing back and forth to and from Hampton Court, their wake rocking the sporting boats at the water's edge.

I knew that place so well. I had courted my wife there, and our first marital home had been nearby in Montserrat Road. The atmosphere was of a gently rural enclave of suburban London. It was to be utterly shattered.

*  *  *

Julian Bailey, a fair-haired athletic Welshman, and an
accomplished rugby player, had been posted to the
response car operating in the Wandsworth area. His
partner was Dave Walther, a much darker, heavily
muscled man. Just perhaps a mile away downriver, the
atmosphere was quite different from Putney. More
commercial, more *London*.

Their day had been equally uneventful as they had
striven to stay cool in the afternoon heat. A few calls,
more false alarms just like the one they were dealing
with now. Just off Armoury Way an embarrassed key
holder was apologising for yet another alarm call,
typically 'set off in error'.

After leaving me, Barry and Barney had 'check-
zeroed' Barry's Glock handgun on the range at City
Road, in company with 'Blue Team' our corresponding
SFO team officers.

Numerous rounds had been loosed down the range,
adjustments made until the sights were deemed accurate, till they were 'zeroed'. Today it would truly matter.
Then Barney and Barry had driven off to meet Barry's
parents, and to pursue Barney's favourite downtime
hobby.

The towering profile of Marble Arch was disappearing
in the mirror, dwarfing the shapes of Barry's parents 'up
from Wales' for the day, standing now waving at the
diminishing shape of the ARV. Barry drove off with a
flourish that lifted dozens of dried leaves from the
roadside of Park Lane. On past the hotels and restaur-
ants, on beneath the towering trees, until they disappeared from view, each from the other. In the two
men was a sense of pride, the father and the son. In the
mother the same instinct to protect that any mother
might feel. The body armour, radios and shields had all
alarmed her, but the guns – she had not liked the guns.

Black, shiny and sinister. She was afraid for her son. Today there would be a nightmare to match the fear.

Barney was in his element, scanning the pavements, woman spotting. 'Mature, long legs and blonde,' he had pronounced. 'That's how I like them.'

Barry responded, 'So Karen's safe from you, then.' Barry's wife was slim, attractive and dark-haired.

'Barry, your wife's very attractive. It's just that I love a sophisticated older woman – like that.' And Barney pointed out a blonde on the footway. A tall, elegant woman swept into the Dorchester from a black Rolls-Royce.

'How many?' Barry enquired, smiling.

'Oh, eight out of ten,' Barney beamed.

Somewhere in central London was a Legion patrol. The crew were made up of several members of the Territorial Support Group, the TSG, descended from the old Special Patrol Group, which had served in earlier years. Travelling with them aboard the huge personnel carrier, and seconded from the Diplomatic Protection Group, were two heavily armed officers. Big Steve would be the acting sergeant for the TSG, that day on antiterrorist duties. In later years he would be Bullseye's victim.

At the end of their day he would, ironically, release the armed officers in central London, and return to the TSG base at Barnes. Their route would take them through Putney.

Somewhere, not far away, two men were making final preparations for a holiday. There were new clothes packed into the suitcases in the boot of the bright-red Escort along with passports, tickets to a destination in Spain. Early in the day it had been left near the foot of the exit from a pedestrian bridge that crossed beside a railway from south to north across the Thames, from Putney.

Then they had begun their final preparations. The old blue Peugeot van lay hidden nearby. The guns and ammunition were checked, the weapons loaded. Robert Knapp fondled the handgun before putting it out of sight in his pocket.

It was a large weapon for a revolver, a .455, rivalling the weapon used in the Highgate Barclays Bank hold-up related in the chapter called 'Blood Money'. He had a mixture of ammunition, some of it strangely adapted shotgun cartridges. Nearby was the odd deerstalker hat. The other, younger, man – The Soldier – had that Italian shotgun.

The relationship between them was the odd product of a shared cell. They had grown to be almost like father and son. The Soldier held Knapp in a kind of reverence. Older by perhaps a decade, Knapp was a 'career criminal' with a history that involved several instances of armed robbery, the telling of which seems to have influenced The Soldier greatly.

Now approaching the autumn of his criminal exploits, Knapp had even worked in offender rehabilitation, but he had been persuaded by the younger man to do one last job, just one.

The Soldier had stepped on to the slope of decline early in life with truanting, minor crime and then armed robbery. For a while, though, there had been stability while Territorial Army pursuits held his attention, moulded and changed his thinking. From that had grown The Soldier image that became his trademark, perhaps his obsession.

On his flesh was a tattoo, a blood-soaked dagger. Above it the word 'Infantry', below it, 'Happiness is a confirmed kill'. In a diary found later was a quotation lifted from a paramilitary book, penned by a CIA

operative: 'The easiest way to achieve complete stra-
tegic surprise is to commit an act that makes no sense,
or is even self-destructive.'

Released from prison, as this new period of freedom
had begun, he had spoken with his father. The promise
given was that he would never go to jail again. But the
meaning of that, as understood by the father, was not
the same as the one intended.

The Soldier tested the sling, then placed all the
rounds in the bum bag around his waist and threw on
the huge swirling coat that would hide it all. In the bag
were cartridges of three different kinds. The first was
birdshot, hundreds of tiny lead projectiles, each of
which would penetrate a man's flesh like a blunt
knitting needle.

Then there was the 'SG' (small game) cartridges
designed to kill anything up to deer. I once heard the
effect of such ammunition described as like being shot
several times with a .38.

The third, and the most sickening, was an adaptation
of the first. Molten wax had been poured into the
collection of hundreds of small pellets within the body
of the cartridge to make them into one solid lump. Only
one purpose for these. If they hit a man, they would just
about tear him in half. And still there was the dagger.

The plan was complete. The 'fence' was ready to
receive the proceeds, the escape route was mapped. As
they drove towards the jeweller's that was to be their
victim, fate was dealing ever stranger cards.

Dinger was in the back seat, maps man aboard Trojan
551. His quiet manner belied a professional experience
spanning years. At Dinger's suggestion Andy, their tall,
dark-haired driver, with Stuart, a solidly built, mild
man, at his side as operator, had piloted the car to
Armoury Way, Wandsworth. It was a route sometimes

used by armed drug dealers, and a minute's run from Putney High Street.

In Lacy Road, just around the corner from Barrett's, the jeweller's shop, two erring youths were being admonished by the crew of a police van. They had been caught drawing graffiti on a nearby shop. The crew, Mark O'Brien and Dave Boyce, were more than enough but, bored with aimless driving, Whisky Two had sidled up nearby with Mark Williams at the wheel. An Astra driven by PC Kevin Sinclair also drew level.

Off Lacy Road runs Cardinal Place. There are few places in London I know better – my wife grew up there. To me, fate was about to be cruel.

As Mark Bradberry and I drove back from north-west London, where I had business, our route took us through Hammersmith, perhaps a mile and a half from Putney Bridge.The old marked Escort I drove was equipped with only one radio. We could hear only one frequency, a shortcoming that would prove pivotal.

In Piccadilly Barry OJ was putting his hand-held multichannel radio to good use. Using the local radio link he tracked down a slim, dark, attractive young woman in uniform as she walked the footway back towards where Eros presided.

''Allo, darlin',' he called as his wife turned smiling to greet him. The evening's agenda was confirmed.

Minutes later he and Barney had negotiated Trafalgar Square into the Strand, the traffic, the people looming busily ahead of them.

The two boys hung their heads sheepishly as the full might of the local law tore them off a strip. Mark Williams swung Whisky Two right out of Lacy Road into the High Street and on towards Putney Hill, while the van crew dispensed time-honoured wisdom to the two youths. Kevin started the Astra.

To the left off the High Street as Whisky Two passed was Montserrat Road, where a light-blue Peugeot van drew to a halt at the kerb. In the driver's seat was The Soldier. In the passenger seat, Robert Knapp. The scene was set for utter mayhem.

The two armed men moved away from the van they had left facing the planned escape route along Montserrat Road, then left towards the river, over the footbridge to where the red Escort waited. Unhurried, they walked back to the junction with the High Street, nonchalantly crossing the road, closing with the jeweller's. No fear, nothing but resolute intent.

The shotgun swung loosely beneath the long coat that defied the late-afternoon heat as they approached the doorway of the jeweller's. Whisky Two had passed by there moments before. Fate yet again played a game.

Inside, at the back of the shop, behind one-way glass, in the relative safety of the office, the manager spoke into a telephone, an ordinary, everyday call to a family member. Then all normality ended as the shape of the two men filled the approach between the display windows, dominating the narrowing walkway that ended at the shop door. To either side of them behind the glass were bright displays of jewellery.

Dozens of small light bulbs shone out from those displays, highlighting the robbers' menacing forms. The strange hat, the sinister coat. Hanging loose now in The Soldier's hand, the ultimate statement of intent, the shotgun. The girl at the counter just a few feet from the door saw them first, and as fear gripped her she ran towards the doorway in one corner, seeking the refuge the manager now enjoyed. In a few strides The Soldier was at the counter, and as the girl took flight for the first of many occasions that day the shotgun blazed.

He had leaned across the counter, the gun tracking her terrified progress. As she turned sharply left into the office, a metal safe yielded to a tight group of lead balls, and debris pierced her flesh. He was quite willing to kill her.

As fear stole the manager's reason, sent his heart into a pounding fever, he spoke a few halting words down the phone. 'I'm being robbed, two men with guns.' But those few words would change everything.

High in the glazed offices of the Met's information room a phone rang. First the deep-brown automated voice of the Speaking Clock: 'At the third stroke the time will be 4.53 precisely.'

Then a woman's voice: 'New Scotland Yard, connecting you.'

Then another female voice: 'Police, Scotland Yard, can I help you?'

'Armed hold-up, 88 Putney High Street.' The voice of an older man.

The woman operator broke in: 'Is that SW15?'

The older man again: 'Yes, JJ Barrett and Sons Limited. they're there now.'

'Your name, sir,' the female voice went on.

'My name is Barrett,' he replied. 'I was on the phone when it happened, that's how I know it happened.'

Quickly now, the operator passed the scant information to a colleague to transmit, to get the 'boys' running.

'Bear with me, I will get someone on the run down there. I need some more details from you.' A pause and she continued. 'Do you know how many of them there are?'

'I don't know anything. I was on the phone and I heard the girl screaming, then the people being told to lie on the ground.'

The same deep-brown voice that broke regularly into every telephone call, every radio message, was there again, marking the time, stamping for us a point in history. 'At the third stroke, the time will be 4.54 and 50 seconds.'

A man's voice intruded into the cars, into that quiet day and into lives that would be affected ever after. Over the radios came words now for some never to be forgotten: 'Whisky Papa 22, Whisky Papa 22, and any Trojan unit. Eight eight, eighty-eight Putney High Street, South-West Fifteen, premises of JJ Barrett, an armed robbery on CAD 6624, MP over.'

Around the corner just yards away in Lacy Road Mark O'Brien and Dave Boyce were just finishing with the two boys. About a mile away, Trojan 551 had just turned towards Putney.

The responses flooded in. 'Whisky Two, MP.' The voice of Mark Williams's woman operator broke in, the first to volunteer. Instantly Barney's voice: 'MP – Trojan 552.'

The acknowledgement: 'Trojan 552, received.'

The TSG units flooded the airwaves in a scramble to be there as voice after voice broke in.

A woman spoke: 'Uniform 517.'

Then a man: 'Uniform 533.'

A deluge of voices, men and women in blue, racing towards the ultimate test of duty.

Having left the armed officers behind, big Steve and his crew aboard the TSG carrier were on the way back to base. Now for them a hair-raising ride through Kensington, Fulham and Parson's Green, as the roly-poly carrier pitched and yawed, bellowing its way towards the scene. In the back the crew fought to don the body armour they had just shed after a long hot day. Shields, kitbags and equipment slid across the floor as the stakes went up. Then frantic words were heard among the many now jamming the radios: 'MP, shots being fired.'

Barry and Barney had spun around in the Strand. They were now facing west. I was perhaps a mile away, but on another radio channel and oblivious to all that was occurring.

Then there was another voice among the many: 'I have just heard a shot fired, Putney High Street.'

As the final words of the bollocking were delivered to the two young boys, Mark O'Brien was still close enough to the open doors of the van to hear the main-set radio bark that ominous message. As he and Dave Boyce turned on their heels the radio was heard again: the feared words, 'shots fired'; the response, 'received by Trojan 551', who were now so close.

An ex-soldier, Northern Ireland, the Falklands, Mark should have known better, but the van was facing the wrong way.

'You turn the van around, I'll run it,' he called back over his shoulder. Once he was into the High Street the robbery was only fifty metres away.

As Dave Boyce and Kevin fought the screaming vehicles through three-point manoeuvres in the narrowness of Lacy Road, Mark O'Brien closed breathlessly with the shop doorway. As natural caution dictated, he paused by a pillar, peering around it into the jeweller's, where the robbers were terrifying the staff, and throwing the jewellery into their bag. Things he believed he would never really see happen were happening before his eyes.

Among the first to volunteer, Barry and Barney aboard 552 barrelled through the confines of the Strand to pass Charing Cross station, then burst blaring into Trafalgar Square, as within moments the unwelcome update that gunfire had been heard was passed over the radio. Instantly a huge dimension of urgency had been injected.

Total focus, total commitment, as the need to be there, to be equal to the task, was suddenly all there was in life. I know that feeling.

Through the myriad tourists, the traffic, cabs, buses, Barry hurled the Rover back and forth, as the time-honoured sound of the two-tones echoed off the high buildings around them. The blue flashes of the roof lights, reflected in the glass and screens of the sea of traffic that stood dumb and impotent in their path, shone back into their eyes.

As a mindset that has to be experienced to be understood took over, he drove the car to where few men ever go: the very edge.

Along Pall Mall they hurtled, and right up to Piccadilly, where a left turn soon plunged them into the dimness of the Hyde Park underpass. Such a short time ago they had passed above this spot and all had been tranquil.

As the sounds magnified against the cold walls Barney fought to retrieve the carbines from the safe in the back. Must be ready.

High on Putney Hill Mark Williams in Whisky Two was leaving tyre rubber all around Tibbet's Corner at the start of the A3, plunging headlong back whence they had just come. The call for a Trojan unit had alarmed him, but then there was an armed robbery, shots fired.

Another ex-soldier, his thoughts were for 'the boys', the mates he'd left in Lacy Road, as he voiced his fears. 'Shit, the boys are still down there, the blokes are in Putney High Street.'

The Rover he was driving was about to get the hiding of its life. Unable to get back down the hill unobstructed, he smashed his way over a concrete reservation, stamped on the accelerator and was gone. 'Fuck the car, help the boys.'

* * *

As Trojan 551 had circuited the one-way system in Wandsworth for the second time a hint of the call to come caused Andy to drive straight on towards West Hill and Putney. The words 'and any Trojan unit' pierced their consciousness. As Stuart in the front came instantly to attention, pen in hand, Dinger in the back strained against the back of the seats, hungry for information, for the content of every syllable.

In moments the enormity of all that was happening was plain, triggering a reaction within the car. At once Stuart had them assigned, while Andy buried the accelerator in the floor, setting the wheels spinning, tyres smoking.

This was to be a day when poor equipment was the fiend sent to plague them all. As Mark O'Brien had watched in horror, the staff were forced at gunpoint to the floor, the manager, the terrified girl and an older woman now, dragged from the rear of the shop.

The shelves, safes and cabinets were rifled by two shouting, screaming, armed men, guns at the ready, as he spoke into his newly issued hi-tech radio to call for help, to tell the world that the very worst possible things were happening before his eyes. That death was dancing a jig so close to him now. The radio spluttered, and then failed.

Forced to be only a spectator, fearful that someone would hurl a police vehicle into confrontation as the robbers came out, yet wanting nothing else more than to access the van's main radio, he was rooted to the spot.

From behind the pillar, and with a silent prayer, he watched as the doors of the jeweller's opened. The long coat swirling, the guns held openly, blatantly, in a challenge to the society they scorned, the two men crossed the road back towards the old blue Peugeot. Still the guns were displayed now for all to see: They had heard the approaching sirens, but with a bag full of stolen jewellery they ambled with total nonchalance towards their escape.

Kevin Sinclair was the first to turn into the High Street as he accelerated hard towards the hill, over-shooting Montserrat Road. The two robbers passed behind him before the terrified manager flagged him down. With him on board frantic efforts to reverse were hindered by dense traffic.

As the figures turned the corner into Montserrat Road Mark O'Brien darted to the corner watching as the two men casually opened the van doors. Knapp was in the passenger seat; The Soldier was to be the driver.

As he watched them Mark heard the Sherpa van drawing close, turning into the same road. Dave could not be allowed to blunder into the two armed men. Breaking cover, Mark signalled to the van, and as it halted he leaped in.

Behind them a protesting car came abruptly to a halt. They couldn't go back. The two men sat praying the blue Peugeot would move, that the gunmen would not look back to where they sat helpless.

Moments later, fighting to get back to the junction, Kevin Sinclair heard the sound of a gunshot as the manager jumped from the car, and ran away.

For an eternity the old blue van had sat motionless. Then, as if all movement were denied them, as if paralysed by the unreality of it all, Mark and Dave, trapped in the police van, watched the driver's door open, the long swirling coat billowing in the warm air.

As The Soldier approached, total disbelief rendered them speechless. In his hands at waist height was the shotgun. When just a few feet from the screen of the van he tipped its ugly mouth upwards towards their horrified faces and fired from the hip. The round was one of those bonded together with wax.

Instantly they were transported to a world of noise, of blood and chaos, as broken glass, pellets and debris rent the air. Mark looked across the van. He could see blood all about Dave's motionless figure, and he thought his mate was dead. At once searing pain racked him. He found himself on the van floor. His kneecap dislocated, the knee bleeding.

It wasn't enough, though, The Soldier wanted more.

Racked with terror, with pain, the injured police officer fell out of the open sliding van door, to lie helpless on the roadway. Beneath the van could be seen the booted feet, the swirling coat: the robber was coming for him. Now came the mortal fear that changes men for ever: the absolute, immediate fear of death.

As Mark lay helpless on the ground, The Soldier emerged from around the van, the long coat suddenly above him casting a shadow across his face, the figure towering. Then the gun, the barrel of that awful weapon pressed hard against the flesh of his forehead, hungry to consume his life.

The eyes high above spoke of total power, live or die. For seemingly long moments he held his gaze, letting Mark plead silently for his life.

Perhaps enjoying the intoxication of it, of a humbled adversary, he turned quietly and walked casually back to the old van, entering the passenger door now. With Knapp now in the driving seat they made off, leaving terror and chaos in their wake.

Fear and anger though are bedfellows. Deep within Mark as he rose, quaking, pained to his feet, the raging creature that anger can be was waking. On pure adrenaline he pushed his own kneecap back into place.

To his immense relief Dave Boyce was moving. Not just the bare signs of life but much more. His anger, too, was rising. Blasted and blooded by a myriad glass fragments and odd separated pellets, and staring through the remains of the devastated screen, he fired up the van and, waiting for no one, not even Mark, he gave chase. Only one thought now. *Let's have the bastards.*

Voices on the radio again: 'Montserrat Road towards Oxford Road, shots fired.' Mark Williams screamed down Putney Hill to the junction with Upper Richmond Road, the words 'towards Oxford Road' registering on his mind. With the speed almost unchecked, he swung right on a course to intercept, leaving broad burn marks curving in his wake as the tyres screamed and the horns bellowed from the slewing car.

Close to overshooting the junction with Oxford Road, he locked up the brakes as at 45 degrees the car skidded, tyres smoking, to a halt. Drinkers on a nearby pavement fled their tables as he fought the car into the turn.

Approaching from the opposite direction but still a distance off was an ARV, Trojan 551, with Dinger, Andy and Stuart aboard. Further away but closing fast were Barry and Barney aboard Trojan 552, now into Knightsbridge with The Scotch House on their right as Barry ran the gauntlet of cabs, buses, dense, twisting, tortuous traffic barely allowing the speed to drop as they accelerated past Harrods' tall façade, the long windows mirroring their progress.

As the end of that vast building drew close a panicking driver threw a small hatchback car into their path. The police car swerved to avoid the impact as its nearside wheels left the ground by perhaps a foot, then fell with a sickening thump as Barry fought with the snaking car.

Leaning stomach down across the backs of the seats, retrieving kit from the back, Barney was not amused, but they were still rolling, getting ever closer. The balance was beginning to swing our way.

\* \* \*

Don St Leger was the inspector, the duty officer of the hour, for the Putney area that glorious sunny day. He was a well liked, well rounded character, almost a sort of father figure to his team. With Sheila Cummings as his sergeant and passenger, they were about to turn from Upper Richmond Road into the gates of Putney police station when the first intimation of the call reached them. Instead, they accelerated on to the junction with Putney High Street, turning left towards the river.

As the wounded van with its equally wounded driver moved forwards, the old blue Peugeot lurched from the kerb into the centre of the road, its exhaust belching clouds of blue smoke, its engine roaring loudly at Knapp's clumsy hands.

Don St Leger swung into Montserrat Road past the horrified motorist who had blocked in the police van. From the chaos that distorted the airwaves, they knew enough to give chase, pausing only to pick up the limping Mark O'Brien. As he slumped painfully in the back of the car, he related breathlessly, almost tearfully, all that had happened.

The robbers turned left into Atney Road, heading, as they had planned, towards the river. This, though, was not how they had meant it to be. Not for them now the smiling satisfaction of success. In convoy behind them was Dave Boyce, peering through the shattered glass of the van's screen. Behind him again, Don St Leger with Sergeant Sheila Cummings and the injured Mark O'Brien, as the short convoy turned left in pursuit towards the river. Hurtling towards another point of interception where Oxford Road meets Putney Bridge Road was Kevin Sinclair in the Astra. Barrelling down Oxford Road behind him were the first armed police officers, Andy, Dinger and Stuart.

Trojan 551 coming in from Wandsworth had turned the wailing ARV right into Oxford Road, tyres protesting, as the same drinkers outside the same pub were treated to entertainment they could not have dreamed of. Distantly they had heard gunfire.

Mark Williams abandoned the area car nearby. Grabbing his body armour he ran towards the fray. His woman operator awaited the armed car and, as Dinger, Stuart and Andy rolled to a halt where Montserrat Road made a junction with Oxford, she was there to direct them.

Kevin Sinclair braced himself. He had made up his mind: if the van appeared in or near Oxford Road he would ram it. Head on if need be.

More elements and more units became involved as the Met's equivalent of a hue and cry went up over the radios. Leaving the scene of that earlier false 'set-off-in-error' alarm in Wandsworth, Julian Bailey and Dave Walther had answered also. As they hurtled towards the scene their route took them along Putney Bridge Road.

The robbers, with Knapp driving, burst on to Putney Bridge Road going east with the pursuit behind them. As Julian Bailey closed with them driving west he realised what would be required. The old blue van hove into view with the raucous bellowing police cars in pursuit. He braced his arms against the steering wheel. Beside him Dave Walther cringed, bracing himself with hands and feet against the dashboard. Only one way, head on impact.

As bewildered pedestrians ducked into doorways or stood transfixed, the distance closed relentlessly. In the old van Knapp turned desperately left again, ever closer to the river and the hope of escape, but the closing police cars had forced him to turn left one street earlier than he had planned. Too much speed, too little skill.

With its front wheels clawing for grip they could not maintain, the van drifted screeching into Merrivale Road. Adding now to the cacophony of sounds was rending metal as it struck parked cars, and came to a grinding halt. Over the air came, 'They've got a shotgun, we have them in sight now, we need a Trojan unit ASAP.'

From Oxford Road the ARV crew had deployed immediately, Dinger and Stuart running back to follow the route along Atney Road down across the junction towards where the crashed van waited. At the scene, though, more things were happening: The Soldier and Knapp were moving. Andy was at the wheel of the ARV rolling down Oxford Road hoping to intercept the fleeing robbers. He could not know they had crashed.

With the police van stationary now in Putney Bridge Road, Dave Boyce watched in frozen anticipation for the next move. Don St Leger rolled his car up to Dave's right a little ahead of him and facing Wandsworth to the east.

Distantly the horns of approaching police vehicles echoed around the scene. Dave was aware of Mark O'Brien appearing on the passenger side as, without speaking, they were both fixated by the opening doors of the crashed van. From it rose polished wood, blued steel. The shotgun, then the hand that held it. They were going to fight their way out.

Swooping in from Putney High Street left into Putney Bridge Road aboard the TSG carrier, big Steve directed his driver towards the scene. As they rounded the corner beyond the police van, beyond Don's car was the crashed 'target' van. As the urge to arrest overcame caution they swept past and level with it. From the passenger door as they drew level came The Soldier, the swirling coat, the shotgun. From within their own carrier came a shout: 'Gun, gun.'

Instinctively the driver stamped on the accelerator. The big V8 engine dragged the heavy carrier forwards. At a distance further on he stopped.

police put the gun down.' But Knapp would have none of it.

As Knapp closed with the Astra Mark circuited around the back of the van, desperate to find a way to stop him, to help the defenceless woman. The suicidal urge to attack grew in him as Knapp leaned into the car. At point-blank range the gun threatened her, as his voice fell from high savage abuse to low resignation. 'Get out of the fucking car.'

The shock and the sound of gunfire had frozen the sergeant's emotion and it held her momentarily paralysed. Drawing his face close, Knapp spoke again, his breath in her face: '*I said get out of the fucking car!*'

As Mark and Dave Boyce reached fever pitch, tripping along the emotional edge of a suicidal attack, Sheila Cummings, unable to stand, opened the passenger door and rolled out on to the footway. Knapp slid into the driving seat, preparing to escape. But 'Boycey' and Mark were not about to give up.

Badly shaken, Don St Leger joined them at the van door. Panting from the fear and exertion that racked him he said, 'Ram the fucker.' Dave Boyce looked at him wide-eyed as Mark leaped in beside him.

In the van the two men's eyes met. From the passenger seat Mark spoke. 'Go on, son, I'm with you, do it.' Knapp's inept driving was there again as he fumbled with the controls of the hijacked police car. In his ears the van's engine screamed as it backed off. With a grinding of gears Dave selected first. The van leaped forwards as with a rending crash it smashed into the stationary car. It's engine revved wildly to the accompaniment of more grinding gears as the now panicking Knapp fought to escape.

Over his shoulder he aimed the revolver at the big van as it backed off ready to assault him again. Towards the scene came a disbelieving Andy alone driving the

ARV. Running down Atney Road came the armed police officers, Dinger and Stuart.

At the northern end of Merrivale Road, turning into Deador Road and the river, harassed by TSG officers, The Soldier was still firing, getting closer to that bridge.

There was another rending crash as the van with that shattered screen roared forwards to impact with the side of the hijacked police Astra again. Still waving the gun, Knapp found a gear, lurched forwards and was off. Within the pursuing police officers, there was now too much anger. They would not let him go. As Andy in the ARV drew level frantically, Justin directed him after Knapp. In a screeching U-turn he tucked in behind Dave and Mark aboard the battered van as they stared out through the same shotgun-blasted screen after a man they intended to make 'pay his dues'.

At the scene of the crash Julian Bailey tried to make sense of the chaos that was left. As they consoled the shaken sergeant and Don St Leger strove to implement cordons and to gather evidence, Julian shepherded curious faces back into safety while, in the distance, The Soldier's shotgun still rang out.

A sweating fat man stood in the doorway of a cab office, cigarette in mouth, as the still-shaken Julian did his duty, cared for his public. While the fear and adrenaline still flowed through him he spoke in even terms to the sweating man. 'Go on, mate, get in there, get out of the way because you just got to protect yourself from what's going on.'

Chewing the cigarette, the fat man sneered at him, then spoke. 'Oh you fucking Old Bill, what are you doing about it? Now you're stuck. You ain't got guns. What you going to do?'

Shocked and speechless, Julian watched as the fat man turned and, laughing, walked away. To this day the hurt remains.

As Stuart leaped into a local car following behind Andy, the convoy of three pursuing cars closed with the fleeing robber. Dinger was alone and on foot, and there was still The Soldier. The Soldier wanted a war.

Knapp pitched the battered Astra into the dip below the bridge approaching Armoury Way as the van harried him like a fighter plane. As he rounded the bend they pushed him ever harder until his limited skill failed him. The car began to drift left. Hitting a kerb, it bounced high and came to a halt, demolishing a set of railings. In a second they were out running forwards as the thought pierced Mark's mind that they were there again, unarmed, facing a man with a gun. No words spoken, no time to think, but they knew. The one that survived was going to bring him down, hard. As the car had crashed, from inside came a loud bang. He had not fired: the bang was the car's inflating airbag.

In a futile attempt to bluff, again Mark raised the long baton to his shoulder, calling, 'Armed police.' Through the driver's window of the smashed car came Knapp. First the hand, in it the huge revolver. Suddenly from behind them came the help they craved.

Andy and Stuart deployed either side of them to confront Knapp. Once more the call, 'Armed police, put the gun down, put the gun down *now*.'

As he raised his eyes, in an instant the bully was fallen. No hero, this man, as the gun clattered to the floor. The hard eyes that watched his every move through the cleft sights of a pistol spoke as loud as the words or even the guns.

From another angle the lethally accurate carbine in Stuart's hands promised an infinity of pain as its sights centred on his most vital organs. He knew. Obey and live, or fight and die. As Mark suppressed his anger, under the cover of the guns he and 'Boycey' searched and handcuffed the humbled robber.

Haltingly he spoke: 'I suppose I'll swing for this.' From within the folds of his clothing came a knife, as, almost pleading, he spoke again: 'I didn't shoot anyone.'

Around them crowds gathered, cameras flashed and whirred as the inevitable amateur video-cameraman seized a once-in-a-lifetime opportunity.

The shock, though, had to come. As a soldier, Mark O'Brien had seen real fighting, the Falklands, Northern Ireland, but it had not prepared him for this here in quiet suburban Putney. Around him a world of media and senior officers attended, while the still-bleeding Dave Boyce received the first medical attention. As screaming ambulances arrived and hordes of spectators invaded space he desperately needed, the walls that surround every act of great courage broke down. From where he stood his legs crumbled and he sat down in the road. Nearby a young woman colleague saw his distress and ran to him. Her arms folded about him, about his grief, as he sobbed out his agony.

In the ambulance as Mark O'Brien confided to Dave Boyce, 'I thought you were dead', both men wept. As they rode towards the clinical tranquillity of the hospital, for others the agony was just beginning. Over the radios came more words to chill, to change men for ever. Dinger's harrowed, tremulous voice: 'Putney Bridge, under fire.'

It was not over yet.

## Part 2 – The True Measure of Courage

The TSG officers played fast and loose with their lives as The Soldier fired at them repeatedly, but they would not let him out of sight. Dinger, now with a second group of TSG officers, converged on Deodore Road as The Soldier headed for the steps leading to the bridge, trying more than once to take innocent people hostage as he walked. No running though. He thought of himself as the military. He would not run, not from the uniforms, but the guns were getting ever closer.

Dinger emerged from a side road almost opposite where, at the base of the steps leading to Putney railway bridge, stood a hard-eyed TSG man. Tucked in, back against the wall, he waved to get Dinger's attention. With his finger pressed against his lips in an unspoken plea for silence, he looked across the width of the road into Dinger's eyes as all words ceased.

Then he folded back his little and third fingers, then the thumb, in the classic mime of a gun. With the same fingers he then pointed repeatedly up the steps. Dinger nodded.

The radios were useless, jammed anyway by the furore created by Knapp's arrest. He was alone and, having deployed urgently from the ARV, he had not stopped to drag a carbine from the safe and load it. Armed with only a handgun, he would have to tackle The Soldier. The steps were killing zones. Two corners, two points of ambush. Two places to die and no one else with a gun to support him.

He knew what was expected of him. He called back to a face he knew well, a man Dinger had worked, trained and run with. Billy was an ex-soldier and paramedic. Wearing body armour and carrying a radio, and being an athlete and a cross-country runner, he was ideal. 'Billy, tuck in behind me. Stay twenty paces back and put everything over the radio.'

The climb up the stairs was a nightmare. A blind turn left, then right, each of which could have been an explosion, a sudden blaze of light, agony, death.

With his heart pounding in his chest Dinger stepped out on to the width of the pedestrian walkway that twinned the railway bridge north towards Fulham. To his left were high, latticed, steel girder works beyond which ran the railway lines between Wimbledon, Earl's Court and thence the northeast. On his right was a handrail, beneath which flowed the grey and murky waters of the Thames, churning foam from the bridge's stanchions.

As a train rumbled by the bridge shook, radios were drowned out. Ahead of him, halfway across, walked a man in a long, olive-green trench coat, billowing in the turbulence the train had caused, exposing the big shotgun hanging loosely now at his side.

Distantly faces were rising to face them from the steps on the north side: three men, one of them wearing a pinstriped suit and a vivid red tie with white polka dots, perhaps a little drunk.

Shaking with fear, his chest heaving with exertion yet tight with anxiety, Dinger raised his gun. Then the classic call: 'Stop, armed police.'

The effect was immediate as The Soldier spun on his heels and fired. Around Dinger pellets played an abstract tune on the ironwork, striking his body armour and arms like vicious stings. The range was extreme, the power almost spent but the contest was even.

At this range with a handgun Dinger dare not return fire. His shaking hands and heaving body would disturb the gun a tiny amount. At the distance away his target stood it would translate into a huge miss. The round would go on perhaps to hit the three men or the houses beyond them.

As the first blast of shotgun fire had rent the air, some builders on a nearby roof had run to the parapet to watch a real-life drama played out. As they watched transfixed they could not know how involved they would be. Their presence, their eyes, would make all the difference. Far below them unarmed police officers were deploying dangerously near the exit from the bridge where a huge steel barrier blocked the road, corralling them as one big collective target.

It had been a really good day's business. By lunchtime the deal was done and it was back slaps all round and down the pub to celebrate. By the time he came out of The Eight Bells he was definitely one over that figure. Swaying gently, he had climbed the steps of the bridge, the red and white polka-dot tie askew. Near the top of the stairs there was shouting, commotion, as the two men following had called him back while they retreated.

No matter, though, he was happy, and there was this curious-looking old man in a tweed jacket who bustled towards him. If he could cross the bridge, why shouldn't Mr Polka Dot?

Dinger was weighing the odds. The long bridge curved gently to his right, diminishing his vision. As he went forwards with Billy behind him the peril grew. The further they went forwards, the more the danger. No cover, nowhere to hide or run. He turned to Billy, pointing down at the murky, swirling water. If the robber advanced on them Dinger was outgunned. They would have to jump.

Then suddenly The Soldier stopped, turned and, dropping to the kneeling position, turned the gun over, fumbling in the bum bag for rounds, going for a reload.

Seeing his opportunity, Dinger raised his gun sprinting forwards to close the gap, to get within striking distance. The gap rapidly closed, in his mind the commitment to shoot, to bring this maniac down. In a split second The Soldier was up, grinning, the gun suddenly aimed. It was a feint. Now he could shoot Dinger.

For the second time that day he enjoyed total power, enjoyed the fear of a helpless enemy as Dinger threw himself to the floor. Then, still grinning, he turned away. Mr Polka Dot was coming closer. The old man in the tweed jacket walked straight past it all.

Mark Williams had run nearly half a mile to reach the base of the bridge, passing the shocked Don St Leger, Julian Bailey and Sheila Cummins on the way. At the base of the steps he saw big Steve, the acting sergeant for the TSG. They weighed the odds.

They were not armed and, although they had body armour, there was no cover crossing the bridge. In the distance they heard gunfire. A few short moments were spent in contemplation as Mark spoke. 'Look we've got the river on one side and the railway on the other. If this bloke comes at us with the shotgun, that's where we'll have to go. I know he's shot at you lot but there could be people lying up there shot or injured or whatever.'

The two men cautiously climbed the stairs as, in his own head, Mark heard words of wisdom. 'This is fucking madness. This bloke's got a shotgun.'

Trojan 552 with Barry at the wheel screamed through Fulham arriving at the north end of the main Putney Bridge blaring, and steaming like a spent horse. What greeted them was a scene of apparent calm, of normality, as Barney left the car at the kerb just short of Gonville Street. He approached two foot-duty officers who appeared quite undisturbed. For long moments the two ARV men remained perplexed.

The Soldier caught the pinstripe suit by the collar, dragging the polka-dot tie up tightly against the man's throat. As he forced the barrel of the gun into the soft flesh below his jaw the robber spoke: 'You're coming with me. If you do as I say you won't get killed.' As fear replaced alcohol, as adrenaline took over, the man rapidly began to sober. Trains rumbled by, deafening; the structure shook.

Edging towards the descending steps, The Soldier threatened first the helpless man, the shotgun barrel pressed ever harder under the man's chin. Then the gun arced back to threaten Dinger, now back on his feet, following.

The shape of the two men, hostage and tormentor, dropped rapidly from sight. For the last few paces Dinger dashed forwards, desperate to know where his adversary had gone, but the steps were empty.

He stared down to the stairwell at the bottom, at a tactical nightmare, a perfect place to be ambushed. He heard the shotgun blaze again, and it was very close. Barry and Barney heard Dinger's voice over the radio, desperate, breathless: 'MP, urgent, Trojan 551. Over.'

The voice of the operator: 'Trojan 551, go ahead.'

Dinger again: 'Putney Bridge, under fire. He's got a hostage, he's got a hostage on the footbridge, he's going to come out the Fulham side of the footbridge. He's got a shotgun to the hostage's head. We are behind.'

His voice was broken by the need to gasp for air. He was desperate, afraid, but he would not let go, not at any price.

Aboard Trojan 552, when they were still running to the call, Barry's driving had reached suicidal proportions as they closed with the wrong bridge. But they had heard only part of the message. One thing they knew for sure, though: they were heading into a gunfight.

The steps descended steeply as the terrified man had stumbled, the polka-dot tie biting into his throat, both choking him and supporting him at once. He fought to clear his head. In split seconds fate had cruelly transported him from euphoria to mortal terror. Ahead of them was a woodyard where workers and a fork-lift driver looked up at them over a high brick wall in disbelief. At the bottom of the steps they were forced to turn left through a long, brick-built, graffiti-ridden tunnel that now passed under the railway. The footsteps echoed, the tie bit deeper.

Step by agonising step, Dinger descended after them, his shoulder hard against the right-hand wall. In his ears was the welcome sound of wailing horns as other units closed with him, but they could not help him now. Behind him still on the bridge, Billy stared anxiously after him.

He knew he was taking his life in his hands. His eyes remained fixed on the entrance to that tunnel, his vision interrupted only by the sights of his raised gun. At any minute The Soldier could emerge and take him to a world of agony, perhaps to die.

At the end of the short tunnel was a right turn along a narrow path next to a tall block of flats, and towards Ranelagh Gardens. Nearby the red Ford Escort waited. Below, where the railway crossed high above the arch over Ranelagh Gardens, was the barrier. Local units were arriving, clinging to the scant cover of their cars where the barrier blocked their path.

The Fulham duty officer was standing from where a man should lead his troops, the front. The inspector was at that barrier as The Soldier emerged with the hapless suited man still suspended by his tie. As he emerged to turn right, and away from them, The Soldier fired again from the hip.

The assembled police officers recoiled as the shot peppered their cover. The inspector stood in the protection of his half-open car door, pellets impacting on the car and all around him. The bonnet, door and screen were all hit. Perhaps by good luck or the presence of street furniture the officer was not hit but badly shaken.

Advancing on the tunnel down those steps, Dinger heard that shot as if it were next to him. He was closing blindly with an armed man who was still firing. As the terrified and the tormentor walked on, The Soldier spoke: 'We're going to a mate's house.'

Over the radio they had heard the mayhem, gunshots in the background. Now there was nothing. Barney tackled the local officers. 'Where is all this happening?' The younger man spoke: 'The other bridge, down there.' He pointed to the railway bridge some 150 yards downstream. Then more gunfire.

He signalled to Barry, still within the confines of the overheated car, pointing towards the footbridge and barrier. With a screech of tyres Barry pivoted the car left through Gonville Street, then right past The Eight Bells. He curved left again and high above him the railway bridge dominated the scene. Outside The Eight Bells drinkers at wooden tables looked on aghast as the car roared by, followed by Barney running headlong in body armour, carrying a carbine towards the sound of gunshots.

Dinger lived an eternity of fear as he walked through the dank, arched tunnel, quietly cursing his echoing footfalls. Ahead of him the half-moon-shaped exit was bright with sunlight. As the sights of his handgun ranged around its shape, he lived an untold agony, waiting for The Soldier to step out, and to fire that terrible weapon.

To walk through that tunnel was enough, but as Dinger had closed with its exit he would have to step out into yet another potential ambush, and he knew that shots were being fired. Moments later he was clear and into the road, his emotions exhausted.

Barry skidded to a halt where the barrier blocked the way. Erected to stop the use of the road as a rat-run, it was now their enemy. A few words were exchanged as he was updated by the shaken inspector. He dragged the remaining MP5 carbine from the car. Ahead of him

Barry could see Dinger and Billy. Sweating in the August heat, Barney was close, still running towards him, cursing.

With the carbine ready, Barry advanced on Dinger to support him, knowing that Barney was close behind. To their right disbelieving workers from the woodyard enquired, 'Are you filming?' High above Dinger, and to his right, those builders had crossed the roof of that tall block of flats to look down on him. He heard a voice calling from high up: 'Oy, copper, he's gone down there.' From the rooftops a distant figure gestured desperately off to Dinger's left, away from the river and into Edenhurst Avenue. He turned following the man's distant directions, feeling then suddenly cold.

He looked down, finding that his groin and crotch were wet. So great was his fear that he had lost control of his bladder, but he was still there, still going forwards. There was a duty to be done; he would do it.

The figure so high above was still gesturing. Reacting to the man profiled now against the sky, Dinger and Billy then turned right into Hurlingham Gardens. Ahead of them another innocent was about to be terrorised.

Mark Williams and big Steve were well across the bridge at this point, when, unknown to any of the pursuers, The Soldier was at the door of a nearby house.

With the terrified hostage he knocked at the door, desperately trying somehow to convince the woman occupier that he was a police officer. She was not so easily fooled, and he then reverted to what he knew best: threats and violence. The chain held, the door was closed, and that was where he was as the searching officers closed with him.

Dinger stood at the corner of Edenhurst Avenue, where a large white box van dominated the corner. Billy was still at his back. The road was lined both sides with parked cars, every one a threat, a potential ambush.

The nearby flats with their low concrete walls, the short front gardens of the houses, hedges, walls, fences – all a nightmare to search.

Above the cars spread the broad leafy branches of a multitude of trees, shading the road with a canopy that created almost a natural tunnel. Distantly came the sound of approaching police cars, but here in the street was quiet suburbia.

Still believing he was the only armed officer, Dinger forced himself from the grip of his shattered nerves. He still would not let the robber go. Leaving Billy to scan about them, Dinger dropped to the prone position and, on his stomach, gun in hand, from beneath the van he looked up and across the road for movement, for feet, but he saw nothing. He had made up his mind. He dominated the centre of the road ready to move forwards.

Then from his left came a whispered voice. To Dinger's eternal relief Barry stood beside him, carbine ready. Over his shoulder to the right was Barney's stoic shape. More whispers till they knew exactly what they were going to do. Three guns, not enough for this search, but better, much, much better, than one man alone.

The street was uncannily quiet, so quiet that even Barry's whisper could be heard from a distance, and it was.

In a garden a few houses further along, screened by a large hedge, was a small dog sitting bewildered on the steps of the Victorian house where the terrified woman occupier had bolted herself in. He looked up, puzzled by the presence of the man in the pinstripe suit and polka-dot tie, and the dark long-coated figure, shotgun in hand.

With no more than a nod, the three began to advance, Barry on the left kerb, Dinger taking the centre of the road and Barney on the right.

Billy was behind in close attendance, still feeding information back over the radio. Leaving the chaos at the exit of the bridge behind, Mark and Steve were rapidly closing with the scene.

Slowly, painfully slowly, they moved forwards as every garden, every bush, every car, became a threat. Scanning left and right looking over, looking under everything.

Searching for movement, a shadow, anything. Occasionally their eyes met, then a shake of the head. Nothing seen.

They struggled to keep the line as their view of each other was broken by the parked cars, barely risking a glance, lest the shotgun should appear. Distantly the footfalls of Mark Williams and big Steve behind them, but they must not look back. In a split second and at any moment, they could be blasted into agony. In the garden the robber brought the gun up, readying himself, while the hostage looked on in horror, wanting to cry out, not daring even to speak.

It will remain in Barry's mind for ever. Not the face – he barely saw his face – but the coat. The swirl of that long trench coat as The Soldier stepped out. Then the flash, burning searing pain, as 140 shotgun pellets penetrated his legs and abdomen. Instantly paralysed from the waist down, Barry fell to the pavement across his own gun. As he lay there helpless, The Soldier paused, perhaps preparing to shoot again or maybe relishing that moment of dominance, of power.

One armed man had followed him across that bridge. Perhaps that was all he believed there was, just one man. He had not seen Dinger there in the centre of the road. Now the contest was even, man on man at a range to make the handgun effective. With his arms and elbows locked in the classic style, the Glock 17 pistol in Dinger's hands jumped first once, and rapidly once again. Bright orange flashes spat from the barrel, the sharp report contrasting with the shotgun's powerful boom.

There was a puff of powdered brick dust from a pillar near the gate where he stood, as The Soldier flinched. Then the second round struck him in the left thigh, high up.

It tore through the limb and pelvis, exiting through his buttocks. A terrible fountain curved up and over a parked car to spatter the centre of the road as a main artery began to pump blood.

An obscene red patch spread rapidly down the leg of his trousers as, dragging the injured limb, he limped back into the garden. Barry's voice rang out across the road as Barney heard words we all dread: *'I've been hit.'*

Barney had seen that same swirling coat out of the corner of his eye, heard the bang, seen the flash. Seeing Barry fall, he thought him dead. Instantly the carbine had risen, but between him and the robber stood Dinger. A slight raggedness in their line and the extreme angle meant that Barney had no chance to reply. Desperately Barry fought to drag himself into an adjacent garden, the only cover a small brick pillar. Parked on the drive was a white Peugeot car, but he did not have the power to move so far. His legs were a pain-racked litany of shotgun pellets, numb and unresponding.

As Barney covered, Billy ran to Barry, dragging the 'medic' pack from his hip, with total disregard for his own safety. Having dragged him further into cover, he turned his back on the threat to minister to Barry's legs. As he cut away the trouser material, the flesh below was peppered with a multitude of blackened and bleeding entry wounds. But as he lay there in absolute agony, Barry drew his handgun to cover across Billy's back. The threat was still there, still moving.

Barney moved to protect them, ducking across the road to cover over the roof of the white car, as from behind and through the hedge came a deafening blast, pellets peppered the white car to Barney's left. The fear grew greater by the second as they realised the robber meant to fight on. Lying helpless, Barry waited for him to come forwards, to finish him off.

Suddenly, Barney's substantial form was there. He had placed himself kneeling in no-man's-land. To shoot Barry again, the robber would have to kill Barney first.

As the carbine rose, ranging about the hedge that separated them, Barney could see two shapes, robber and hostage. He could not tell which one was his enemy.

Dinger had crossed over to them, and picked up the superior weapon, Barry's fallen MP5 carbine. With that tucked into his shoulder he went forwards and right with only one intention. He would end all this fear, this horror now. If the robber was moving he would kill him. As he ducked away, to his and to Barney's absolute horror, a sound penetrated their consciousness in a way that blanked out all other thought, all other noise. Click, click, click. Behind the hedge The Soldier was reloading.

Unable to separate one shape from the other, Barney prepared himself for a final desperate assault. Taking the carbine by the stock, he braced himself to break through the hedge, determined to bring down whoever he found, reasoning that at least perhaps no innocent would die. Across the road Dinger raised the carbine, when to his horror he found the sights were smashed off.

Barney strode forwards wielding the carbine as a club and, as Dinger redrew his handgun, there came another shot, different from the rest. Muffled, contained.

Both men reacted. Barney dropped to his knees as Dinger dived for cover behind a parked car. Through the hedge Barney could still see two silhouettes, one standing, the other kneeling. Then slowly the man on his knees toppled and fell. The second figure moved haltingly forwards as Barney's carbine rose to meet it.

As his finger curled around the trigger, his whole being tensed for the ultimate act, the sights tracked the shape closing with the hedge. At this range he could not miss, but it would be a split-second decision. The face that rose above the leafy hedge was not above a swirling trench coat, but complemented at the neck by a red and white polka-dot tie.

'Who are you?' Barney said as he fought to defuse the enormous tension that racked his being.

'He got me,' replied the quaking man.

'Where is he now?' Barney asked.

'He's down there.' He pointed towards the fallen shape, and added, '*Dying.*'

Unable to think of a more forceful way to get the innocent man out of danger, Barney shouted, 'Get the fuck out of there.' Dinger had moved to the centre of the road and directed him away.

As Barney skirted around the fences towards the point where the robber lay, Dinger in the centre of the road called to him, 'He's still got a gun, he's still breathing.'

By the time he had reached the gate a terrible sight greeted Barney. Half turned across the tiled path lay The Soldier, still holding the gun pointed towards the gate, finger on the trigger. Nearby spare rounds were laid out ready for reloading. Edging forwards, Barney covered the fallen man with the carbine until he was able to pull the gun from his limp hand, and throw it clear.

To the left of the path built into the tiles was a shallow gully that ran thick and red now with congealing blood. His left thigh was soaked in blood from

Dinger's shot, a finger damaged somehow by a glancing round.

Who knows what thoughts invaded his mind in those last moments? But the remaining rounds stood regimental nearby as testament to his intention to fight on. Then perhaps the pain, the futility of it all, had suddenly been so terribly obvious. In his last moments he had placed the barrel of the shotgun in his mouth and pulled the trigger. The muffled sound of the last round fired was the product of it spending itself within his head.

Although it was patently obvious the man was dead, with due deference Barney checked for a pulse, but there was none. The head and face were a parody of what they had been moments earlier. His palate was destroyed and his face had split vertically along the bridge of his nose, and then collapsed inwards leaving the area concave. Only one eye was visible. Barney cannot forget. Wherever he went the one eye watched. Sometimes he sees it still.

When The Soldier had promised he would never go back to prison, this was what he had meant.

As help arrived in droves, Barney walked back towards Barry, now writhing in agony. Dinger sat desolate in the centre of the road. Raising his eyes to Barney, he asked, 'Is it over?'

Barney placed a hand on his shoulder. 'Yes mate, it's over. You're all right.'

Senior officers arrived by the dozen as flying squad cars appeared along with other ARV crew and a paramedic motorcyclist, as that same damned barrier thwarted an ambulance fighting to get there. As morphine eased Barry's pain, he was lifted gently into a squad vehicle and rushed to hospital.

Mark Williams and big Steve had been very close as the last shots were fired. Able to distinguish between the sounds of the weapons, and knowing the last round Mark heard was the shotgun, they had feared the worst as they ran to the scene. Mark's abiding memory is of Barry's absolute agony at every movement, of Dinger's utter distress. He spoke to him. 'Thanks for helping us, mate. Thank you.' Then he and Steve walked to where the robber lay. 'The smell of death, like a mortuary,' he said. He will never forget it.

Months later he saw Barry again recovering in a nursing home. To him also: 'Thanks mate, thanks for helping us.'

Julian Bailey and a local sergeant had left the scene in Putney Bridge Road to drive north, to do whatever they could. As they had approached along Edenhurst Gardens, distantly the last flurry of activity was in progress. At the scene the lasting impression was of Barry's extreme pain, the shock and fear in his face. Then as he was driven away the sudden total quiet, like an early morning, still, birds singing, a sort of hum.

## The Aftermath

The last few miles passed quickly as Mark Bradberry and I talked. On the radio, over the phone, nothing. He was eager to get back for an evening out. On the back seat sat a quantity of paper that would require a good few hours of my time.

I turned the car towards the big green gates as the passenger door swung open for Mark to clamber out, to open up and get us into the yard and him on his way as soon as possible.

At the stairwell he broke off left towards the armoury, rushing to unkit while I walked towards the base room, the pile of papers in my hands. Gerry Calnan, base man for the day, walked out towards me, his face betraying the concern he sought to mask. He raised his hands almost defensively, palms towards me, as if anticipating some emotional eruption.

'Barry Oldroyd-Jones has just been shot. It's not life-threatening. It's all right, it's not life-threatening.' It was a moment for me frozen in time.

Another one of my people shot, and this time it was worse. Gerry's gentle diplomacy did nothing to calm the volcanic emotion I suddenly felt.

'And the shooter?' I asked, strangely angry, even with Gerry, with the whole world.

'Dead,' he replied. 'Dinger shot him.'

'Good,' I retorted. 'I hope he died in fucking agony.'

Much later, at the coroner's court, when I saw the pain etched into a middle-aged woman's face, I was to regret having made such a hasty remark.

In moments Mark and I were back in that car as we hurtled across London to the Charing Cross Hospital, perversely retracing the route that such a short while before we had casually driven while mayhem and carnage were being acted out.

At the doors to casualty two ARVs waited, the crews alive with every emotion.

They, as I did, acutely suffered the feeling of failure, that we had not been there in that street to help, maybe to prevent all of this. Jake's barely contained Celtic fury almost overtook him as the anger he felt could find no enemy on which to vent itself, and he boiled in his own frustration.

But their feelings, deep as they were, were a fraction of my own. I was their sergeant. Whether or not I could have been there, I had at one point been so close.

I knew the locations so well. Perhaps I could have saved Barry this agony, the others their distress. Maybe even The Soldier's parents a bereavement. But he was on a mission. It is a question that for the rest of my life will torment me. If I were given the chance to go back and be in that street in the hope of a better ending, I swear to this day that I still would.

As I crossed the reception area to where Barry lay, his pain rising as the morphine wore off, the staff looked with deference at me, while Mark did his best to placate the crews hovering nearby, to deal with the administration. I approached his hospital trolley as he awaited the first urgent surgery; if he had not been moving I would have thought him dead, so ashen were his features.

Within minutes Karen was whisked in past the first gathering of media, as Mark and I reassured her, 'He's hurt, Karen, but he'll be all right, he's not going to die.' I left them together, a huddle of emotion. Minutes later high in the building, as Barry was transferred to a side ward, his parents and brother arrived, his mother's face an essay in distress, his father torn by concern for them both.

I spoke to them. 'He needs you to be strong for him. His life's not in danger. You can be very proud of him.' Her eyes cleared, her back straightened, and she walked into the room. His father's eyes spoke to me of much more than any words could ever convey.

In the days that followed there was surgery, much suffering and unwanted intrusive attention. All the days of his life the pain will be there as the remaining pellets, over a hundred, fret and aggravate his flesh. He has endured surgery several times since that day, and regularly will again.

When he kneels to play with their two lovely children, the pain takes him back to that street. Still sometimes in the night, a man in a dark swirling coat comes to torment him.

Several months later I was present at the inquest, as were many of the people involved. In the witness box men in uniform flushed and shed tears. Some recoiled as the big gun was produced, still stained with now aged blood. Women on the jury cried.

As the story was recounted, the terrible fatal injuries described, I watched a middle-aged couple seated on the benches in the well of the court. The man tried vainly to comfort his inconsolable wife as she recoiled at every word, as if a great invisible hand were striking her, driving her down. Later, at the conclusion, when the inevitable suicide verdict had been reached, I spoke to them in a small anteroom. I told them who I was and said, 'Neither my men nor I would have wished this upon you. We are truly sorry for your pain.'

Only the man answered. The Soldier's mother was too distraught. His eyes, though, were quite gentle, but resigned, as if the story were only ever going to end somehow like this. In a half-smile he merely said, 'Thank you.'

Dinger's luck sadly got worse, and he went on to be seriously injured in a car accident. Thankfully, he has now recovered and is working in an area much removed from SO19. I owe to Barry, and to Dinger, for talking to me, for revisiting the most awful fear, a most humble debt of gratitude.

I know it took great courage for them to revisit that route with me, to speak those words, see the photographs, hear the tapes, to live it all again. As Dinger and I crossed that bridge together, descended those steps for the first time since that fatal day, as we passed through the arched brick tunnel out into the light, thoughtlessly I said, 'This is a terrible place to be ambushed.'

His eyes filled and that was when in a faltering voice he said, 'I was prepared to die.'

Later, when more composed, he said this: 'Some people have said to me I was lucky to be involved in a real gunfight. They are so stupid. You tell them I was afraid, that I pissed myself. Tell them it is a dirty, filthy, horrible business.'

Rarely in over thirty years of police service have I been so moved. By my own definition, real courage is not being unafraid, a bold seeker of combat. But to be terrified, truly, mortally afraid, believing you may die, and yet to do, through a sense of duty, what is right – *that* is the true measure of courage.

There is little that I can add except to say that throughout my service I have investigated many armed robbery incidents, but never before have I come across such sustained violence and the total disregard shown by two dangerous criminals for the lives and safety of uniformed officers who were acting in the execution of their duty.

*Detective Superintendent Craig*

The courage they displayed under the most trying of circumstances, knowing they could be confronted by an armed gunman, who had and would not hesitate again to discharge his weapon at them is worthy of the highest praise and recognition.

*Detective Superintendent Malone*

On 27 February 1995 Robert Arthur Knapp was sentenced to twelve years' imprisonment for his part in the robbery and following events. After sentencing, the judge, the Common Serjeant of London, made the following comments to the prosecuting counsel: 'Mr McGuinness, before I leave this case, from what you have told me of the facts, it seems to me that Police Constable O'Brien and Police Constable Boyce acted with exemplary courage. They deserve to be commended and they are commended, and I will rely on you to convey that through the appropriate channels to them.'

Early in 1995 the coroner for the western area of Greater London, Dr John Burton, while recording the verdict of suicide upon the death of the man known to you as The Soldier, made the following comments: 'It is not for me to award commendations. However, having heard of the events of Tuesday the second of August it is clear to me that a very large number of police officers were on the scene to contain it. Most of them were unarmed. Many of them took serious personal risks, with little or nothing to protect themselves, in order to ensure the safety of the public. All of them did what they could and I trust that anyone concerned with considering commendations for the officers involved will bear in mind the serious danger that they put themselves in whilst carrying out their duties.'

In the writing of this story I have gratefully received the co-operation of a large number of people, for many of whom the recounting has been a painful and difficult experience. To each and every one I extend my profound thanks. There follows a list of the unprecedented number of awards and commendations won on that fateful day . . .

## The Awards

Police Constable Mark John O'Brien – High Commendation and Queen's Gallantry Medal
Police Constable David Boyce – High Commendation and Queen's Gallantry Medal
Police Constable William Morris Hilton – High Commendation and Queen's Commendation for Bravery

Police Constable David McKinnon – High Commendation and Queen's Commendation for Bravery

Police Constable Barry Oldroyd-Jones – High Commendation and Queen's Commendation for Bravery

Police Constable Philip David Alston – High Commendation and Queen's Commendation for Bravery

Inspector Edward Alec Lawther – Commissioner's Commendation

Police Constable Sean William McGachie – Commissioner's Commendation

Police Constable Stephen McNally – Commissioner's Commendation

Police Constable Sarah Ward – Commissioner's Commendation

Inspector Doneraile Charles St Leger – Commissioner's Commendation

Police Sergeant Sheila Cummings – Commissioner's Commendation

Police Constable Julian Bailey – Assistant Commissioner's Commendation

Police Constable Andrew Nicholson – Assistant Commissioner's Commendation

Police Constable Stuart Andrew Brogan – Assistant Commissioner's Commendation

Police Constable Daniel James Tiller – Assistant Commissioner's Commendation

Police Constable David Walther – Assistant Commissioner's Commendation

For his part in the incident, in that he remained calm and controlled throughout his ordeal, trying through measured conversation to calm the armed man, Mr

Jonathan Pike, the hostage, was recommended for and received the honour of the Binney Award.

And let us not forget all of those other police officers who were also present at this incident, and, regardless of their actual involvement, went to the scene in the full knowledge that they may be confronted by an armed man who was prepared to fire, and had indeed already discharged that shotgun. If their only commendation lies here, I hope that they will feel that their willingness has been recognised.

# **12** Our Darkest Hour

I SUPPOSE IT WAS THE ELEMENT of shopfloor humour that first put me on my guard. I was the sergeant and Andy the new man, a ready smile and a wicked gleam in his eye. We are always defensive, us 'supervisors', until we get the measure of every new face.

Slowly though the ground was broken for a friendship, arising from a mutual love of sports cars, tempered by time and a host of jobs. I knew that we could clash on some issues, yet be fraternal over others: such is always the product of a man who sticks to his guns when he believes he is right. What was plain was that he was a character, one of the many ingredients that make up a successful relief, which it was.

When I asked him for something, I got it. Bits of equipment appeared as if by magic. I recall an occasion when a village in Kent became a miniature battleground for warring gypsy families: shotgun fire exchanged between them, and the local police driven out. In response to a call for armed assistance Keith and I hurtled out of the Met along motorways towards the scene, visualising and requesting all the possible kit we might need. Night vision, floodlights, an armoured Land Rover; shotguns, more carbines, shields, dogs – all manner of things. It was Andy's voice that came reassuringly back over the radio in response. 'Yep, got all that sarge, where do you want us?'

His involvement was total. He loved the job, the department, the ARVs, the relief and his friends –

largely the same thing – and he loved a 'wind up'. Most of all, though, he loved his wife. Their privacy, home, holidays and life together were sacrosanct.

The most poignant of his relationships was demonstrated by the time and care he gave to his close friend Deane, who sustained gross spinal and skeletal injuries in a road accident.

As time moved on, the Armed Response Vehicles grew in numbers and stature and a south base was opened, close to Lambeth Bridge. By the nature of the building and facilities, the men posted there bonded ever more closely. In this atmosphere, their fraternity, and Andy, thrived.

While I operated from the north base at Old Street, I would still see him occasionally at the bigger jobs, or when the relief as a whole went training. Down south, Pete and Ray presided over events, and suffered the rigours of Andy's wicked humour. It was the colourful way things went on until that fateful night duty.

I had dwelled on my thoughts for too long. It was a Friday evening of a long weekend's leave before nights. Sue and I sat in the warm ambience of the restaurant as, whenever we could, we would seize an opportunity for some R&R. Time to talk, to relax, to be like other people, just for a while. But I couldn't settle or concentrate my mind. My thoughts were elsewhere ... I couldn't drag them back.

Nights, life in limbo. That strange feeling that I was not part of the rest of society. Sleeping while the world scurried about its business. Coming home on quiet roads, the early sun in my face as the night's news was related through the car's speakers, maybe telling me what I already knew. Often because I had been part of it. So many times; the light mornings of summer, the dank depressing atmosphere at the beginning of a winter's day, as night duty after night duty had passed, some eventless, an agony of lost sleep. Others frantic, tumultuous, as events swept over us that I will never forget.

This week coming I would travel alone while Keith basked in the sun on some foreign shore. I would miss the voice, the face, and the humour. In the car as we travelled, we would discuss this problem or that. When we ran with the horns blaring to one job, burning this generation's version of the blue lamp on the roof, two heads were better than one. We would plan, anticipate, prepare.

This coming week I, alone, would be the duty officer. Mine would be the first responsibility for every and any immediately occurring firearms incident in the whole of the Metropolis. I had been there before, I would cope. Yet I couldn't put it out of my mind. I was fretting, I didn't know why.

I turned over in my mind the many things that might occur and how I would deal with them. Silently I sat imagining situations, finding answers, until Sue's voice brought me back to the real world. 'Am I eating alone tonight?' I was staring blankly at her with unseeing eyes.

'I'm sorry sweetheart,' I said, forcing a smile, and we enjoyed a good meal. It did no good, all that speculation. It would not help with what was to come.


George the rifleman loved motorcycles. Anything that was a gadget, that could be polished, plated, honed, refined, altered or modified, won a place in his affections. That was perhaps why he loved the rifles. So polished, so precise.

There had been a succession of bikes over the years including big Harley Davidson's, but now it was a powerful Japanese 'V' four. It was bedecked with every reflective safety stripe you could imagine, but it made no difference. A man in a dark Volkswagen realised his mistake, as he swung off suddenly from the roundabout, recognising his exit at the very last moment. The motorcycle was in his mirror but he had not seen it.

George's injuries were gross. The concussion alone left him with lifelong hearing damage, while the impact chipped and damaged his collar bone and shoulder blade. The nerves in his shoulder were affected, and the mobile phone in his breast pocket was driven into his chest, breaking several ribs. Below the knee his left leg was broken in four places.

When George woke up in hospital a towering shape loomed over the bottom of the bed. 'You know you're late for work, don't you? This will cost you cakes' (the standard relief fine for poor punctuality). But the eyes were kind, those of a friend: Andy.


Jan could see the shape through the frosted glass of the front door. Every policeman's wife dreads it. A man in uniform to say those things that are most feared. In the firearms' department that fear is more intense, the dread more likely to have foundation.

As the door swung open Andy's outline filled the entrance. 'He's not going to die.' He was immediately at pains to remove the most burning fear. 'He's had an accident a little while ago. They have cleaned him up, and I have come to take you to see him.'

As the shock sunk in, he consoled Jan while they pulled some of George's things together, then drove to the hospital. There he left them alone and went away to deal with the paper aftermath.

In the journeys to and from the hospital that followed, he was always there ferrying Jan back and forth in his old Ford. Pete and Ray cut him the slack he needed to be there for her. That was the way we did things.

Some while later, George was released to go home, heavily plastered and bandaged, But the pain in his arm grew relentlessly as it began to swell and discolour. Very rapidly he found himself back in the same hospital under the threat of losing his arm. He had developed a blood clot.

Jan drove herself there in a kind of trance as fear gripped her. She left her husband in the care of the doctors but fatigue, shock and lack of food took their toll and, during the drive home, she crashed. Limping the car home she telephoned Pete. He knew who was best placed to help, and called Andy.

On the morning of that fateful Monday, with the prospect of a night duty just hours away, Andy was there again, just as he had said he would be. Somehow different today though, looking tired, a little drawn, but he dismissed it.

As the journey passed, Andy seemed strangely concerned about the old Ford. 'It's an old car,' he had said. 'It might pack up.' It was strange, because it had run faithfully up until then. The conversation with Jan grew deeper, more personal than ever before. He began to talk about how long he had left to serve in 'the job', that he would not serve a day longer than his '30' and that after he would devote all his time to his wife and home.

'My Dad died young you know,' he confided in Jan, 'and my Mum had a struggle bringing us up. Just like George and his accident – you just never know what's going to happen.' Then, brightening up a little, he and Jan began to speculate on holiday locations for Andy's next break. At her home he straightened out a little of the damage on Jan's car. Leaving her feeling uneasy and puzzled, he drove off.

The weekend passed all too quickly, the unsettled feeling never being too far away. As the light began to dim I found myself back in my old car again, heading in towards the city, and the north base at Old Street.

Soon I was labouring down those familiar steep stairs bearing armfuls of kit and a huge responsibility. As I turned the corner in through the door, to be embraced by the welcoming bustle of a shift change, I remember thinking, '*Here we go.*'

Not only would I be the duty officer for the whole Met, but also base sergeant, section sergeant for the north base and anything else that happened to fall to me, so I resolved to delegate. I grabbed Barry OJ to fill out the duty binder, while the boys sorted themselves into crews. Grateful for their co-operation, I turned my attention to other things. From the clamour of our small base room came a voice, 'Are you duty officer tonight sarge?' I confirmed that I was. 'Phone call, south base.'

Leaving the banter and the tea drinking behind me, as the kit and guns were carried out to the cars, I answered the phone. It was Mike 'the headmaster'. Confirming again that I was the duty officer, he said in a typically level voice. 'Andy Pearce has stopped breathing.'

I had, moments earlier, passed through a room full of good-natured men, the familiar sounds of the equipment rattling, the body armour, guns, voices. Now this would be an ocean of heartbreak and, in those first split seconds, I could not comprehend it.

'So, what's happened? Has someone nicked his overtime?'

Mike's monotone voice gave nothing away as he said again, 'No, I'm serious. Andy has stopped breathing, they're working on him now.'

The saddest episode in the history of my relief had begun.

Steve's week had been a good one. He had literally soared as he tried his hand at paragliding. Soon he was going to put himself through the rigours of a course that would be physically exhausting and in preparation for that he had a programme of training. Tonight, before duty, he would 'run the bridges' – a circuit devised by the relief, and commonly used by many of them.

This was a very sociable group, and they did not run alone. Steve phoned Andy and, though Andy said he didn't really feel up to it, he agreed to meet Steve early and go with him on that run.

At home Andy confessed to feeling a little sick, but Shelley's advice not to run was ignored. He patted his stomach. 'Got to get rid of this before the holiday,' he joked.

Andy had made several journeys back and forth to the car, carrying shirts, kit, and books. Having kissed Shelley goodbye he walked to the old Ford, and dropped into the driving seat.

Suddenly he got back out of the car and walked back towards his wife. Holding her gaze, he spoke: 'I just want you to know, Shelley, that I really, *really* do love you.'

Surprised by this unusual, extra assertion of his feelings, she smiled as Andy's strong arms held her closely, strangely tight. 'And I love you too,' came the reply. Then he climbed back into the car. As he started the car, a cloud of blue exhaust smoke filled the air and he turned to share a laugh with her. The car lurched away, and he was gone.

In the base at Lambeth, Steve mocked Andy's 'scrawny legs'; Andy retaliated, saying Steve's short stature and Lycra shorts were effete. Andy, in truth, wore something similar, but more significant was the logo on the back of his training shirt: an unofficial emblem, and something very close to Andy's heart, a large bronze-coloured Trojan horse.

From the base they ran out along the river's edge with Big Ben off to the left. On past County Hall then the Festival Hall, until they passed over Blackfriars Bridge, to return along the north side. They ran along the Embankment, past the Houses of Parliament, over Lambeth Bridge and back into the base. Nothing that hadn't been done by them both untold times before.

In the base room, around the lockers and showers, more of the night duty-relief were appearing, some hot from the gym, others preparing for the night ahead. Nearby was Tony 'Carrot', and young Darren. It was his first night on the relief. Andy walked ahead of Steve into a parade room, saying 'I'll check the corre's [correspondence] tray, and see what our duties are.'

When he was only a few feet away through an open doorway, Steve became aware that Andy was gasping, fighting for breath.

Tony is a fit man, no doubt of that. He had run from Chelsea with a pack on his back, and the heat was getting to him too but, as he conversed with Andy, while Steve flicked through some papers in the next room, Andy's increasing distress became apparent. Tony tried to calm him, believing that heat exhaustion was making Andy hyperventilate, making him panic. 'Try to calm yourself down,' he pleaded.

'I can't, I can't get my breath.' For long moments Tony supported him while Steve rushed back into the room. Then Andy's eyes changed, glazed over, and Tony held him as he began to collapse.

For moments Steve was stunned by what he saw. 'You twat, what are you doing?' he joked, expecting the standard humour but, as their eyes met, he could see Andy's face changing. 'That's not right,' he thought. 'This is serious.'

Steve and Tony took his arms to support him. Andy tried to speak. Then, as he lost consciousness, they eased his sturdy frame to the floor. Steve turned him into the recovery position and, using the resuscitation skills we had all been taught, he checked for breathing. There was nothing. Tony felt for a pulse. Young Darren stepped in to help while Tony grabbed the phone, calling for an ambulance. Tony Amey watched aghast, and Blond Billy hovered, stunned, nearby. More faces began to appear as the relief paraded for night duty. Still almost disbelieving of the situation, expecting Andy's terrible sense of humour to be the culprit, Steve began to administer mouth to mouth, but this was no joke. Through the door came 'Nicky Boy' and Ray.

At the car ramp outside Charley, the late turn sergeant rolled to a halt. Bringing the Rover gently to rest he carried his kit in through the double doors. As he entered the main parade room, the crisis was at first too much to take in. Then the faces, Steve's urgent efforts to get Andy breathing, Darren's fight to pump blood through his heart, brought the searing reality of what was happening home to him.

As the roar of a motorcycle heralded the arrival of a paramedic, Charley tasked Tony to check the call for an ambulance and meet it, to bring it up through the complex of ramps to where they were. The arriving ambulance crew set up lines and monitors, joining the fight. Then, lifted high by many willing hands, Andy was carried to the waiting ambulance, but the signs were not good. The valiant efforts of his colleagues and the medics had kept his circulation going, his colour good, but his heart would not restart.

On my instruction, Phil 'Twelve Hits', hurtled around the M25 to pick up Deane, to rush him towards Old Street. Deane and Andy had grown to be inseparable as members of a territorial support group. It was a friendship which had continued when they transferred to the firearm's branch. As I had spoken to Deane over the telephone, the effort to measure my words had been enormous. 'Deane, Andy's collapsed and it's not looking very good.'

Still disbelieving, I made my way to St Thomas's hospital where stunned faces greeted me. In a cubicle the hospital crash team fought with every ounce of their skill, and every resource to bring him back. I watched them for moments before walking back to the doorway where Steve waited, desolate, his glistening gaze exposing his fears.

The young sister's eyes moist with tears betrayed the agony of it all as, in a halting voice she said, 'We couldn't save him.' She paused. 'My husband's a copper.' She spun on her heels. Taking a few steps away from me, glancing over her shoulder, she said, 'I'm so sorry.'

I did not in truth know what to do. So many things had crossed my mind, so many possibilities that I had tried to anticipate for this week, but not this. I had walked through the door of Old Street into a nightmare.

Outside in the ambulance bay, Charley and I wrestled with our responsibilities. He would do the paperwork, I would care for my blokes. Back in the casualty department the same sister approached me, hers eyes a fund of kindness. 'Do you wish to see him?'

My last vision of Andy had been his prone figure as they fought to save him. I entered a small anteroom where he lay on a trolley, looking almost unchanged from life. Only the stillness of his form, his unblinking eyes made it a tragic lie. On his lips was the same wry grin that was his trademark in life. I held his still-warm hand, and said what quite simply was in my heart: 'This is out of order, Andy. So out of order; so unfair.'

Minutes later Shelley arrived, her eyes downcast and bewildered as Ray ushered her in through the casualty door. In a small room the young sister told her the terrible truth. I wanted to take her pain, to bear it for her, but in this I was powerless. The sister took her to where Andy lay, leaving them alone.

\* \* \*

As the truth emerged, Phil diverted to the hospital, using every device to keep the news from Deane. He desperately wanted the security that the friendship of his colleagues would give. The marked car swung on to the entrance ramp. Charley was waiting, blocking Deane's path to the hospital door, knowing what must now be said: 'I'm sorry, Deane, he's dead.'

Deane walked towards where Shelley waited. Overwhelmed, he fought through his own agony to comfort her. 'Have you seen him?' he asked.

Moments later, Deane was led gently to the anteroom and stood where I had spoken those words to Andy's still form minutes earlier.

In the small hours of the morning, Jan was disturbed by the telephone. As she shook herself from sleep she was afraid that something else had happened to George, but the breaking voice was his. As he told her of the tragedy that had befallen us all, she reflected on the conversation she had held with Andy so few hours earlier.

Charley and his relief, bless them, stayed on duty while the devastated 'C' relief tried to make sense of it.

At a meeting the following night much was said, about us, about Andy. Even if, as he fell, he had landed on the surgeon's table, unless there had been a new heart there for him, he could not have been saved. The fight to keep him alive had been so sustained, his colour was so good, that the hospital staff believed Andy had collapsed only moments before. But it did not help.

If he had been shot, killed in a car crash or a fall, the relief could have accepted that more easily, but not this. No, this was not anywhere in their thinking and they were terribly hurt. They still are.

Days later, Deane with two other of Andy's old friends, Danny and Bernie, went to where he lay. They cracked open a new bottle of scotch, and filled four glasses. As they talked over old times, across deaths divide the four men held a sad toast.

'Whatever we had, we *still* have.'

The small church nestled at the end of a long gravelled drive that rose gently towards its boundaries. Near the gates, the coach and personnel carrier full of immaculate uniformed men stopped while we stepped down.

The burden would have been all Ray's, but that would have been unfair. Although there exists a format for a force funeral, much falls on the shoulders of the deceased officer's immediate supervisor, in this case it was Ray. I had offered with my heart in my mouth to speak from the pulpit. With the burial party to organise and the greater part of the event his responsibility, Ray, with some relief, accepted.

At the roadside bareheaded ARV crews stood to attention, paying their last respects as the cortege, escorted by six motorcycle outriders from the Special Escort Group (a service usually reserved for politicians or heads of state) passed them. Within the churchyard Shelley waited with her parents, managing a smile as we passed, but I could find no words.

Slowly and tenderly, Andy's friends carried him forwards with soft, regulated steps. Carrot was there for him, and Steve, the familiar smile fallen from his face. Above their shoulders, the force flag was draped, decorated with a profusion of flowers starkly at odds with the black-and-white, chequered band of his duty cap.

As the last notes of 'Endless Love' faded, Deane told of the deep friendship he and Andy had shared for so many years. Then, bravely, and to a church filled to overflowing, Shelley spoke of her love for the man she had lost.

Then with great apprehension, I climbed the steps to the pulpit; hundreds of faces stared back. Fighting for control, I remembered the support Andy had so often given me. So focussing on that terrible night when John O'Grady had died, I related the most powerful example.

'It was at the conclusion of one of our most serious incidents to date, where shots had been fired, police and public put in fear, and I had felt the weight of responsibility heavy on my shoulders, that Andy had said with a smile as he withdrew, 'I think you did really well.' It was what I needed to hear.

'A relief is only the sum of its parts. Andy chose to play an active part because he wanted it to work, and it does. He wanted it to work because he believed in certain things being right, in the shared convictions of which you are all aware. We will continue to strive for those things and then, in a way, Andy will still be at your shoulders as he always was. That would be a continuing tribute he would understand.'

I stepped down from the pulpit feeling hollow. As the clergyman moved forwards to fill my place, faces rose to meet me, on them supporting smiles. The relief had always been close. Now it was bonded as never before. Later 'Shaky Jake' touched my arm. 'If I die doing this job,' he said, 'I want you to speak for me.' It was perhaps the most profound thing anyone has ever said to me.

As the blessing was given, the hush fell again, and I moved forwards to help Ray and his party.

The words of 'Death is nothing' were spoken as I struggled through the packed church. Then Shelley's haunting musical gesture – the lyrics of 'One Sweet Day' – told again of her loss.

'I know you're shining down on me from heaven, like so many friends we've lost along the way. I know one day that we will be together, one sweet day.'

Without exception, this was the hardest, the most emotional episode for me to write. I was unsure even if

I was right to do so, but as I progressed, I was reminded again of how much these people of mine care for each other and that, in all the evil and violence there is in this world, the hope given by profound love can still inspire us.

Charley said some things that meant a lot. 'When I wrote the report, it didn't seem enough. Andy's years of service became just a few written words. It's not enough, doesn't reflect the man. While we accept the risk of being shot, giving a hundred per cent, a hundred and ten per cent, getting to people because they need us; we accept that. We don't expect this, no, *not this*.

'The funeral, it was very moving. What you said, that was the man. If I am going to go, that's the way I want it. It looked good, very supportive of Shelley.'

She was so good. She held her head up high and dealt with it.

'Like a Trojan.'

# Epilogue

IT'S OVER. I know that it's true yet it's still unreal. I could roll out of bed tomorrow morning at a godforsaken hour for an early turn, and it would still feel normal. I could open that locker and put on the same kit, load and holster the gun, drink the tea, drive, deploy, make those decisions.

But it is over.

The locker is empty now, or someone else has their kit hanging there. The messages, the bits of aged graffiti, they're still there. The gun's still there somewhere, but now it's in younger hands.

I will miss so many things, so many feelings that are hard to explain. When Keith and I would return from 'down south' over one of the bridges, or perhaps even when I was alone and duty officer, the sight of London's heart profiled against the skyline would always move me.

Tower Bridge, with HMS *Belfast* grey and menacing, moored at its feet, profiled in the blood red of a rising sun and reflected in the waters of the Thames. It sounds very poetic, I know, but that's how it felt. The knowledge that for a while, should the worst happen, and the firearms branch be needed, it was my call; that whatever the incident, if it was guns, my phone would be the first to ring.

I'll miss the 'debriefs', the banter and the sound of the guns returning to the safes at the end of a job, rack,

rack, clack. The ripping sound of the peeling Velcro as the body armour comes off. The misty breath in cold night air as we unkit, the sound of the radios. Tea in plastic cups, steaming, laughter, men I would, I did, trust with my life, smiling.

The surge of blood as sirens wail, and the words heard over the radio telling you that this job is for real. Wide-eyed children as you pass, a collage of noise and colour. The enormous respect that the department enjoys among our uniformed colleagues on division.

The responsibility disproportionate to my rank as the most senior of police officers asked advice. The resources mustered in a moment just for the asking.

I remember a radio message when we were searching a multistorey car park near Hatton Garden, looking for armed robbers. As high in the information room, the fear of a stray round going skywards crossed the supervisor's mind, there came a suggestion. 'Trojan 500, do you require an air exclusion zone?' Well, you don't get an offer like that every day, do you? So I said, 'Yes.'

The feelings it generated, being armed and uniformed out there in the streets of London, to have control of it all – they all come back to me when I dwell on it for a moment.

I will miss my colleagues, 'the boys', more than anything else. It has been a huge compliment, being allowed to be part of their lives, to share in their happiness and help in times of misfortune. Everything from the loss of a parent to car-crash and gunshot injuries, from marital strife to personal ambitions, some realised, some dashed. In the celebration of birth, the mourning of a death, they allowed me to share with them, and it has been the most enormous privilege.

The lack of sleep, the conflicts and the confrontations pale into insignificance now, as in the greater plan of things I realise that I have seen and done more in a few short years than some men could hope for if they lived through two lifetimes.

So what will I do now? There is not a huge demand for firearms tactical advisers out there in civvy street. Perhaps I should for now concentrate on catching up with half a lifetime's domestic bliss. I can definitely be at home this Christmas. I can have Sunday lunch on Sunday, socialise, go to the theatre, the cinema, watch a film, but if I do I can make a lie of most of what I see, because I know the reality.

What I should do is pay back the debt I owe to the woman who has always been there for me when I needed her, when so often I was deployed somewhere and she needed me, yet coped anyway. Behind every great man, they say, is a good woman. And I'm not great: just lucky.

What I *am* going to do is walk my old bull terrier, restore the sports car I have kept since my youth, travel a little, enjoy life if I can.

I suppose, though, what I could do is write a book – or should I say *another* book? We'll see. I vaguely remember a work of Rudyard Kipling's being transferred to celluloid. It was *The Jungle Book*, the story about Mowgli, the boy who is raised by the wolves. At its end Gobind, the old storyteller, alludes to the fate of one of the characters and a child asks, 'What happened to him?' The answer given was, 'Ah, but that, my child, is another story.'

# Glossary

**ACPO** Association of Chief Police Officers.

**AFO** Authorised firearms officer.

**Area car** fast police car, with two-man crew. Operating within the limits of a particular district or area.

**ARV** Armed Response Vehicle.

**asp** extending steel baton.

**ASU** IRA active service unit; or Air Support Unit (helicopter).

**baby** portable door-opening ram.

**ballistic blanket** large, heavy, flexible sheet containing bullet-resistant material.

**birdshot** shotgun round containing a multitude of small lead balls.

**blue on blue** accidental armed contact between friendly forces.

**boarded** to go before an interview board of senior officers.

**CAD** Computer-aided dispatch.

**call sign** the title by which any police unit can be identified, usually prefixed by the area or department from which it operates: e.g., Trojan 500.

**carbine** short rifle-type weapon.

**carrying** armed.

**casevac** casualty evacuation.

**check-zeroed** range-testing and adjusting a weapon until it is deemed sufficiently accurate.

**CID** Criminal Investigation Department.

**'C' relief** the group of firearms officers to which I was primarily attached.

**CROPs** Covert Rural Observation Posts.

**D6**  title of the first Metropolitan Police firearms unit.

**D11**  title given to the firearms unit subsequently.

**DA**  deliberate action.

**DC**  detective constable.

**DCI**  detective chief inspector.

**DI**  detective inspector.

**dig-out**  term used for an early-morning raid to effect an arrest.

**Divisional Support Unit**  carrier-borne unit of police officers, usually raised locally to target specific problems.

**DPG**  Diplomatic Protection Group.

**Dragon light**  powerful hand-held lamp.

**DS**  detective sergeant.

**end-ex**  end of exercise.

**enforcer**  second-generation door-opening ram.

**ER**  emergency response.

**expo**  explosives officer.

**FAP**  final assault position.

**Federation**  Police Federation (police officers' union).

**FME**  forensic medical examiner.

**Forward Control**  SO19 control point.

**Glock**  Austrian firearms manufacturer.

**Glock 17**  9 mm self-loading pistol, now carried by virtually all SO19 officers.

**Heckler & Koch**  German firearms manufacturer.

**HEMS**  Helicopter Emergency Service.

**India 99**  call sign for the force helicopter.

**IR**  information room (central control, New Scotland Yard).

**Lab**  Forensic Science Laboratory.

**LAS**  London Ambulance Service.

**Lee Enfield**  British firearms manufacturer.

**mag**  magazine to contain ammunition for a specific firearm.

**Met**  Metropolitan Police Force, or reference to its area.

**MOE**  method of entry.

**MP**  call sign used when addressing information room over the radio.

**MP5**  Heckler and Koch 9 mm carbine.

**OIC** officer in charge.

**on blues and twos** driving to a call with blue lights and two-tone horns employed.

**OP** observation point.

**PERME** Propellant, Explosive and Rocket Material Establishment.

**PFX** hand-held radio, capable of receiving main-set (information-room) calls.

**PIRA** Provisional Irish Republican Army.

**plasticuffs** plastic handcuffs strongly resembling industrial cable ties.

**PR** personal radio.

**PT17** forerunner of SO19.

**relief** A group of police officers who regularly work and are rostered together (designated E to F within SO19).

**Remington** American firearms manufacturer, famous for the production of pump-action shotguns.

**rowdyism** term used to describe a patrol tasked to deal with drunkeness and disorder.

**RVP** rendezvous point.

**SFO** specialist firearms officer.

**SG** shotgun ammunition containing a dozen projectiles resembling large ball bearings.

**shooter** slang expression for a firearm, or term to describe an offender who has opened fire, probably where injury has resulted.

**shot** police-speak for an authorised firearms officer.

**slot** to slot an enemy. Military slang term to describe shooting and killing.

**Smith & Wesson** very well-known American firearms manufacturer, best remembered for the production of early revolvers.

**SPG** Special Patrol Group.

**stick** broad term for staves, batons or truncheons. Also describes a small file of men, usually preparing to go forwards.

**strapping** filling in on a team or relief.

**TI**  target indication. A means to describe a firearms-incident scene for tactical purposes.

**tooled up**  armed.

**Trojan**  prefix to the call signs of all SO19 units.

**TSG**  Territorial Support Groups.

**up behind**  slang term for close follow/surveillance of a suspect.

**yardie**  Jamaican gangster.